WITHDRAWN
UTSA Libraries

# A LABYRINTH OF IMAGERY:
## RAMON GOMEZ DE LA SERNA'S
### *NOVELAS DE LA NEBULOSA*

MIGUEL GONZALEZ-GERTH

# A LABYRINTH OF IMAGERY:
# RAMON GOMEZ DE LA SERNA'S
# *NOVELAS DE LA NEBULOSA*

TAMESIS BOOKS LIMITED
LONDON

Colección Támesis
SERIE A - MONOGRAFIAS, CXX

© Copyright by Tamesis Books Limited
London 1986
ISBN 0 7293 0234 2

DISTRIBUTORS:

Spain:
Editorial Castalia,
Zurbano, 39,
28010 Madrid

United States and Canada:
Longwood Publishing Group,
27 South Main Street,
Wolfeboro, New Hampshire 03894-2069, U.S.A.

Great Britain and rest of the world:
Grant and Cutler Ltd.,
55-57 Great Marlborough Street,
London W1V 2AY

Depósito legal: M 43014-1986

Printed in Spain by Talleres Gráficos de SELECCIONES GRÁFICAS
Carretera de Irún, km. 11,500 - 28049 Madrid

for
TAMESIS BOOKS LIMITED
LONDON

LIBRARY
The University of Texas
at San Antonio

*In memory of my wife, Betty,
who ingeniously helped me to
put the original ideas and words
together.*

The true poet must be tragic and comic at once, and the whole of human life must be felt as a blend of tragedy and comedy.

(SOCRATES, in Plato's *Symposium*)

Devo al suggerimento di Octavio Paz che i poeti non abbiano biografia e che la loro opera sia la loro biografia, l'averla raccontata come se si trattase di una vita imaginaria.

(ANTONIO TABUCCHI, *Donna di Porto Pim*)

# TABLE OF CONTENTS

I wish to thank the University Research Institute of the University of Texas at Austin for financial assistance in the publication of this book.

# INTRODUCTION

It cannot be denied that one of the outstanding contributions of Ramón Gómez de la Serna, the one most universally praised, is the easily recognized, extremely brief and aesthetically poignant kind of text he called *greguería*. Critics and historians who stop there, however, totally misjudge the range of his originality and tend to restrict his meaningful production to the period between the two World Wars. Ramón's work as a whole is not trivial imagery. All one has to do is read carefully his more recondite essays, such as «Las cosas y el 'ello'» and «Las palabras y lo indecible», certain passages in his literary biographies, and his more ambitious novels to comprehend the notions and concerns which lie behind his dynamically imagistic, basically humorous and metaphorical style.

Humor and metaphor were characteristic of avant-garde writing throughout Europe. They came along with the turn of the century, with the spirit of a new and youthful world. Roger Shattuck suggests that in France before the First World War «humor, a genre that can command both the directness of comedy and the subtler moods of irony, became a method and a style» and that «the future of realism in the arts of the twentieth century may lie in the ease with which it can sustain the carefully timed commentary of humor».[1] Although I tend to agree with the latter statement, I believe that there is another side to the question, namely the ease with which different kinds of humor in the arts survive the test of time or, more precisely, of given periods of time. For example, there seems to have come with the aftermath of the Second World War a schism in our general attitude toward literature, a schism brought about by the makers of literature themselves. In other words, humor, which had been during the war years a desperate refuge for everyday sanity, became something undesirable, particularly if the reader was not «in on it»; literature had to be at least thematically *engagée*. Not until Ionesco and Arrabal do we again find serious humor in literature, bizarre as it may be, without reaching the extremes of Genet, Beckett and Artaud. As Shattuck explains the phenomenon, «the ultimate modern transfor-

---

[1] ROGER SHATTUCK, *The Banquet Years: The Arts in France, 1885-1918* (New York: Doubleday and Company, 1961), pp. 33-34.

1

mation of the comic may render it no longer laughable, for the comic has delivered itself into the hands of the *absurd*».[2] And when we consider that, as Shattuck himself points out, «existentialists have invoked absurdity as the essential human condition»,[3] we come upon the line of separation between Ramón's two humorous nebular novels of the twenties (he had not coined the term yet) and the two of the thirties and forties. If, as Shattuck suggests, there is «a method of humor based on logic perpetually reversing its terms»,[4] which is quite the one Ramón used in his aphoristic and some of his discursive *greguerías,* his version of the absurd consists precisely in presenting human life in a dreamlike stasis which is suddenly liberated by a commotion such as death, the ultimate absurdity. This may be the kind of humor Shattuck attributes to Alfred Jarry by saying that «humor offers both a form of wisdom and a means of survival in a threatening world».[5]

It is unfortunate that Spanish and, until recently, Spanish American literature have been so neglected by American, British and even other European literary critics and historians engaged in broad sweeps. It is regrettable that there should be no cognizance of a writer such as Ramón in Bradbury and McFarlane's *Modernism, 1890-1930.*[6] The only Hispanic writers mentioned are Calderón de la Barca, Miguel de Unamuno, Juan Ramón Jiménez, [García] Lorca, Neruda, Borges, and Paz. Ortega y Gasset is quoted several times. British and American channels for this cognizance can easily be traced. Similarly, there is no recognition of Ramón, though there is no imperative reason for it, in Shattuck's study of the French avant-garde. It is somewhat less excusable to find such an absence in Renato Poggioli's *Teoria dell' arte d'avanguardia,*[7] where García Lorca, Góngora, Jorge Guillén, Eugenio d'Ors, Ortega y Gasset, Pedro Salinas, and Guillermo de Torre are taken into account. This choice, too, can be explained, and it is a pity that no Spanish American writer is present. Yet even more surprising is the fact with ample opportunity and reason Octavio Paz, who has elsewhere, as we have seen, praised him, does not mention Ramón in *Los hijos del limo,* which makes me suspect he has not yet taken the time to assess the full import of the Spaniard's achievement.[8]

[2] SHATTUCK, *The Banquet Years...*, p. 34.
[3] SHATTUCK, *The Banquet Years...*, p. 34n.
[4] SHATTUCK, *The Banquet Years...*, p. 237.
[5] SHATTUCK, *The Banquet Years...*, p. 248.
[6] MALCOLM BRADBURY and JAMES MCFARLANE (eds.), *Modernism, 1890-1930* ([Harmondsworth]: Penguin Books [1978]).
[7] RENATO POGGIOLI, *Teoria dell' arte d'avanguardia* (Bologna: Società editrice il Mulino, 1962); *The Theory of the Avant-garde,* translated from the Italian by Gerald Fitzgerald (Cambridge, Mass.: The Belknap Press of Harvard University Press, 1968).
[8] OCTAVIO PAZ, *Los Hijos del limo: Del romanticismo a la vanguardia* (Bar-

Twenty-five years after writing the brilliant book cited above, Roger Shattuck, in an amusing and touching piece described by the magazine where it appears as «a conversation on a train, in which literature is shown to have left life for language, and a professor fights the 'metaphysical picaresque'», reconsiders through one of his speakers as follows:

> Modernism is not a period, like the Victorian era. It's not a proper school or movement, like Surrealism. It has no geographic character or associations, like Der Blaue Reiter. It serves no heuristic purpose, like Baroque or Imagism. It's the weakest term we've had since Symbolism... But best of all, worst of all... modernism embodies a disabling contradiction. It has cancer. The only general characteristic of the modern era is the celebration of individual experience, of particular feelings in particular circumstances, not repeatable. Every epiphany is sui generis. The term modernism tries to make a category of items that will not fit into a category...[9]

And through the other:

> There is no such thing as modernism. There are only professors talking about it in order to keep their tenure in the culture.[10]

The truth of the matter is that from early times civilized man felt the need of analysis and grouping. As culture has become more sophisticated so has the need. The history of art and its criticism is one of change and oneupmanship. Octavio Paz has referred to what he calls «la tradición de la ruptura»[11] (admittedly after Harold Rosenberg's *The Tradition of the New*). The natural evolution of things, however, may have reached the point of diminishing returns. This seems to be Shattuck's recent veiled complaint, and at the end of the present study I will try to substantiate my conclusion that in the decades of the thirties and forties Ramón was able to anticipate the ultimate consequence of the «anything seems possible and probable» kind of twentieth-century literary text which began with Strindberg, developed in Gide, caught fire with Borges and Robbe-Grillet, and seems to have culminated (at least for Shattuck) in García Márquez.

It is, therefore, at this particular juncture that Ramón Gómez de la Serna should achieve the larger recognition denied him until now even by Hispanists. Americans and Europeans alike have not had the problem to the same extent that Hispanic people have with their coming of age in the arts and movement away from the provincial and into the main-

celona: Editorial Seix Barral [1974]); *Children of the Mire,* translated by Rachel Phillips (Cambridge, Mass.: Harvard University Press, 1974).
[9] ROGER SHATTUCK, «The Poverty of Modernism», *The New Republic,* Volume 188, Number 10, Issue 3,556 (March 14, 1983), pp. 25-31.
[10] *Ibid.*
[11] PAZ, *Los hijos del limo...,* pp. 15-35.

stream of a developing Western civilization. Today Spanish America is as sophisticated in the arts as anyone, but that was not the case fifty years ago and certainly not at the time Ramón was opening up the Spanish literary language with deep furrows of expressive intuition and folk-usage. The rediscovery of Gómez de la Serna has been delayed by events more logical than those advanced by some of his commentators, such as his apparent carelessness. Guillermo de Torre, once the spokesman for Spanish Peninsular avant-garde and later Ramón's best though somewhat laconic critic, suggested the following: the language factor (Spanish is not internationally «prestigious»), the remoteness of Ramón's last place of residence (Buenos Aires), and his noncommittal yet intellectually unpopular political stance (traditionalism). Although these could have been valid reasons in the forties and fifties, it is more likely that something else is at the bottom of such neglect. Of course, the international prestige of a culture or its novelty among the *cognoscenti* is indeed a factor. It is thus culturally understandable that Apollinaire, Jarry, Breton and Cocteau should still be so admired, even among Spanish-speakers, at the expense of Gómez de la Serna who, in my opinion, was just as original and imaginative.

Among the sixty novels published by Ramón there are four which he set aside as especially significant and called them *novelas de la nebulosa* («Novels of the Nebula»). These works of peculiarly imaginative fiction constitute a tetralogy in ascending order of technical and structural skill. So far, to my mind, they have been, especially the last two, either misunderstood or unduly neglected by the critics. The style which had crystallized in the microcosmic *greguería* expands its sphere of activity in these narratives, the *nebulosa* thus becoming a macrocosmic counterpart. Some might argue that in the course of this study I have treated the four individual works in a somewhat informal manner. I remain convinced, however, that rather than engage in more formal methods at this time, a combination of summary and *explication de texte* is the most effective way to lead to a final «interpretation» of these highly unusual prose works, for in this case, if quantification of patternings is useful at all, the reader must first become familiar with this totally unorthodox vision and language.

The commentaries and interpretations provided here may be best understood when preceded by sufficient exposure to Gómez de la Serna's hallmark of style, namely his aphorisms, of which I give a close account in another study now in preparation. Other than that, I have endeavored to provide a practical as well as theoretical preamble on certain issues involving the novel as a genre and its critical application to Ramón Gómez de la Serna in order to approach most effectively those which I consider his most difficult and most original narrative constructions.

4

# I

# A GENERIC SETTING FOR RAMON'S NOVELS

It is my contention that Ramón Gómez de la Serna's *greguerías* evince a style of writing and not merely a specific literary genre. The present work attempts to demonstrate, through the analysis of some of Ramón's works of narrative fiction, particularly those which he called the *novelas de la nebulosa,* that we are dealing with a kind of narrative whose technical virtuosity consists at least as much in the textual aspects as it does in the structural, considering that his «gregueristic» vision applies to the language even more than it does to the plot. Gonzalo Torrente Ballester says that «las greguerías de Ramón adoptan a veces apariencia novelesca», and wonders: «¿Sólo apariencia? Nos inclinamos a creer que sí. Sería altamente útil averiguar el funcionamiento de su imaginación puesta en el trance de escribir una novela...»[1].

Compared with how much has been written on Ramón's aphorisms, the critical material devoted to his narrative fictions amounts to very little. Federico Carlos Sainz de Robles comments as follows:

> ... la greguería que es un culto ardiente por la imagen —línea y color— y por la paradoja —sugestión y sorpresa—... ha terminado *por apoderarse* de su creador, fanatizándole, obligándole a utilizarla lo mismo cuando escribe biografías que cuando escribe novelas, ensayos, obras escénicas. Hasta punto tal, que de muchas de sus obras pudiera afirmarse que son *greguerías eslabonadas*...
>
> Ha escrito... novelas extensas y novelas cortas, raras, extravagantes, sugestivas, dislocadas, felices en las imágenes, desorbitadas en el lenguaje, y en muchas de las cuales se adelanta a los más audaces y extraños novelistas extranjeros actuales...[2]

This critic points out the importance of the *greguería* in Ramón's narrative works but mistakenly places the emphasis on the gregueristic phrase, instead of the overall gregueristic vision of the work which, in his second paragraph, he correctly identifies by means of descriptive adjectives: strange, eccentric, metaphorical, illogical.

---

[1] *Panorama de la literatura española contemporánea* (Madrid: Ediciones Guadarrama [1956]), p. 306.
[2] *La novela española en el siglo XX* (Madrid: Pegaso [1957]), pp. 169-70.

Angel Valbuena Prat, to give another example, thinks of Ramón's fictional narratives as «mundos de gérmenes en movimiento continuo, de metáforas irónicas, de constante creación del idioma en giros y juegos que recuerdan —con su diferencia— el estilo barroco del siglo XVII».[3] The quantity of such impressionistic criticism is apt to increase. And Melchor Fernández Almagro, one of the most circumspect of Ramón's critics, says of him that he

> hace novela, a su manera, claro es, sirviéndose de su gran invento, la «greguería», aparato de extraordinaria precisión, que lo observa y transfigura todo. No es el ingrediente más indicado para la confección de una novela. Pero la «greguería» responde a una visión de conjunto que el novelista utiliza para «greguerizar» personajes, situaciones, ambientes, en línea de arriesgada originalidad. No cabe transposición más ingeniosa y más veraz del alma de Madrid a plano tan desconcertante como la conseguida por Gómez de la Serna en *La Nardo*, así como *El doctor inverosímil* o *El incongruente* anticipan formas muy típicas del humorismo que hoy priva, dentro y fuera de España.[4]

And this is all he has to say about Ramón's «novels», although he adds in the same article: «su arte literario es personal e intransferible. La 'greguería' comienza y acaba en Ramón», this being a «modo de descomponer la realidad y de rehacerla —poética más que humorísticamente— en imágenes...».[5] What Fernández Almagro says is not long in words, but it is not short in significance. Put in another way, what he says is this: Ramón not only writes novels but is a novelist; quite unconventional, to be sure (in 1914!), using a stylistic device not ordinarily recommended for such a purpose yet one which creates a total metaphoric vision of great originality that transforms all the constituents of the novel, thus having a disconcerting effect on the reader. It can be inferred from Fernández Almagro's statement (if the *greguería* is a «mode of decomposing reality and remaking it —more poetically than humorously— into images», and if Ramón uses this device as a «vision of the whole» to transform «characters, situations, and settings») that the process employed by Ramón ultimately to produce his «novels» is one of rendering images into a narrative sequence. Does this mean, then, that Ramón's so-called novels are manifestations of his style simply structured as novels? Offhand, as far as I am concerned, the answer is yes, to a greater or a lesser degree, depending on the particular work. But just as it is necessary to analyze the aphorism as a literary genre and to fit the short or capsular *greguería* in its structure, I attempt here something more complex: first, to explore the novel also as a literary genre and, second,

---

[3] ANGEL VALBUENA PRAT, *Historia de la literatura española,* vol. II, p. 975.
[4] «Esquema de la novela española contemporánea», *Clavileño* (Madrid), núm. 5 (septiembre-octubre 1950), p. 24.
[5] *Ibid.,* pp. 24-25.

to see if what Ramón calls his novels can actually fit in its structure.

I will not presume to be either scientific or exhaustive in my considerations of the novel, generally considered to be the newest and most flexible of established literary forms. On the other hand, I cannot skirt the problem. What is a novel? And how did Ramón understand the term? Let us take the second question first. In his delightfully capricious autobiography entitled *Automoribundia,* Ramón says that he, prior to 1914, «creaba innumerables artículos periodísticos y escribía novelas y libros futuros», and that one day he decided that «había que escribir una novela larga, algo sostenido, con título novelesco. Hasta que no lograse eso no sería escritor».[6] It is thus evident that, like most modern prose writers, Ramón felt compelled to produce a novel and that his ideas involved not only length but also a sustained theme. He thus tells of the results:

> Así, por esa perentoria obligación, nació «La Viuda Blanca y Negra», escrita en el verano madrileño con la obsesión del crimen, los celos y el aire trasnochador verbenero.
>
> En ese mecimiento veraniego y con su invierno de reverso, escribí mi primer novela larga...
>
> La crítica lenta, dedicada a más ingentes tipos de influencia política o de escritores jaleados por el público, apenas dice nada de mi novela, y queda como un acta de bodas en la sacristía de alguna biblioteca amiga.
>
> No aceptan de ningún modo ese año ni muchos después —los bastantes para frustrarme como novelista, aunque yo no me doy por frustrado— esa forma de novela que en el futuro no será sino así.[7]

So we find in Ramón's album of memories this courageous confession which is quite revealing. His first novel, *El ruso,* appeared in 1913. His second novel, *La viuda blanca y negra,* though not published until 1917, after his third one, *El doctor inverosímil,* had already appeared (first edition, 1914), was long ignored by the critics, a fact which the author acknowledges as having had some sort of adverse effect on his novelwriting. And yet we know that he went on to produce many other «novels» of the same general type; by 1948 he looks back on *El doctor inverosímil* as a «novela curiosa que podría ser de público».[8] Ramón evidently thought that the psychoanalytical theme of this work explained its relative popularity.

The question of what is a novel is a particular dilemma for a Hispanist. On the one hand, he has heard repeatedly that the novel actually begins with Cervantes' *Don Quixote.* On the other hand, he labors at a disadvantage in this field, particularly with respect to the contemporary, for apart from Ortega y Gasset's admirable contribution there is little that

[6] RAMÓN GÓMEZ DE LA SERNA, *Automoribundia* (Buenos Aires: Editorial Sudamericana, 1948), pp. 290-92.
[7] *Ibid.,* p. 292.
[8] *Ibid.,* p. 294.

applies to the problems of theory. Menéndez y Pelayo and Montesinos, for example, are —for reasons of methodology and subject-matter, respectively— too far in the past. Francisco Ayala's *Reflexiones sobre la estructura narrativa* (to which I will refer in short) is a very useful synthesis but justifiably draws most of its examples from older literature. Now, the Academy Dictionary defines *novela* as an «obra literaria en que se narra una acción fingida en todo o en parte, y cuyo fin es causar placer estético a los lectores por medio de la descripción o pintura de sucesos o lances interesantes, de caracteres, de pasiones y de costumbres». Quite obviously, this definition is too vague, for it can apply to any form of fiction. Julián Marías, a philosopher who prides himself on his knowledge of literature, understandably dissatisfied with such a definition (and following the views of Ortega y Gasset, as we will see later), asserts that «la acción es necesaria a la novela, pero no es lo sustantivo... sino más bien los personajes y el mundo ficticio en que éstos viven»: he explains that «lo peculiar de la novela no es la narración, sino la descripción... pero no se trata de la descripción de cosas, sino de la vida de esos personajes y de su ambiente»; however, «lo decisivo es la narración misma, la presencia dinámica de los personajes en su mundo» and (perhaps with Ramón Fernández[9] in mind) «la novela... no maneja el pasado absoluto, sino que envuelve cierta actualidad o, al menos, un pasado que, por ser el nuestro, aparece como actualizable».[10] Marías' effort is helpful in its possible application to Ramón's fictional narratives, insofar as it stipulates that the novel should not deal primarily in the description of things but in that of the characters' life and environment, not always a clear-cut distinction. And yet, one gradually finds in the course of examining the work of critics and theorists of the novel that differentiation is precisely the method by which they try to decide, as specifically as they can, what a novel is.

Turning to English, one is confronted with this definition of the term novel in Webster's *New Collegiate Dictionary:* «a fictitious prose tale of considerable length, in which the characters and actions professing to represent those of real life are portrayed in a plot»; it is succinct in its approach, as a dictionary definition should be, but obviously not devoid of theoretic flaws. It can be rewritten even more succinctly as follows: «a long prose fiction whose characters and their plotted actions imitate real life», in which case the theoretic emphasis is placed more clearly where it was intended: on length, plot, and mimetic quality. Will these aspects suffice to distinguish the novel from other forms of prose fiction?

[9] See his essay on Balzac in *Messages* (Paris: Gallimard, 1926; English translation, New York: Harcourt, Brace, 1927).

[10] *Diccionario de literatura española* (Madrid: Revista de Occidente [1953]), page 507.

Depending on their intention, English and American literary critics have distinguished various fictional forms. Wellek and Warren state that «the two chief modes of narrative fiction have, in English, been called the 'romance' and the 'novel'»,[11] noting that, as early as 1785, Clara Reeve distinguished them as follows: «The Novel is a picture of real life and manners, and of the time in which it is written. The Romance, in lofty and elevated language, describes what never happened nor is likely to happen».[12] For this lady, it would seem, as well as for the critics who quote her, the difference between these two modes is merely one of literary verisimilitude, the highest level of Aristotelian mimesis. Let us bear in mind, however, when the original statement was written, as well as the fact that humanity and dehumanization in art have been historically variable factors. Myth made possible the epic, which in turn gave rise to the romance (in Spanish literary history, the «libro de caballerías»), which in turn was modified into the novel (in Spanish, Cervantes' *Don Quixote*).[13] This does not mean that romances are not written any more, regardless of language; in these the key aspect is neither length nor mimetic quality but plot. For reasons of literary and linguistic history, Spanish does not ordinarily use cognate terminology to distinguish between the two modes mentioned thus far. With regard to Spanish literature, the term *romance* immediately suggests an octosyllabic poem in the manner of the medieval popular ballad, rather than the Academy Dictionary's «novela o libro de caballerías, en prosa o en verso». There is undiminished interest in the fact that German, French, and Italian use the terms *Roman, roman, romanzo,* respectively, as compared with Spanish *novela* and English *novel*.

Northrop Frye differentiates among four fictional forms: novel, romance, autobiography, and a kind of satire which he prefers to call anatomy. «The essential difference between novel and romance lies in the conception of characterization», he says; «the romancer does not attempt to create 'real people' so much as stylized figures which expand into

---

[11] *Theory of Literature*, p. 223. Of this work, Chapter 16, written by Austin Warren (from which my quotation is taken), has been reprinted in ROBERT SCHOLES (ed.), *Approaches to the Novel* (Scranton, Pa.: Chandler Publishing Co., Revised ed. [1966]), pp. 5-21.

[12] *Progress of Romance* (London, 1785). Quoted in Wellek and Warren, *Theory...*, p. 223.

[13] In his *Reflexiones sobre la estructura narrativa* (Madrid: Taurus, 1970), Francisco Ayala suggests another interesting trajectory. Since myth also made possible the folktale, which in turn gave rise to the startling anecdote, which in turn was modified into the short story as we know it today, Ayala says with respect to the «protonovela» *Lazarillo de Tormes:* «El tiempo que Lazarillo pasó bajo el poder del ciego (probable núcleo original de la obra) es una sucesión de anécdotas...; pero el autor las dispuso con arte tan sutil que, en lugar de aparecer como cuentas ensartadas... adquieren una secuencia orgánica... dentro de un proceso vital», and in its third *Tratado* or chapter, «el escritor se mueve en el terreno de la novela moderna, que él mismo acaba de descubrir...» (pp. 69-74).

9

psychological archetypes», whereas «the novel tends... to expand into a
fictional approach to history... As it is creative history, however, the
novelist usually prefers his material in a plastic, or roughly contemporary
state...».[14] Autobiography also «merges with the novel», according to
Frye; «we may call this very important form of prose fiction the confession form», and finally comes «the Menippean satire, also more rarely
called the Varronian satire» or «anatomy» (after Burton's title), which
«deals less with people as such than with mental attitudes».[15] Such a
differentiation has been formulated by this critic because when speaking
of *Gulliver's Travels* «surely everyone would call it fiction, and if it is
fiction, a distinction appears between fiction as a genus and the novel as
a species of that genus».[16] In other words, Swift's famous book is not
a novel; Frye has found it catalogued according to the Dewey decimal
system in a section labeled «Satire and Humor». The case is similar
to the one stated by Maurice Z. Shroder who, while justly taking to
task the compilers of a literary manual for their initial treatment of
the novel («a fictional prose narrative, of substantial length»[17]), says that
*Lancelot, Pilgrim's Progress,* Ballanche's *Orphée,* and *Finnegans Wake*
all fit such «definition» yet would not «qualify as novels were we to
compare them with *Don Quixote* or *Madame Bovary, The Egoist* or *The
Ambassadors...* that are unquestionably novels and nothing else».[18] The
same critic begins his own disquisition as follows:

> When we speak of «the novel» in general terms, we are —willingly or
> unwillingly— accepting the assumption that genre has more than a theoretical
> reality...
> The reluctance to provide more explicit and more substantial descriptions
> of the novel may reflect the admirable desire to avoid the pitfalls of
> prescriptive theories of genre.[19]

But in view of Frye's and Shroder's work, as well as that of others, I,
for one, cannot help feeling that the main problem is neither neglect nor

[14] NORTHROP FRYE, *Anatomy of Criticism* (Princeton: Princeton University
Press, 1957), pp. 304-06. The essay entitled «Specific Continuous Forms (Prose
Fiction)» has been reprinted in ROBERT SCHOLES (ed.), *Approaches to the Novel,*
pp. 29-42; it is also included in PHILIP STEVICK (ed.), *The Theory of the Novel*
(New York: The Free Press [1968]), pp. 31-43, under the title «The Four
Forms of Fiction».
[15] *Ibid.,* pp. 307-09.
[16] *Ibid.,* p. 303.
[17] BARNET *et al., A Dictionary of Literary Terms,* p. 59. However, it must
be said in all fairness that the treatment as a whole is quite good for a handbook.
Shroder also refers to the French equivalent: «Une fiction en prose d'une
certaine étendue» (ABEL CHEVALLEY, *Le Roman Anglais de Notre Temps),* acceptable to and quoted by E. M. FORSTER, *Aspects of the Novel* (New York:
Harcourt, Brace and World [1966]), p. 6.
[18] «The Novel as a Genre», *The Massachusetts Review,* IV (1963), 291-308;
reprinted in PHILIP STEVICK (ed.), *The Theory of the Novel,* pp. 13-29.
[19] *Ibid.*

pusillanimity on the part of writers, but the difficult critical prospect which crystallizes in Frye's statements: «the forms of prose fiction are mixed»,[20] and «the novel has combined with each of the other three» forms; moreover, «exclusive concentration on one form is rare».[21] Wayne Booth has criticized Frye's general approach. My feeling is one of being left by Frye in a state of enlightened difficulty, not so much because his «ten types are of limited use as a basis for judgments on technique»,[22] as because the basic four of those ten types are perhaps so rare that they cannot be found. Of course they can, Frye will answer: «When we start to think seriously about the novel, not as fiction, but as a form of fiction, we feel that its characteristics, whatever they are, are such as make, say, Defoe, Fielding, Austen, James central in its tradition, and Borrow, Peacock, Melville, and Emily Brontë somehow peripheral».[23] Such a conclusion was undoubtedly reached after a great deal of study on the subject which immediately concerns us. But how can we know there is a novelistic tradition, if we are not sure of its characteristics? And if we do not know this, how can we isolate the novel form from any other forms of fiction? This is where Frye's technic comes in; it is based on perception and ingenuity. It is actually brilliant. Still, if it leaves us with Henry James at the vanguard of novelistic tradition, we might be doomed. The crucial question is whether novelistic tradition can evolve and, in fact, has evolved vertically, into newer modes (Frye's own word), or only horizontally, into undifferentiated prose fiction through the admixture of the other nonnovelistic fictional forms. According to Frye, Joyce's *Ulysses* «is a complete prose epic with all four forms employed in it, all of practically equal importance...».[24] We are saved, we think, if we interpret the adverb «practically» as suggesting that the novel form is still uppermost and thus ultimately claims the great work. But

> The forms we have been isolating in fiction, and which depend for their existence on the commonsense dichotomies of the daylight consciousness, vanish in *Finnegans Wake* into a fifth and quintessential form... traditionally associated with scriptures and sacred books, and treats life in terms of the fall and awakening of the human soul and the creation and apocalypse of nature. The Bible is the definitive example of it; the Egyptian Book of the Dead and the Icelandic Prose Edda, both of which have left deep imprints on *Finnegans Wake,* also belong to it.[25]

And, paradoxically, the novel suddenly seems lost to the past. Yet, despite the significance and weight of the evidence that leads to such a conclu-

---

[20] FRYE, *Anatomy...*, p. 305.
[21] *Ibid.*, p. 312.
[22] WAYNE C. BOOTH, *The Rhetoric of Fiction* (Chicago and London: The University of Chicago Press [1965]), p. 37n.
[23] FRYE, *Anatomy...*, p. 304.
[24] *Ibid.*, p. 314.
[25] *Ibid.*

sion, there should be other possible answers. If the novelistic tradition suggested by Frye is more than a hypothesis, where has it gone since Henry James in English and, say, Galdós in Spanish? We must remember that Frye has cautioned us that the essential difference between novel and romance (and, it follows, confession and anatomy) lies in the conception of characterization (of this he is sure, regardless of what may be the other characteristics of the novel). Indeed, as Wayne Booth has pointed out, this method of differentiation results in «groups of works still unmanageably large and heterogeneous, groups distinguished from each other less by an induction from their common effects than by a deductive classification of the materials presented...»,[26] which takes us back to Shroder's complaint. There is no doubt in my mind that the source of the difficulty still in question is inevitably a matter of preconceived notions and the use of corresponding terms. For example, regarding contemporary Spanish literature, Juan Luis Alborg states: «Nuestros novelistas, en general, creen... que una novela no puede consistir sino en un nudo argumental dotado de interés y en unos tipos humanos consistentes... porque todas las grandes novelas que podría citar cualquiera son eso exactamente...»[27] (Disregarding questionable details, this seems to refer to such a novelistic tradition as suggested by Frye.) «Donde yerran, sin embargo, es al creer que una novela no puede ser ya más que eso y que cualquier otra condición o la mezcla de otras sustancias perjudica o corrompe su naturaleza»; he rounds it off thus: «ya está fundido el molde para toda la eternidad, y quien se sale de ese tiesto es un heterodoxo de la literatura.»[28] According to this critic, then, the novelistic tradition can evolve vertically into newer modes, and even the horizontal evolution through formal admixture does not alter its essence. Frye thinks of post-Jamesian continuous fiction as a mixed form of prose fiction and refers to Joyce's *Ulysses* as «a complete prose epic»; Alborg is of the opinion that contemporary works of fiction (presumably continuous), regardless of form or content, are the products of novelistic evolution and, therefore, merely newer novels. We have seen that other Spanish critics, even while voicing reservations, refer to Ramón's sustained fictions as «novelas», despite the common use of the term *narración* as the equivalent of undifferentiated prose fiction. The fact is that the word *novela* is very frequently, popularly, and indiscriminately used in Spanish without much regard for what it really means. Anything sentimental is usually considered a «novela»; take, for example, the way Alejandro Gómez refers to his wife's view of marriage, in Unamuno's *Nada menos que todo un hombre*. Today, television «soap operas» are

---

[26] *The Rhetoric of Fiction*, p. 37.
[27] JUAN LUIS ALBORG, *Hora actual de la novela española* (Madrid: Taurus [1958]), p. 29.
[28] *Ibid.*

called «telenovelas». And it would seem that, despite professional interests, Hispanic literary critics have often tended to exhibit the same linguistic peculiarity regarding the word *novela* as the layman.

I have already mentioned the scarcity in Spanish of sound theoretical material on the novel. Alborg offers the following comment:

> Como lo novelesco es un género que en realidad no ha sido todavía definido, no cabe en buena lógica precisar qué cosa es una auténtica o una falsa novela, qué temas le son propios y cuáles ajenos, qué caminos convenientes y cuáles equivocados. Hasta el momento no cabe duda que la novela ha procurado de mil modos —adoptando las más proteicas posturas, abriéndose a todo, caminando hacia las metas más dispares— el hacer imposible su propia definición; y ahí precisamente está su fuerza, puesto que no conoce la literatura ningún otro género tan rico. Todo ha cabido en ella: narración, psicología, paisaje, intimidad, aventura, pensamiento, ciencia, estética, religión; y nada digamos si se atiende al modo con que el mundo ha sido reflejado desde el realismo más crudo hasta las fantasías más audaces.
>
> Sin embargo, en líneas generales puede decirse que la opinión común y el juicio de la mayoría de los críticos han convenido en afirmar que una novela auténtica es un relato bien contado, *objetivamente contado,* es decir, consistente en una acción humana y real, sostenida por personajes dotados de vida propia y, en consecuencia, enteramente desligados de su autor.[29]

After the first hurdle (to define the novel as a genre and to determine what is a true novel amount to the same thing), Alborg's paragraphs are clear and meaningful. There is a novelistic genre, but, at least so far, it defies definition (cf. Shroder above); it is the richest of literary genres and has made use of all possible forms and contents (cf. Frye above), but the freedom inherent to the genre is being curtailed by certain public (including some critical) demands. This last opinion brings up the important opposition (particularly in regard to Ramón) between mass taste and modern art, which was so perceptively developed by Ortega y Gasset.

Both Ortega's views on modern art and his views on the modern novel are widely known. At Ortega's *tertulia* which took place in the editorial offices of the *Revista de Occidente,* some of those views may have reached Ramón's ears before appearing in print. This is not to say that they would have determined Ramón's novelistic structure, however; one must remember that his first «novels» were published as early as 1914 and 1917. In *Ideas sobre la novela* (1925), Ortega y Gasset states that the formulation of his views on the novel was prompted by conversations with Pío Baroja regarding the technique of novel writing. Unlike Croce, Ortega accepts the novel as a genre which, however, he believes to be in decline for lack of new themes (he reminds us that the

[29] *Ibid.,* p. 51.

13

term *novela* is related to *novelty),* but whose last hour should be its finest. To achieve this, the modern novel needs to discard all but a minimum of plot and action and adopt a maximum of vivisection and contemplation; presentation instead of narration, atmosphere instead of ideology. The novel is a dense, heavy type of prose fiction; it is the opposite of the tale or short story. It moves slowly; an observation which impressed Baroja, who «ahora se ha propuesto hacer un libro de *tempo* lento, como digo yo».[30] It must eclipse everyday reality, «gigantesca síntesis de nimiedades», with its own reality, «denso cerco de menudencias claramente intuidas»,[31] in which the reader is absorbed. This abridgment of Ortega's views on the novel would apply perfectly to Ramón except for one item which I have deliberately left out. Ortega's ideal novelist is Dostoevski, and the reason for this preference is the Russian novelist's development of his characters: «En sus comienzos pudo creerse que lo importante para la novela es su trama. Luego se ha ido advirtiendo que lo importante no es *lo que* se ve, sino *que* se vea bien algo humano, sea lo que quiera.»[32] Here Ramón does not qualify. Despite Ortega's erstwhile encouragement of Ramón in other literary endeavors, his judgment regarding the latter's novel is implicit in the following paragraphs:

> Desde el punto de vista humano tienen las cosas un orden, una jerarquía determinados. Nos parecen unas muy importantes, otras menos, otras por completo insignificantes. Para satisfacer el ansia de deshumanizar no es, pues, forzoso alterar las formas primarias de las cosas. Basta con invertir la jerarquía y hacer un arte donde aparezcan en primer plano, destacados con aire monumental, los mínimos sucesos de la vida.
>
> Este es el nexo latente que une las maneras de arte nuevo en apariencia más distantes. Un mismo instinto de fuga y evasión de lo real se satisface en el suprarrealismo de la metáfora y en lo que cabe llamar infrarrealismo. A la ascensión poética puede sustituirse una inmersión bajo el nivel de la perspectiva natural. Los mejores ejemplos de cómo por extremar el realismo se le supera —no más que con atender lupa en mano a lo microscópico de la vida— son Proust, Ramón Gómez de la Serna, Joyce.
>
> Ramón puede componer todo un libro sobre los senos..., o sobre el circo, o sobre el alba, o sobre el Rastro o la Puerta del Sol. El procedimiento consiste sencillamente en hacer protagonistas del drama vital los barrios bajos de la atención, lo que de ordinario desatendemos...[33]

---

[30] José Ortega y Gasset, *Meditaciones del Quijote; Ideas sobre la novela* ([Madrid] Espasa-Calpe, Colección Austral [1964]), p. 159. Actually, in his «Prólogo casi doctrinal sobre la novela» to *La nave de los locos* (Madrid: Caro Raggio, 1925), Baroja «replies» to the «fórmulas del ensayista» (Ortega's) regarding the novel.

[31] *Ibid.,* p. 206.

[32] *Ibid.,* p. 167.

[33] José Ortega y Gasset, *La deshumanización del arte* (Madrid: Revista de Occidente, 9.ª ed. [1967]), pp. 48-49. Cf. Guillermo de Torre, *Problemática de la literatura* (Buenos Aires: Losada [1958]), p. 71: «más exacto que hablar de deshumanización hubiera sido hablar de antirrealismo o desrealización. El vocablo 'deshumanizado', por no sé qué desliz asociativo mental, parece aludir

How can one turn the «outskirts of attention» into the protagonists? By directing the reader's attention, through a novelistic technique, not merely to the trivial among human actions (Ortega has advocated this) but to areas beyond ordinary human awareness, in other words, to the realm of the inanimate. Is this not contradictory to Ortega's requirement of the human element in the novel? After all, is this not what Ortega is describing as «dehumanization»? Apparently so, and it will be a point of controversy in any attempt to classify Ramón's «novels» as novels according to the theories we have been summarizing, including Frye's. But a great deal more needs to be discussed before one can reach a final conclusion.

Taking up the question of the novel where Ortega y Gasset left it, Francisco Ayala makes many incisive observations on its various aspects. He begins by stating that a work of literary art, by virtue of being made of language, is always forced to «say something» that goes beyond its aesthetic intent. If Góngora, that prodigy of literary immanence, seems ultimately trivial, «¿qué no ocurrirá con menos afortunados y más radicales experimentos vanguardistas como la escritura automática o las palabras en libertad? Se trata de destruir el idioma como instrumento discursivo...»[34] (These are, by the way, techniques closely related to the *greguería*.) Ayala defines the literary work of art, or poem, as «una configuración de lenguaje imaginario» which «alude por necesidad a un concreto acontecer en el tiempo... Podrá ser enteramente ficticio ese contenido, pero no por serlo dejará de presentar la realidad histórica de un ser humano viviendo en tensión temporal».[35] And yet, as language, the common property of the members of a culture, transcends the aesthetic intent of an individual, that individual attempts to surpass his mortal condition through the very individuality of his art. The poem is a world by itself, «un ámbito cerrado en sí mismo, pese a cuantas referencias al mundo exterior sean indispensables», among which is the language in which it is written, a system of «significaciones convencionales... De otro modo, se nos escaparían aquellas resonancias que responden a la experiencia colectiva y modulan una idiosincrasia».[36]

If the writer removes his language too far from the conventional, it will, like a foreign language, become unintelligible. In that separate world of poetic fiction, mimesis takes place, not a «copia fiel de los aspectos sensibles de la realidad, sino reproducción creativa de ésta en la esfera

al sujeto, al artista, no al objeto, la obra en sí. Habría sido, pues, nada superfluo aclarar —evitándose ociosas polémicas— que lo deshumanizado en aquellas obras —valederas por sí mismas, y no solamente como síntomas de un estado espiritual— no era el artista, sino la materia artística con que manipulaba.»

[34] FRANCISCO AYALA, *Reflexiones sobre la estructura narrativa* (Madrid: Taurus, 1970), pp. 9-10.

[35] *Ibid.*, pp. 11-13.

[36] *Ibid.*, pp. 18-20.

15

de lo imaginario».[37] Here we have a «new» or «rival» reality to seduce the reader, just as Ortega recommended. How is it to be created? Through a verbal structure, says Ayala. «A la estructura de la obra literaria... pertenece esencialmente un sujeto que habla: el poeta», but «la configuración de lenguaje en que la obra está realizada lo absorbe, integrándolo... en el mundo imaginario donde funcionará como elemento capital de su estructura».[38] Every original writer injects himself into his work, taking such a basic position within the narrative structure that the same story told by a different writer would be actually another story. This aspect of contemporary literary theory has a direct bearing on what, conventionally, we have called style, and in a work of prose fiction it fluctuates most often between structure and characterization. «La presencia del autor ficcionalizado en el cuerpo de la obra de arte literaria puede manifestarse», according to Ayala, in «la figura de un personaje dado dentro de la trama, personaje secundario quizá, casi siempre el protagonista»;[39] there are many possibilities, including that of an omniscient, godlike narrator. And, however tenuously, every poem tells a story, Ayala says, and «argumento y forma han de ponerse en juego para dar la expresión más idónea a las intuiciones del poeta, y éstas serán originales si consiguen, mediante recursos expresivos utilizados, manifestar la índole única de su visión del mundo».[40] Finally, just as Ortega had argued that «la novela ha de ser hoy lo contrario que el cuento»,[41] Ayala submits that this is in fact how it is, due to a difference in structure, thought by the master to be «lo más hondo de... toda creación artística».[42] How does the structure of the novel differ essentially from that of the tale? Although he regards every literary work of art as an «ámbito cerrado» (and those are also Ortega's words[43]), Ayala considers the structure of the tale closed and that of the novel open. He says in effect:

> Quizá la diferencia de enfoques... (enfoque sobre situación o caso, o bien enfoque sobre la vida humana individual en cuanto proceso abierto hacia el futuro) pueda servirnos para intentar una distinción de principio entre el cuento y la novela, capaz de superar el criterio de la longitud del relato, demasiado mecánico y a todas luces insatisfactorio...
> Atenidos a aquella distinción, podríamos buscar el origen del cuento... en los relatos míticos que expresan la perplejidad frente a las vislumbres numínicas, mientras que la novela derivaría de otro tipo de relatos primitivos: los que, con valor de paradigmas, establecen la trayectoria y el destino de dioses y héroes, dando lugar a la epopeya. En la práctica (y tal

[37] *Ibid.*
[38] *Ibid.*, pp. 20-22.
[39] *Ibid.*, pp. 27-28.
[40] *Ibid.*, p. 57.
[41] *Ideas sobre la novela*, p. 169.
[42] *Ibid.*, p. 181.
[43] *Ibid.*, p. 200.

vez desde el comienzo) ambos modos de relato aparecen combinados, pero
si se les aplica el principio ordenador propuesto resultará posible desextri-
carlos...[44]

While I agree that length is not a suitable criterion for defining the novel,
it is obvious that it furthers its possibilities; I refuse, however, to be led
astray in the consideration of additional subgenres, such as the novella
and the novelette. There is in Ayala, as in Frye, a view that continuous
fiction is a mixed form; but this emphasis is on structure: the tale has
a closed structure and is associated with the enigmatic; the novel has
an open structure and is associated with the paradigmatic. Furthermore,
a novel may contain one or more tales within itself. With respect to
characterization, where, according to Frye, the difference lies between
the novel and the romance, Ayala observes that in a tale or short story,
«los personajes que entran en esa estructura no tendrán otra significación
que la que ella les presta, ni más entidad que la necesaria para servir de
soporte a la intuición de aquel misterio».[45] Hence one can infer that in
the writing of fiction, according to Ayala, intent determines structure
and structure directly affects characterization; there is no need to concern oneself with subject-matter and sources, for there are really only
two forms of fiction: the novel and the tale.

There is for us, however, a further question about the open structure
of the novel itself. To consider it, I will begin where two other critics of
the novel join hands. Ramón Fernández, certainly one of the most subtle
literary critics of the first half of this century, in his collection of essays
entitled *Messages* submits a critical method («philosophic criticism») for
studying «the philosophic substructure of a work», that is, «the body of
ideas which, organized by a hypothesis, supplies an explanation of the
essential characters of that work by relating them to the problems of
general philosophy which may be implied by them».[46] This method is
justified by the belief that «aesthetics must be an imaginative ontology».[47]
Fernández refers to the aesthetics of the novel at the time of his writing
(1926) as «still very confused», and embarks on a study of Balzac by
distinguishing between the novel and the recital *(récit)* which, he says,
«are interchangeable as to their object», but differ radically in their
methods. «The novel is the *representation* of events which *take* place in
time, a representation submitted to the conditions of apparition and
development of these events. The recital», on the other hand, «is the
*presentation* of events which *have taken* place, and of which the repro-

---

[44] *Reflexiones sobre la estructura narrativa*, pp. 69-70.
[45] *Ibid.*, p. 67.
[46] RAMÓN FERNÁNDEZ, *Messages*, trans. Montgomery Belgion (New York: Harcourt, Brace [1927]), p. 15.
[47] *Ibid.*, p. 7.

duction is regulated by the narrator in conformity with the laws of ex-
position and persuasion».[48] Thus «the recital is ordered around a past
and the novel in a present not verbal but psychological».[49] Fernández
substantiates his thesis with convincing examples that explain why the
novel is, curiously enough, difficult to define and yet easy to recognize:
«the linking-up of the sensory and psychological representations is not
dependent upon reasoning or an order of production other than that of
life, and... the characters are... seized by a kind of intuition analogous
to that whereby we are put into relation with living individuals».[50]

By applying what Fernández says about the recital to the period novel,
Edwin Muir comes into at least partial agreement with him in an approach
which brings all forms of continuous prose fiction essentially under the
generic term *novel*. In the book entitled *The Structure of the Novel,* he
offers this breakdown of the genre: (1) the novel of action, in which
«the characters are designed to fit the plot», (2) the novel of character,
in which «the plot is improvised to elucidate the characters», (3) the
dramatic novel, in which the characters and the plot «are inseparably
knit together», (4) the chronicle, in which «human life is not set against
fate or society, but against human life in perpetual change», (5) the period
novel, in which «society is essentially an abstract conception, not an
imaginative reality», and (6) the novel of later development (particularly
James Joyce and Virginia Woolf), which is «more in the pure aesthetic
tradition of prose fiction than the work of the preceding generation»,
taking its «development from an earlier and traditional form».[51] The
foregoing divisions all correspond to differences in structure, since it
happens that the same structure cannot contain what the differences
entail; in other words, each type of novel must have a different structure.
Not unlike Frye, Muir admits that «there are of course no novels purely
of character or merely of conflict; there are only novels which are pre-
dominantly the one or the other». But he unequivocally states: «This
predominance, however, is always salient and always sufficient.»[52] And
not unlike Ayala, he recognizes that, although not exclusively consisting
of it, the novel (like any other literary work) has a plot, and one can
infer from Muir that the plot precisely is the key to its structure. «To
say that a plot is spatial does not deny a temporal movement to it», he

[48] *Ibid.*, p. 63; italics mine.
[49] *Ibid.*, pp. 63-64.
[50] *Ibid.*, p. 69.
[51] EDWIN MUIR, *The Structure of the Novel* (New York, 1929). I quote from
the Harcourt, Brace and World (Harbinger Book) edition [n.d.], pp. 27, 29, 41, 97,
122, and 133, respectively. Although it was meant partially as a view contrary
to E. M. FORSTER'S *Aspects of the Novel*, Muir's book is an interesting treatment
of the different types of novel enumerated above, particularly with respect to
the structural effects of time and space.
[52] *Ibid.*, p. 62.

explains, «any more, indeed, than to say that a plot is temporal means that it has no setting in space. Here, once more, it is all a question of the predominating element».[53] As a summary example, Muir submits that «if the sphere of the character novel is space, the sphere of the dramatic novel time, then, so it has been suggested, that of *Ulysses* is a sort of space-time».[54] This is a most illuminating insight into the nature of prose fiction, for it is on that basis and no other that the modern novel can be judiciously scrutinized in its complete aesthetic fulfillment.[55]

Fernández's description of the novel as a narrative that takes place in a psychological present time, and Muir's differentiation between temporal and spatial novelistic structures together can lead us directly into the question of the novel's presumed openness. We have seen that Ayala suggests a distinction between the tale and the novel on the basis of closed and open structures, regarding the first as the narration of an anecdote, the second as that of life as a process open to the future. Now, the existence of this future-oriented life process can be appreciated only if one employs criteria such as Fernández's psychological present and Muir's symbolic space-time continuum, of which the former is a most peculiar fourth dimension, a dimension of fictional openness that a later critic of the genre, Alan Friedman, attributes solely to the twentieth-century novel. There is no doubt that instead of an absolute openness of the novel in general as opposed to the absolute closedness of the tale, suggested by Ayala, it is now a question of a sort of «relative» openness —the closing of the narrative and the unclosing of its illusion— which is consciously achieved through modern novelistic devices. This is how Friedman begins his criticism of the post-Jamesian novel:

> The traditional premise about the design of experience which was profoundly, if variously, embodied in the eighteenth and nineteenth-century novel, was the premise of a closed experience... Modern novelists turned to create experiences that promised from the outset, threatened all along, and finally did indeed come to an end while remaining still unchecked —in extreme cases, still expanding...
> ... the seeds of change... were carried across national and literary boundaries. Gide's *The Counterfeiters,* Verga's early *The House by the Medlar Tree,* Kafka's *The Trial,* Mann's *The Magic Mountain* —any of these might serve to illustrate the formal openness of experience in fiction.[56]

---

[53] *Ibid.,* p. 64.
[54] *Ibid.,* p. 126.
[55] This notion of spatial as well as temporal development is of the greatest importance for the study of modern literature, as has been subsequently explained by JOSEPH FRANK («Spatial Form in Modern Literature», *Sewanee Review,* LIII [1945], 221-40; 433-56; 643-53), among others.
[56] ALAN FRIEDMAN, *The Turn of the Novel: The Transition to Modern Fiction* (New York: Oxford University Press [1970]), pp. xi-xii.

The critical view is enlightening. Once again, one can only regret that an otherwise well-informed, intelligent critic does not, or cannot, bring Spanish examples to bear on such important literary problems (particularly in a case such as this, since Ramón's *El novelista,* so similar to Gide's book, precedes it by three years). Friedman accepts the novel as a genre, a genre having the «ability to depict not only the exterior world of action, but the interior world of character —and one crucial thing more, the relation between them».[57] And the novel, he tells us, has a structure, which constitutes its organization of experience; a structure, furthermore, which «is always and only in motion», in other words, «a flow, a journey, a process».[58] Chapters later, he continues: «in certain extreme cases —Lawrence, Joyce, Faulkner, and beyond— the expanding process of conscience remains not merely unclosed but unclosable»,[59] because life is an open experience and, if the novel is to really reflect life ethically as well as aesthetically, the novel must be also an open experience.

How is such a feat performed? In fact, how has it been performed in every great novel which, in one way or another, anticipated the new tradition? First of all, I would say, by the installation of a motor-force within the novelistic structure, which Friedman has characterized as constantly and inevitably moving. That force precedes all conscious invention such as situation, character, or intrigue; it comes from the fictionalization of the author himself, as Ayala has pointed out, an act that will make him an essential factor in the structure of his narrative. This presence of the author in his work has various facets and has been the object of different attitudes throughout literary history. Percy Lubbock, in a study which deals mostly with Henry James, states that «the art of fiction does not begin until the novelist thinks of his story as a matter to be shown, to be so exhibited that it will tell itself».[60] He is undoubtedly correct, insofar as the direction of the narrative needs to acquire a certain autonomy, but the story is obviously not going to *write* itself and as long as he is writing it, the novelist is not only going to have something to say about it, he is going to be saying it. How much he actually *says* and how he does it is, of course, of the utmost importance. Complete authorial objectivity is impossible since, as Wayne C. Booth points out, the very «act of narration as performed by even the most highly dramatized narrator is itself the author's presentation...». Characters? «The author is present in every speech given by any char-

[57] *Ibid.,* p. xiv.
[58] *Ibid.,* pp. xv-xvi. See also ALBERT S. COOK, *The Meaning of Fiction* (Detroit: Wayne State University Press, 1960).
[59] *Ibid.,* pp. 184-85.
[60] PERCY LUBBOCK, *The Craft of Fiction* (London, 1921). I quote from the Viking Press Compass Book edition [1957], p. 62.

acter...» Style? «Every recognizably personal touch, every distinctive literary allusion or colorful metaphor, every pattern of myth or symbol; thay all implicitly evaluate..., they are imposed by the author.» In short, «though the author can to some extent choose his disguises, he can never choose to disappear».[61] Thus the author of a work or works will always be the same (insofar as a human being in the process of living can ever be the same), but that same author will never be «the same» with respect to his work or works or, most especially, *in* his work. This «implied author», to use Booth's term, the variously fictionalized versions of the real author will oscillate between the demands of his narrative and the propensities of his personality. Although he ultimately rejects the equation, Booth admits that, broadly speaking, the terms *style, tone,* and *technique* «are sometimes used to name the core of norms and choices» which he calls the «implied author».[62] Realizing, like Ortega and Ayala, that the reader also undergoes a certain «fictionalization» and hence must establish a relationship with the narrator, Booth proposes the term «subplot» for the story of that relationship; I in turn will submit the term «substructure» for the function of that relationship, since without it the totality of the structure will never be realized. Needless to say, exactly what the structure and the substructure are will depend aesthetically on the author alone; how near or how far he wants to appear in the course of his narrative, that is, how much he wishes to «intrude» is his right and privilege, which has a great deal to do with the element of autobiography in fiction.

As we have seen, Frye makes autobiography or confession one of his four divisions of continuous prose fiction, but for him prose fiction is, except very rarely, a mixed form. For Ayala, literature, broadly speaking, is autobiographical since «la operación actual de producirla... se cumple a base de fragmentos de la experiencia viva del autor...».[63] Which means that autobiography does not have to be the record of a life already lived but a manifestation of a life in the process of being lived. And, as we have already surveyed, not only is life a process but the novel is a process too, so that the parallel can be carried over to the life of the author, both the implied and the real author. The autobiographical element in the new mixed form of prose fiction, that is, in the new novel, has sought and found more subtle modalities than the straight confession and the direct commentary. The result has been a devious and imaginative kind of personalization or stylization attained by means of complex structural devices. Different as Joyce and Ramón are, for example, their life experience with language in the act of literary creation and recreation

---

[61] BOOTH, *The Rhetoric...*, pp. 18, 19, 20, respectively.
[62] *Ibid.*, p. 74.
[63] FRANCISCO AYALA, *Reflexiones...*, p. 14.

is a constant reminder to the reader of the author's presence and power. In Ramón's case it might be more than that, for reasons of life style and method of composition. He himself admits an autobiographical content as such in many of his novels; rather humorously, he asserts that «autobiografía hay... en 'El novelista', en 'El Secreto del Acueducto', en 'La Mujer de Ambar', en 'La Viuda Blanca y Negra', en 'La Nardo', en 'La Quinta de Palmira', en 'El Gran Hotel', warning the inquisitive reader, futhermore, that in all his other books «también hay algo autobiográfico» and invites him to read them all so that he can have the total picture of the author's life.[64] Since the statement appears in *Automoribundia,* one must assume such to be the main autobiographical stream, of which all the others are tributaries. Sister M. Albert Mazzetti believes that *Automoribundia* «provided a frame of reference by which to measure his other works»[65] of biographic intent. In this respect, I find her judgment indisputable. Moreover, Ramón's entire literary production is, in the strictest sense of the word, personal. His novels are just as much a reflection of his personality and his life as his autobiography. But, by the very nature of their «genre», that is, the intent of the author and the disposition of the linguistic materials of which the works consist, the novels posses a greater autonomy, as it were, a greater imaginary dimension: no historical facts need to be consciously preserved, omitted, or distorted.

Both Frye and Friedman have suggested that the novel of the old English tradition ended with James; the corresponding Spanish tradition probably ended with Unamuno. (Of course, there is no equivalent of James in Spanish, just as there is no equivalent of Unamuno in English.) The Generation of 1898 was, ultimately, a heterogeneous group of ideological writers primarily concerned with a bankrupt system of social and political values; even their metaphysical preoccupations stem largely from their cultural disillusion, a sort of nineteenth-century *engagement.* This is not to take away their literary originality, and certainly the group includes such an aesthete as Valle-Inclán. My point is that simply as «literature», they did not take to the writer's activity as did later individuals in conscious or unconscious agreements with the literary tenets of, say, a Mallarmé. Hence in contrast, after a youthful and brief revolutionary period, Ramón's deepest concern, and what he thought the only way for a writer to make his true contribution, was to devote himself to the one thing he really knew how to do, and that was simply to write, an activity which enabled him to achieve, aesthetically at least, the highest fruition of personal reality. With him and others began, if I am not mistaken, a new narrative technique described by Juan Luis Alborg as «vuel-

[64] RAMÓN GÓMEZ DE LA SERNA, *Automoribundia,* p. 11.
[65] Sister M. ALBERT MAZZETTI, p. 3.

ta de espaldas al mundo y encarada hacia el propio 'yo', más preocupada por vaciar la personalidad del autor que por capturar hechos externos, más dedicada al 'cómo' que al 'qué'...».[66] The same critic quotes the Hungarian novelist Manes Sperber, who marvels at the paradox of the contemporary writer's ability to interest a reader in a book that seems basically written for himself, a phenomenon which he describes as «universal intimacy». And Alborg ends with this comment:

> Creo que éste es el secreto de lo que debe ser una novela de hoy después de su liberación de lo anecdótico, a manos del reportaje visto o escrito. La *intimidad universal* ya no producirá las grandes creaciones de la novela popular de tiempos pasados, pero será capaz de darnos, en cambio, ese libro donde en torno al eje de una acción, siempre indispensable, podrán darse cita la gracia literaria y el calor entrañable de un ser humano que de modo más íntimo, más eficaz y gustoso que en la obra de puro contenido intelectual, se manifiesta en la belleza de la ficción.[67]

That the whole of this statement can apply to Ramón is debatable, I realize. Having started writing while still so young, he is an anomaly that cannot be easily compared with the Spanish writers of the succeeding generations except retroactively. Thus it may be said that he anticipated certain themes and techniques much in vogue today, though he would never allow himself to become involved socially or politically in his novels. Neither did he abandon his pseudo-fantastic subject matter, induced by his search for the 'para-real', in order to arrive at a neo-realism à la Sánchez Ferlosio, for example. It is interesting to note that Ramón has such novels as *El turco de los nardos* (which takes place in Buenos Aires) and *Piso bajo* (which takes place in Madrid), where a more or less conventional structure seems to emerge. But the true norms of his novelistic technique lie elsewhere.

It would be extremely difficult and, for my purpose, not sufficiently useful to include all of Ramón's novels in this survey. Consequently, I have chosen to study at some length the four which he personally considered his «gregueristically» normative works of prose fiction. He called them «novelas de la nebulosa», and they bear the following titles: *El Incongruente* (1922), *El novelista* (1923), *¡Rebeca!* (1936), and *El hombre*

---

[66] JUAN LUIS ALBORG, p. 55. Alborg does not actually take Ramón into account in this evolution of the Spanish novel; his survey is quite contemporary and begins with Camilo José Cela. In a much less important work (AGUSTÍN DEL SAZ, *Novelistas españoles* [Barcelona-Buenos Aires: Librería Editorial Argos (1952)], p. 58), we find the following meagre consideration: «llegamos al novecentismo cuya cronología, en realidad, no comienza hasta 1918 con la crisis de la primera guerra mundial de este siglo. Hacen concesiones a los vanguardismos Valle-Inclán y Azorín; pero se consideran iniciadores y cultivadores consagrados de las nuevas formas novelísticas a Benjamín Jarnés (1888-1949) hacia la novela poemática como 'Paula y Paulita' (1929); y a Ramón Gómez de la Serna (nacido en 1891) con la novela humorística como 'Gran Hotel.'»

[67] *Ibid.*, pp. 77-78.

*perdido* (1947). It is strange that the critic who has a very accurate, though too brief, description of Ramón's narrative technique does not mention any of these works. Juan Chabás, in effect, says:

> ¿Es Ramón Gómez de la Serna un novelista? Nadie que dude ante esta pregunta podrá dejar de reconocer que, buenas o malas, definibles o no como formas genéricas acabadas, Ramón ha escrito múltiples novelas...
>
> Las novelas de Ramón... nacen de una greguería, que prolifera y se desenvuelve en varias anécdotas en torno al núcleo central..., o bien, crecen desde una pequeña narración hasta el abultado tamaño de la novela grande, no por interna pujanza de desarrollo, sino porque Ramón comienza a tirar del tema y de la anécdota como el prestidigitador que saca de su boca innumerables metros de cinta; es un procedimiento reiterativo, acumulativo, que a veces le da a Ramón felices resultados, gracias a su ingenio sagacísimo.[68]

Although it may turn out that everything Ramón ever wrote should be regarded as undifferentiated prose fiction, if we accept Frye's larger term, I shall endeavor to consider the four works listed above as belonging to that troublesome genre, the novel. Now, after a rambling investigation,[69] what can I concretely say about it? That it is written in prose, extended to an indefinite length, and conceived as fiction can be taken for granted. In his introduction to one of the best collections available on the subject, Philip Stevick says of the novel that

> Traditionally, it is flexible and indeterminate in its form... With a genre so eclectic and various as to include *Emma*, *Moby Dick*, and *Malone Dies*... the demands that theoretical criticism be appropriately flexible are so considerable as almost to inhibit theory altogether.[70]

A Hispanist would have to think of a gamut that includes *La gaviota*, *Fortunata y Jacinta*, and *Rayuela*, to take just three examples. For my purpose, I will use the following «practical description» of the genre, aimed at the idea of novelistic structure: a narrative based on the invention of character which unfolds as the author continues to become aware of its possibilities of independence, as it were, from himself. This most important aspect of a dual control technique seldom has been pointed out when speaking in such vague terms as «character development». It means that in writing a novel, the success of the author *as a novelist*

---

[68] JUAN CHABÁS, *Literatura española contemporánea, 1898-1950*, p. 389.

[69] The important works on the theory and practice of the novel are, of course, numerous and obviously I could not bring them all to bear on the present discussion; many are included in the bibliography and further references to those mentioned so far and to others can be found in the remainder of this study.

[70] PHILIP STEVICK (ed.), *The Theory of the Novel* (New York: The Free Press [1968]), p. 2.

will depend on his ability to invent *at least one character* and on his ability to discover that *character's possibilities of autonomous behavior.* The relative degrees to which these abilities are applied in a given novel will determine its structure. Beyond that, there is little doubt in my mind that the novel *sub specie aeternitatis* will continue to resist definition.

## II

## *EL INCONGRUENTE,* OR THE IMAGE OF DESTINY

As early as 1924 Ramón complained in print that «de *El Incongruente* nadie ha dicho una palabra».[1] Since then, however, critics have variously judged the work and even have classified it. With respect to its content, it has been called «la novela del donjuanismo»;[2] with respect to its technique, it has been assessed as «an abortive attempt at a surrealist novel».[3] In my estimation, neither is the first statement warranted by the mere inclusion of frequent amorous adventures in the story, nor is the second statement accurate with reference to the poetic and humorous aspects of its presentation.

As a novelistic structure, *El Incongruente* is sustained sometimes by a tenuous story line, sometimes by a bare yet basic theme, but always by the image of the protagonist, whose name is simply Gustavo, occasionally given the epithet of the Misfit. Gustavo, the narrator tells us, is «un caso agravado del mal del siglo, de la incongruencia».[4] This is, in effect, the aspect of modern life that Ramón, as in his aphorisms, wishes to emphasize. The structure, the central theme, and some of the characteristic and circumstantial details have at least an apparent basis in previous works of literature. Like *Lazarillo de Tormes, El Incongruente* begins and ends with peculiar arbitrariness; it begins with a reference to the incongruous circumstances of the protagonist's birth and ends with his absurd marriage. The element of chance that permeates the story, when regarded as positive, as it could be in the comparatively carefree time when it was written, becomes that of fate or destiny, and the humor can envelop even that: Gustavo «se fue a casar a los diez y ocho años; pero no se

---

[1] *Pombo II*, p. 507.

[2] GUILLERMO DE TORRE, preface to R. GÓMEZ DE LA SERNA, *Cincuenta años de vida literaria,* p. 22. The fact that the protagonist of the story is on one occasion mistaken for a «señorito Juan» is as meagre textual support of this opinion as any.

[3] PAUL ILIE, *The Surrealist Mode in Spanish Literature* (Ann Arbor: The University of Michigan Press [1968]), p. 156.

[4] RAMÓN GÓMEZ DE LA SERNA, *El Incongruente* (Buenos Aires: Editorial Losada, Biblioteca Contemporánea [1947]), p. 10. Henceforth, all quotations are from this edition.

casó porque en el descorchen del *champagne* mató a su suegro con el corcho de una botella y la novia se negó a dormir ni una sola noche con el asesino de su padre» (p. 15). But Gustavo the Misfit is neither a poor servant boy nor a blind man; he is a *señorito* without profession or obligations; his parents, to whom reference is made early, do not actually figure in the story, which is reminiscent of Unamuno's *Niebla,* and the girl who makes the deepest impression on Gustavo but whom he does not marry is, like the beautiful jilt that haunts Augusto Pérez, a piano teacher (incidentally, Gustavo is a near-anagram of Augusto). Yet, while *Niebla* (1914) is, in the simplest terms, a sad story, *El Incongruente* (1922) is a happy one; both are «experimental» novels for their respective authors.

The nine «movements» made up of groups of chapters in the narrative are the following:

1.   (Chapters I-II) Family background and delineation of the protagonist's nature. He is «predisposed» to the absurd. However, he is also imaginative: «Una de las cosas que tenía costumbre de inventar de pequeño es que él era Periquito...» (p. 9), which is significant to the whole narrative because, at the end, he again has the notion of being like someone else. Almost from the beginning we are told that «Gustavo veía ya la vida con tranquilidad, pues se hallaba conforme con su destino. ¡Qué lo iba a hacer!» (p. 13). But Gustavo is not just the resigned victim of incongruity, he also thinks incongruities, a fair sample of which is found in the second chapter; these are, of course, gregueristic aphorisms jotted down in his «gran libro *Mayor*» (p. 20), in a manner analogous to Ramón's own method of composition.

2.   (Chapters III-IV) Contemporaneous adventures and juvenilia which «characterize» Gustavo's incongruous life. It affords good opportunities for the author to exercise his humor and fancy as well as interesting new approaches to narrative technique, details of which have been ignored by previous critics. The third chapter, entitled «La llamada», which reveals that Gustavo is sought by women at least as much as he seeks them, opens thus: «Le llamó por el balcón aquella señora» (p. 21), with a gratuitous slur in the form of the demonstrative adjective where one would expect the indefinite article. Such idiomatic manipulation, also found in the aphorisms, is quite frequent in *El Incongruente* and anticipates perhaps less whimsical analogues in contemporary fiction like, for example, Carlos Fuentes's *Aura.* Also like his aphorisms, Ramón's narrative is rich in suggestions, especially when playing upon reality, happiness or eroticism, as it does frequently. There is no sight «más inesperado, más incongruente, más grato» (p. 23) than the eyes of a beautiful woman on the other side of the peephole in a door. What we have here, of course, is something not unlike Ramón's aphorisms; after all it

27

is a gregueristic image, but it is deeply injected into the narrative; it is not merely a superficial adjunct. We begin to see that Gustavo is something like the personification of the *greguería,* a walking incongruity that transforms reality with his very presence. Gustavo «lo sospechaba todo y lo temía todo»; the door opens and a blonde appears: «¿Rubia, cuando la asomada que le había llamado por el balcón era completamente morena? No era la misma. Ni era aquél el piso. Aquélla era una aventura distinta de la primera.» The only safe place for such a rendezvous is the stairwell, a place absurdly nonexistent: «El se sentía fuera del mundo en aquel margen de la vida» (p. 24); thus we find here an early suggestion of what Ramón would develop into his humorous ontology. There is also a fictional parallel of the principle of the *greguería,* the now familiar Ramonesque problem of the instability of being: «Sentía... la maravillosa delectación que sentiría el del nicho de abajo si recibiese viva y besuqueadora a la mujer besuqueadora del nicho de arriba.» Ramón is not exploring surrealistic techniques; his path is that of humor and fantasy. Discovered with the blonde by her husband, he is immediately exonerated by virtue of its happening in the limbo of the stairwell.

3. (Chapters V-XIV) A rich variety of episodes, mostly of a fantastic nature, such as particularly to justify Ilie's inclusion of *El Incongruente* among what he calls «intellectual fairy tales».[5] The chapter titles are thus indicative: «En el salón de los figurines», «La casa predilecta», «Aquella Nochebuena», «La cacería», «El baile de máscaras», «El peón perdido», «La impaciencia», «¿Un Velázquez? ¿Un Leonardo?», «Detrás de los decorados de teatro», «La lluvia torrencial». Highlights of these are the following: the image of gratuitous movement («iba descartando sitios», page 31), the anticipation of the epithetical protagonist of another novel (the Lost Man —«se escapó por la noche oscura, alejándose de su casa, yendo no se sabía por dónde, porque de frac era un hombre perdido», page 32), and the constant theme of encounter and surprise, including the incongruous, as a possible source of happiness (it should prove interesting, in the proper place, to study carefully Ramón's notions of eudaemonics).

4. Chapters XV-XXII) The first group of chapters which has a truly narrative, not merely thematic or imagistic, continuity. At the beginning of this movement —in the chapter «El día optimista»— Gustavo awakes to the song of a mechanical bird, demonstrating both an infantile aspect of Ramón's imagination and a mechanistic factor in his world of ob:ects. A sudden doubt in the mind of the protagonist: «la incongruencia hará que el día más feliz de mi vida esté vacío de acontecimientos» (p. 73). But the feeling of happiness overcomes his apprehension; in fact he goes

[5] ILIE, p. 152.

to have his picture taken in order to capture his look of *felicidad*. In the next chapter, he goes back to the photographer's studio to see the proofs and, to his amazement, finds that in the photograph, at the other end of the divan where he posed, there appears an unknown girl. How did it happen? The same plate was used somehow to take their pictures at different times, and yet «resultaron los dos como retratados al mismo tiempo» (p. 81). Who is she? «Una señorita pianista... Vive con su mamá.» As much as he would like actually to meet this woman, Gustavo decides that her circumstances are such that «era inútil probar la aventura... Siempre sería curiosa aquella fotografía en la que resultaría retratado con la que no conoció nunca» (curiously enough, unless taken in the Biblical sense, the verb phrase will prove inadequate when referred to the thirty-second chapter).

5. (Chapters XVIII-XIX) Episodes closely associated by the amatory theme. The use of the pun in the aphorisms is operative here too: Gustavo receives a telegram from a widow in Segovia (cf. *El secreto del acueducto*) inviting him to stay with her; she ambiguously signs her name Socorro (p. 84). The woman indulges in gregueristic language («Hoy ha amanecido el día nevado de minutos... Tengo la cabeza llena de segundos...»), a habit which disquiets even Gustavo. Finally he learns how it happened that she sent him the telegram: she picked out his name from the telephone directory moving her finger down the list with her eyes closed; Gustavo feels cheated and suddenly leaves his fortuitous paramour. Sunday —Gustavo feels— is like a temporal cage with chance locked out. «Los objetos de su cuarto estaban más quietos e inmóviles que nunca, pasando su domingo en un mayor descanso que el de los otros días» (p. 88). Suddenly there is a ring at the door: it is a maid on her day off who somehow felt that she must comfort him. «La besó, encontrando el sabor de la carne cruda, carne de 'falda'» (page 89), an example of Ramón's humorous sensualism found in all his works, particularly in *Senos* and *El chalet de las rosas*.

6. (Chapters XX-XXV) Another group of chapters joined together, partly by narrative continuity, partly by imagistic devices. During a traffic congestion (in 1922!) Gustavo sees a woman riding in an automobile: «la mujer del traje de *charmeuse* negro» (p. 91; again the gratuitous reference, this time by using the definite article); she offers to take him to his house and, after he gets out of the car, he notices on the door a coat-of-arms. Gustavo goes to an expert in heraldry in order to identify it, for he feels as if he has been run over not by the woman's car but by her beauty. He is offered an introduction to the lady's house by the son of her husband's tailor. The lady rejects Gustavo's attentions, and he is so humiliated that he decides to leave town by the quickest means possible, which he considers to be a motorcycle. Thought leads to action, but he neglects to find out how to stop the

machine: «se dirigía sola a alguna parte, con un sobre cerrado del Destino en su cartera» (p. 101; those were still the days when special delivery letters were brought on such a vehicle). The motorcycle finally runs out of gas (?) as he arrives in a strange town, whose description once again demonstrates Ramón's range of fantasy and is an unintentional analogue of his narrative technique: «aquella profusión de espejos en los balcones parecía dejar más solitarias las casas, pues así rechazaban toda intimidad, toda profundización, todo secreto...» (p. 102). Finally someone appears, the «Intérprete Único», who informs him that he is in the city of the wax dolls. Gustavo has always wanted to marry a wax doll (it is interesting to remember that Ramón actually had a life-size wax doll imported from Paris, which he kept in his study; see *Pombo II,* pp. 530-31, and *Automoribundia,* plate IV), and the «interpreter» offers to introduce him to the local beauty queen. The doll speaks; the «interpreter» explains that they all speak because they are not exactly wax dolls but wax women, whom one meets just before they turn into dolls. She accepts Gustavo's marriage proposal, but Ramón actually offers a parable here: an exchange of individual resignations that neutralizes, on the one hand, the ravages of time and, on the other, the incapacity for physical love; aesthetics is all and this is as profound as Ramón gets. Gustavo goes home to make arrangements for his marriage («partió por los caminos desconocidos, tardando mucho en dar con el camino de la vida», p. 108), but afterwards he cannot find his way back to the city of the wax dolls, «teniendo al fin que desistir de volver a encontrar la más bella mujer del mundo» (p. 109). The twenty-fourth chapter —«Psicología de la moto»— includes a long list of greguerístic descriptions of a motorcycle. Still on his motorcycle, Gustavo comes upon «el pueblo alegre», which he enters like a champion racer being given a grand, bacchic reception. A boy offers to take Gustavo to his sister who, like everyone at home is playing the Gramophone (it is the age of the *Gramophone),* and man and woman go through the usual Ramonesque dialogue: «¡Así es que me querrá siempre!» she says; «Siempre», he agrees (p. 117). But before a wedding can take place, Gustavo realizes he has been a bit hasty, leaves an apologetic note of gratitude, and rides out of town on his motorcycle, until he arrives at a fishing village with secluded beaches, the perfect place to get away from destiny: «Allí estaba como al margen de su propia novela, pues sobre aquella cenefa arenosa del mundo, las cosas se neutralizaban» (p. 120); for a while Gustavo thinks he has escaped from incongruity but he soon realizes that he is on the «playa de los pisapapeles», where these objects possess a life of their own (Ramón himself collected paperweights; see *Automoribundia,* plate XXIII).

7. (Chapter XXVII «Sus sueños») Naturally, Gustavo's dreams are «incongruous», but not in the manner in which the subconscious is

usually approached. This constitutes the crux of Ilie's criticism of the book as an aborted piece of surrealism. Actually, these «dreams» are in some way an anticipation of the kind of vision now called psychedelic; for example, Gustavo's image often appears multiplied by six (p. 123). On the very year that *El Incongruente* and four other works by Ramón were published, he had a photograph made showing five views of him sitting at a table; it appeared in the magazine *Buen Humor* (see *Pombo II*, p. 489, and *Automoribundia*, plate II). There are, of course, women in Gustavo's dreams: they do not merely offer themselves to him, they offer him instant children. «Entre las prendas de su sueño había una que se repetía en los palacios, en las habitaciones particulares y hasta en los trenes, y era un armario de luna del que salían, por decirlo así, todas las aventuras» (p. 124). He dreams of being old and gradually becoming younger until he winds up a baby (cf. Otto Rank's theory of birth trauma and the unconscious desire to return to the womb): «acababa su vida en la hora precisa del final, por el revés, cuando volvía a perderse en el vientre materno para morir antes del parto.» In his subconscious, as modern psychology would put it, lay the secret of his being: «Había, como en su vida, en sus sueños muchas llamadas, porque el modo de atacar la incongruencia, lo que subvierte la lógica, es la llamada» (pp. 124-25), and those calls are from women who, naturally, represent life, and that is why, Guillermo de Torre notwithstanding, this is not really the story of Don Juan but that of the quest for the other half through the «natural» motivations that bring man and woman together.

8.   (Chapters XXVIII-XXXV) A third group of chapters which have a truly narrative continuity, although two of them (XXIX-XXX) are a sort of interpolation telling of an incident in court due to a false seduction suit brought by a girl and her mother. Not knowing why, Gustavo orders dinner for two from a restaurant and subsequently invites a widow living in the same building. Permission must be granted by her dead husband through spiritual means. In the course of the evening, the house mysteriously catches fire; the widow dies, but Gustavo obtains the attentive gratitude of two girls he saves. It is characteristic of Ramón's novel that it does not follow a logically explained course of events; the reader must supply whatever is actually needed to «complete» the narrative; for example, we find (as in a comic strip or movie cartoon) that in Chapter XXIX, «Citación del tribunal», Gustavo already lives in another apartment. The narrative in this interpolated chapter is unusually strengthened by an act of reasoning directed toward the future: «Mañana, no tendría más remedio que despertarse temprano. Colocó el despertador en hora y dio a la cuerda del timbre...» (p. 137); this is rare in the book, and the following chapter provides the court scene from which he emerges victorious, for he is not a habitual seducer: his

31

name (!) appeared in the indictment because it was probably given by an acquaintance who did not know he was on a vacation cruise at the time the crime was committed. «Gustavo respiró porque la Providencia que ayuda a los que son perseguidos por la incongruencia le había salvado una vez más» (p. 140). The author renews the action cut off by the interpolation; Gustavo has become the lover of a general's daughter whom he saved from the fire and is being pressured into marriage. His desire, however, is really for the other girl he saved, the nude who fainted and «a la que puso la tarjeta en la juntura de los senos, en el bolsillo ideal» (p. 141). When again he finds this beautiful girl with the beautiful breasts, he proposes to her, but she is fatally ill, and he must resign himself to marrying the general's daughter. On the day of the wedding, Gustavo thinks of not showing up, but the invited guests might pillage his apartment and the thought of his paintings turns him conservative. He wonders: «¿La incongruencia que perseguía su vida, no se acabaría con el matrimonio?» (p. 144). In the church, to his surprise and that of everyone else, it is suddenly apparent that there are two brides. The unexpected one is none other than the pianist who had mysteriously appeared in the photograph of chapter sixteen (the image reprise serves as an emphasizing device), and the question of choosing between the two women provides Gustavo with an excuse not to marry either and he leaves for Paris. On the train another reprise takes place; he recognizes «aquella rubia de su aventura en la caja de la escalera» (p. 149; see chapter three). He meets another widow and decides to court her. There is in the narrative some use of personification or Ruskin's «pathetic fallacy», so frequent in the aphorisms: «El vagón restaurant, que se compunge tanto cuando tocan a vaciarlo, estaba alegre... El tren avanzaba por sitios que se asombraban de ver el coche restaurant...» (p. 153). The widow spurns his marriage proposal and he goes on to Paris where, at the hotel, he finds a letter waiting for him from a dying friend of his father: «Gustavo tomó un automóvil y se fue por la película de los automóviles hacia la casa del agonizante» (p. 157). One could not wish for a better example of Ramón's awareness and use of imagery. The dying man wills his estate to Gustavo, an estate which mysteriously and subtly diminishes as the chapter ends, but there is enough for him to live a life of luxury and adventure in the French capital. At an art museum, Gustavo is mistaken for a man whose portrait hangs there and immediately afterward a woman takes him to her mansion and disrobes for him; he feels compelled to reveal that he is not the man in the portrait and, therefore, not a truly rich man: «Gustavo se fue atemorizado ante la ira de aquella mujer modelo de sombreros, de zapatos, de ropa interior, de trajes matinales, de trajes vesperales, de trajes fuera del tiempo y del espacio» (p. 164). Once again Gustavo is thwarted by something beyond his power, something represented by a woman but in effect an ideal suggesting Ramón's notion of the nebula.

9. (Chapters XXXVII-XLI). The action still takes place in Paris but the narrative sequence becomes more tenuous. This final movement includes a variety of episodes, from the morbid to the beautifully *cursi*. In his hotel room one night, Gustavo is relieved by having escaped from «aquellas mujeres casuales que, sin tener en cuenta que eran las mujeres casuales, querían ser sus mujeres para toda la vida. ¡Todo para toda la vida, cuando él era *el Incongruente!*» (p. 180). The retrospective device here is employed as a means of abridging the narrative. Gustavo decides to return to Madrid the next morning, «pues allí la velocidad de la incongruencia era menor». The notion of velocity is found frequently in Ramón and is of particular importance to his method of recording perceptions. Gustavo's attitude toward his problem is not simple: «si él se hacía acompañar siempre por gentes distintas; si él se prestaba a toda casualidad, era por evitar mayores complicaciones, para que hubiese testigos frente a toda incongruencia excesiva.» Here is an excellent manifestation of the whimsical irony that permeates Ramón's humor. Gustavo *is* a psychological abstract of his creator (cf. Ramón's reference above to autobiography in his novels): «Tenía un gran miedo de que se atreviese todo con él, ya que era el predestinado a soportar todos los atrevimientos de que están deseosas las cosas.» If Gustavo is a fictional counterpart of Ramón, their encounter with things takes the form of physical incongruity for the one and of imaginative association for the other. As Gustavo is about to fall asleep, two young women appear; no amorous threat, they are merely the «forgotten» actresses that dwell behind the curtains of hotel rooms, the stage-struck maidens, old before their time, who play their parts when no one is watching from *this* side of their unreal theater, brought into existence when the curtains have been drawn.

The last chapter, entitled «En el cinematógrafo, 'Ella' a su lado y el 'film' del Destino», must be considered separately and at length. Gustavo, despairing of what has been happening, goes to the movies: «se solía escapar de la incongruencia en la atmósfera muerta del *cine,* donde no sucede nada; el sitio vano, vago, engañoso, en que no hay acción ninguna, sino una especie de contemplación absurda» (p. 182). What happens in the movies is *expected* make-believe. Furthermore (according to Ramón's metaphorical perception of movement), Gustavo, in the movie house, feels as if he were on a means of locomotion (see chapter thirty-four: «la película de los automóviles»).

«De pronto apareció una película norteamericana, de la que era él el protagonista, él, con su mismo rostro, su misma expresión, todo lo mismo... ¿Cómo podía ser él aquel personaje de película, cuando nunca, ni en sueños, había pasado por aquellos parajes ni había reconocido a aquellas gentes?»

«Pero el caso es que, a medida que pasaba la película, se sentía más el mismo en el gran espejo» (p. 183). Gustavo thinks that the incongruity of his life has reached its climax; he feels like «el mártir de la incongruencia, algo así como el redentor de los pequeños incongruentes; el que, como hijo otra vez de Dios, iba a conseguir, gracias a la gravedad de sus incongruencias, el perdón de su padre y señor para todas las insignificantes incongruencias de los hombres». Serious humor and a metaphorical penchant have led to an association of the concepts of sin and incongruity, as it has been evident throughout the book that incongruity or chance is something from which one can suffer as well as derive pleasure. Despite the irreverent extreme of the analogy, it is clear that there is more to this work of Ramón's than a collection of ingenious and humorous metaphors; the moral content of the narrative, meagre though it is, has begun to emerge.

Gustavo wishes he could recognize the women in the movie, particularly his leading lady. The more he studies the situation, the more he becomes convinced that, rather than real people, those playing the parts in a movie are «representantes ideales, fantasmas de otros seres vivos que vivían su vida, sin mezclarse con el *cine*. Por eso él, que tenía tipo y alma de personaje de *cine* en un film lleno de peripecias, de esquinazos del destino, de casualidades, de incongruencias, había sido escogido entre los tipos humanos para representar ese papel» (p. 184). Charlie Chaplin, he reasons, is merely the representative of the innumerable Chaplins scattered throughout the world, living obscure existences. His «theory» (pp. 184-85) is that there is a *Doppelgänger* relation between a movie character and a real person. This, incidentally, not only emphasizes Ramón's idea of human types, but also shows quite clearly his technique in the use of the image as a basis for a «character» in a narrative.

At this point the woman sitting next to him entwines her leg around his, «como si fuese una maciza enredadera... La serpiente de aquella pierna se liaba a la suya...» (p. 184); the phrasing is more imagistic and sensuous than allegorical. When the house lights come on, Gustavo sees that the girl, who had had her leg wrapped around his until that moment, looks exactly like the movie's leading lady. For her part, she has already remarked on his resemblance to the leading man, as she explains that she does not customarily wrap her leg around those of men who sit next to her. «Nuestro destino —dijo él— está fotografiado en el resto de la película... No tiene remedio...» When the lights go out again for the second and final reel of the film, Gustavo has placed his arm around her waist, and she has once again wrapped her leg around his. «Ya se conocían. Ya no sentía él tanta extrañeza por las cosas que sucedían, que no eran tan extrañas, porque eran las que tenían que suceder. Era fatal. Ahora sí que no intentaría escaparse al Destino» (p. 186). The leading characters get married in the movie. When the lights come on again Gustavo and his girl, much to the displeasure of the audience and knowing that «reality» is about to break in, are kissing each other. Out in the street, «se sintieron unidos para siempre» (p. 187). The girl takes Gustavo to meet her mother, who (in accordance with the limitations of the *Doppelgänger)* is not a double of the mother of the movie's leading lady. «Después, todos fueron preparativos sin ninguna peripecia, y a los pocos días se casaban en el Juzgado de Paz, acabando en aquel mismo instante la incongruencia del *Incongruente,* la vida novelesca de Gustavo» (p. 188). Gustavo's suspicion, expressed in chapter thirty-two, was correct: the incongruity that constantly stalked him has ended with his marriage; the Platonic doctrine of the halves searching for each other has been incongruously fulfilled. But, is it not true that the real and ironic reason for this end is the ending itself? What has ended, in fact, is the «life» of the protagonist, in the author's own words, his «vida novelesca», that is, the novel.

It is interesting to note that Ramón himself thought that *El Incongruente* «abría un nuevo camino en la tramazón novelesca y que era la primer novela de la fantasmagoría pura y desternillada».[6] By 1947, he states: «fue la más innovadora de mis novelas» and «no ha pasado inadvertida para las nuevas generaciones...».[7] As a matter of fact, Ramón specifically uses the word «novela» in the first chapter story, saying of Gustavo that «no se podrían contar todas las incongruencias de su vida. No; yo sólo intento escalonar unas cuantas, y que se le vea vivir y producirse, y se imagine el lector todo lo que pudo pasar en los otros días que no se reseñan» (p. 14). Ilie interprets this as a reason, perhaps even an apology, for a weak narrative structure: «the novelist should adopt the technique of haphazard selection; the hero's disposition is uniform anyway. Moreover, the structural arrangement of these random incidents ought to be gratuitous.»[8] I regard Ramón's statement rather as signaling his intention to create an open narrative, actually the only kind that his method of composition can produce, but it was extremely innovative to theorize about such narrative possibilities when he did. To be sure, we are dealing here with the sort of fiction based on fantasy and whim, of large abstractions and small concretions such as the stuff fairy tales are made of, yet also the modulations found in contemporary writing, provided it is endowed with a consistent, humorous and hence self-critical vision; we are therefore confronted not with the behavior of

---

[6] *Pombo II,* p. 539.
[7] Preface to *El Incongruente,* p. 7.
[8] ILIE, *The Surrealist Mode...,* p. 154.

35

social types but of a particularly ingenious mind at creative play, not unlike the labyrinths of Borges or even Cortázar's *Rayuela*.

Nevertheless, despite the elements of narration cited above, we find in *El Incongruente* the essence of *ramonismo* expressed (though the author does not admit it) even in the author's own words, thus:

> No había gentes, figuras, sucesos en aquella habitación. Todo estaba pasmado en su silencio, en su disimulo inmóvil. Hubiera sido algo artificial prescenciar la exhibición de los personajes de aquel comedor. No. Sólo decorados, adornos y cosas en el aparador y en la mesa, naturalezas muertas distintas... (p. 43)

III

## *EL NOVELISTA,* OR THE IMAGE OF INSPIRATION

With this work,[1] Ramón demonstrates that his idea of literature is generically closer to the novel than one might have anticipated. Because this is a large work, I propose to employ in this chapter a more detailed method of critical synopsis.

CHAPTER I.   Corrige las pruebas de *La Apasionada.*

As in *El Incongruente,* the narrative is in the third person. The reader is immediately introduced to the novelist, Andrés Castilla. When we first see him, he is indulging in gregueristic considerations, such as the relative quality of the time measured by a wall clock and a pocket watch: «El reloj hondo, en el que sonaba un eco y una repercusión de ataúd» does contrast with «el reloj juvenil, chiquitín, de un níquel optimista y jovial» (p. 9), two frequent moods in all of Ramón's writing. Castilla is about to correct the proofs of a second edition of his novel entitled *La Apasionada,* a book inspired by a personal love affair. His first impulse is to make not corrections according to typographical precision but rectifications according to the reality of disillusion, for the woman he loved he now knows to have been a cheat. He thinks: «el público espera ya mi personaje, tal como fue concebido... nadie me perdonaría la modificación de su carácter...» (p. 10); despite this, we have sample paragraphs of a story within a story. He justifies this by saying that after five years the text required a certain up-to-dateness. But after superficial additions, the novelist decides it is useless and instructs the printer to proofread against the first edition; an old novel is like an old love, both should be forgotten. He turns to his current work...

[1] R. GÓMEZ DE LA SERNA, *El novelista* (Buenos Aires: Editorial Poseidón [1946]). All quotations are from this edition.

CHAPTER II. *El barrio de Doña Benita.*

Another story within the story. The section of Madrid that bore that name received it from its founder, the widow of a wealthy dairy farmer, a frightened recluse who established the *barrio* to protect herself. Here we have the familiar Ramonesque anecdote based on the whimsical and bizarre. The old woman dies; her descendants do not take proper care and the neighborhood deteriorates. Suddenly, the novelist introduces an interesting character-possibility: «Rafael, un joven explorador, un meditativo muchacho vestido de luto... tomaba café en el *Café de la Verdad*» (p. 16). The residents place their faith in him to appeal to the authorities for improvements, but his frequenting the *barrio* is due to the fact that he once saw there «la muchacha más guapa del mundo» who was «indudablemente, la blanca hija del trapero» (p. 16). This fragment of the novel comes to the end of written composition and simply continues in the mind of the novelist (now in the narrator's words): he imagines how the girl must have looked when appearing behind her garden gate. With regard to Andrés Castilla:

> Su despacho estaba muy obscuro, pues la luz del novelista no debe esparcirse mucho por la habitación.
> El novelista estaba en ese momento que, siendo el más claro y verdadero de la novela, anega en su propia realidad y hace pararse a ver lo que pasa, aprovechando la intensidad de las miradas, con ruin egoísmo de transeúnte, olvidando la pluma. (p. 17)

CHAPTER III. El crítico y la inspiración.

The novelist has instructed his servant not to let anyone in, but a critic tricks the servant and gets into the house. Once there, critic and novelist converse. The novelist's last work, the critic opines, has not been popular because in the course of four hundred pages no character smokes a cigarette: «no se dice eso que hace descansar la tensión del público y que basta que el escritor diga de cualquier personaje...» (p. 19). When the critic leaves, the novelist has another visitor, Inspiration, who brings him the sketch of a novel on a roll of papers: «Andrés leyó en ellos largo rato, aunque cualquier lego en cosas del espíritu hubiera dicho que no leía nada, porque los papeles estaban completamente en blanco, escritos con la tinta simpática de la Inspiración...» (p. 20). After Inspiration departs, the novelist decides to change the original title of the work and to add a paragraph at the beginning, continuing on page 28. The result is a novel entitled *Cesárea,* which is the name of the protagonist because of the way she was born. A sample passage is provided, as well as some thoughts on how the novelist will proceed.

CHAPTER IV. El protagonista de *La resina.*

The novelist has an unexpected visitor, who turns out to be, he says, the central character of a novel which had as a setting a pine forest and the pine resin industry. «El novelista, como hombre que acepta la imaginación, sabía que aquel hombre podía estar unido a él por vínculos profundos, aunque insospechables...» (p. 24). The character gives his name as Alfredo, «aunque no me llame así; por más que también estoy en la A, pues yo soy Alberto... Usted me puede llamar Alfredo... Yo se lo consiento sólo a usted...». When the novelist marvels at the coincidence of a real man's life with that of his character, Alberto-Alfredo replies: «No es coincidencia, señor, sino que es un caso completo que ha llegado a sus oídos y usted lo ha propalado...» (pp. 24-25). What does the man want from him, the novelist inquires. He needs help in his real life; he has acted according to the plot of the novel and now it is the novelist's responsibility either to find him a job or to give him part of the money earned from royalties: «Dicen que esa es su mejor obra... Por lo tanto, yo soy su mejor personaje» (p. 25). The novelist can do nothing but agree to help; after all, the man was «el personaje de su vieja novela, al que no podía convencer de su inexistencia real anterior al libro...». The novelist had always feared that some day one of his characters would show up like this, despite the fact that he considered them «tipos comunes, tipos que no había aceptado hasta que no se había dado cuenta de que eran tipos genéricos, tipos que se podía encontrar uno en cualquier parte». There is little doubt that Ramón indulges here in a 'greguerization' of the concept of fictional reality; the situation is a rather obvious Ramonesque parody of Unamuno's *Niebla;* instead of killing his protagonist, however, this novelist decides about his that «tenía que ayudarle a vivir» (p. 26). Another echo: «Ya había llegado uno, el primero y no el más esperado. Mas temía que se presentase aquel feroz grandullón de su novela *Fratricida»,* a capsule 'greguerization' of the theme of Unamuno's *Abel Sánchez.*

CHAPTER V. *La novela de la calle del Árbol.*

This chapter is almost in its entirety a narrative sketch, poetic and pseudo-*costumbrista* in nature, dealing with the street on which Andrés Castilla is supposed to live in Madrid. It is comparatively long; the bulk is called the «primera jornada de *La novela de la calle del Árbol».* It is written in the first person singular and includes: (1) descriptive details such as the sunlight reflected in the windows as in mirrors (cf. «El pueblo alegre», *El Incongruente),* flirtation of women on balconies and staircases (also *El Incongruente),* cinderella girls and bored women,

39

imaginative projection of the author's idea of behavior between men and women, the passing of time in the suburbs heralded by the sound of clock chimes, and (2) narrative motifs such as the anecdote of one of Andrés Castilla's own love affairs, reminiscent of Gustavo el Incongruente's: «Un día reñimos. Ella salía con la madre ya en tren de noviazgo seguro y oficial, y yo, cuando las vi, eché a correr por miedo al matrimonio» (p. 32).

CHAPTER VI.  En la jaula de la calle.

The novelist spends two weeks at home finishing this novel; his only distraction —and source of material— is his balcony, from which he sees everything that happens on the street. As he proofreads his manuscript, we are given a sampling of paragraphs, some of which are almost gregueristic aphorisms. A significant one, especially in the context of this book, is the following:

> Un cuerpo garboso.
> Y otro.
> Y otro.
> Hay a veces verdaderas procesiones.
> Nos acordamos de todo en el balcón.
> De viajes, sobre todo.
> De aquella vendedora de caramelos en aquella estación como en otra de aquel libro que hubiéramos querido leer. (pp. 37-38)

CHAPTER VII.  Otra tarde de otro día.

The novelist leaves one afternoon before dark his «casa oficial», his home; he is the owner of four other houses, of which only the study has been furnished, where he conducts different observations and seeks different inspirations: «Desde que sintió la vocación de novelista había comprendido que un verdadero novelador necesita encontrar las perspectivas de la ciudad desde distintos sitios, llegando a ser de ese modo distinto novelista y distinto personaje del arte de novelar en distintos cuartuchos con balcón a otras luces y a otros barrios» (p. 40). Some aspects of the «implied author» suggested by Wayne Booth (see p. 235) are present here. The novelist is writing four different novels each in the four different «casas pobres» (an extension of Ramón's own table with several chairs and «works in progress»). In those other houses which he kept secret, the novelist «se sentía inexistente e inencontrable. Su mayor felicidad. Era como un muerto dentro de cierta inmortalidad». Here too we find a manifestation of Ramón's notion of a parallel reality: «La entrada en el portal de su casa modesta y destartalada le hacía dichoso. 'Ya estoy fuera del mundo', pensaba...» (p. 41; see also *El Incongruente* and the discussion of it in the previous chapter). In the particular house he visits that afternoon, he is writing a novel —*La Criada*— about a servant-girl named Micaela, for he is very much concerned with the injustices perpetrated by society on domestic help. The thematic approach to the subject is at first reminiscent of Ramón's earliest work —*Entrando en fuego*— in which there is an obvious social concern. It is not surprising, however, that we find in the fragments offered here five successive aphorisms based on themes of domesticity, followed by some very realistic dialogue between two servants. And then: «El novelista hizo una pausa y se asomó a la noche. Le acongojaba la desgracia de las criadas, sobre todo a aquella hora en que coincidía la hora triste de su novela con la hora triste de la realidad...» (p. 44). His plot will be very basic and picaresque: «Bastaba con que su protagonista pasase por muchas casas y viese la tragedia de las otras compañeras y sufriera su propia tragedia» (page 45). It would be a sad story because «su Micaela buscaría la casa de la felicidad y de la cordura sin encontrarla» (p. 46).

Chapter VIII.   El usurero sarcástico.

The novelist goes to a moneylender; it is not the first time he has done this, since he cannot live on his royalties. What happens is an ironic commentary on everyone concerned: the moneylender offers to *pay* him for every letter he writes him asking for a loan; Andrés Castilla cynically agrees, his reasoning —sarcastically sound— being that there is «ese deseo del público de coger en renuncio a sus grandes hombres y tener en la mano la prueba de su miseria y su necesidad» (p. 48). Castilla, however, does not like moneylenders as characters of his novels.

Chapter IX.   Cocimiento de la novela.

We are back with the novel entitled *El barrio de Doña Benita*, which is almost finished; Rosario, who turns out to be a great-granddaughter of Doña Benita, is engaged to marry Rafael, the stranger hated by all the men of the *barrio*, including the priest, for having won the interest of the local goddess. The novelist, in new fragments of his novel, develops the plot and the characters in a way which is essentially a development of the narrator's thinking about the *barrio*: an enumeration of impressions attributed to the various characters as signs of their behavior. At this point it is convenient to differentiate between «the novelist», who is a character in the novel, and «the narrator», who is, of course, the particular aspect of Ramón involved in the writing of this novel (not the «whole» Ramón). The narrator, through the novelist, gives the *other* characters (those restricted to the fragmentary novels of which the novelist is *said* to be the author) an imaginary dimension: Rosario, an air of mystery; Rafael, a problem. The young man knows that to marry the rag-dealer's beautiful daughter is to bury himself in the *barrio*. Rafael «no acababa de comprender el alma de aquella mujer», as «el novelista caminaba con cautela hacia el capítulo en que descubría la aciaga verdad, que hacía a aquella muchacha tan verdadera y tan arrebatadora y tan mujer» (p. 53). Ramón's literary eroticism manifests itself once more as the novelist offers further development: a young man of his acquaintance tells Rafael that Rosario has been dishonored by her own brother, whose existence has been kept secret from him and who lives in America; Rafael starts to leave but returns to the *barrio,* more attracted than ever by the thought of Rosario; he takes her in his arms and their kisses preclude any possible recrimination. Rosario's beauty triumphs over worldly depravity, but Rafael cannot look forward to complete happiness.

CHAPTER X.   En busca de personajes.

«El novelista buscaba sus personajes con verdadero ahinco. Los buscaba en plena vida para que no tuviese que decirle nadie que eran muñecos de trapo» (p. 56). There are both irony and a revelation of technical results in this statement. The novelist is said to advertise in the newspaper for characters, «encontrando... materiales superiores a los que podía haberle prestado la imaginación». Of course, there is a greguerístic process here, but there is also a revelation of why believable characters are not Ramón's objective; the characters he presents in his novels are simply the images of those he has seen and has taken from real life, including himself as the novelist: «Gracias a ese procedimiento, recogió de viva voz impresiones que no habría podido inventar nunca.» There is a reprise of *El Incongruente:* regarding a certain type of young man, the novelist visualizes that «parecía que el destino les perseguía y les desbarataba todas las combinaciones» (p. 57). There is also a reprise of Ramón's novel entitled *Gran Hotel,* published also in 1922. And at least one narrative version of an aphorism can be found: «Se veían también muchas señoritas de esas que llevan una piel de corderito, el cordero que mataron por Pascua en el pueblo lejano.» As the title of the chapter states, the main theme, an important one for the whole book and thus developed in Ramón's peculiar style, is the novelist's search for characters. «'Un novelista es un verdadero detective', se decía Andrés» (p. 58); and hence «usaba todos los procedimientos posibles para cazar los personajes de sus novelas» (p. 59). There are 'greguerizations' of echoes of older writers. While inquiring for someone at a certain house, the novelist is confronted by an impressive lady. «Era, sin duda, un protagonista de novela, en el traje de la verdad», the narrator comments. «Andrés habló con ella, pero cuando la dijo que era novelista ella se echó a llorar, rogándole que no dijera nada y sobre todo, que no la matase al final de la novela» (p. 58; cf. Unamuno's *Niebla*). On a different occasion Andrés comes upon yet another woman, the result being that «engancharse en los flecos de un mantón de Manila es una manera de tomar una participación espontánea en la vida» (p. 59). But the novelist still depends on Inspiration and is anguished when she fails to keep an appointment. The chapter ends with this exceptionally good gregueristic image: «Aquellos días en que faltaba la Inspiración a la cita le dejaban enfermo, desabrido, suicida, jugando con el cuchillo de la cena como con un terrible puñal» (p. 60).

CHAPTER XI. Exaltación del farol.

This long chapter begins by telling how much Andrés Castilla is fascinated by street lamps. (Ramón himself had one installed in his study, a picture of which is found in *Automoribundia*, plate VI, followed by the corresponding anecdote on page 341.) Also reminiscent of Ramón's own desire to write his first novel (see my Chapter II) is the fictitious novelist's gregueristic conception of his literary talent: «¡Si yo pudiera hacer una novela con un farol sería un gran novelista!... ¡Hasta que yo no escriba esa novela no seré un verdadero novelista!» (p. 61). His idea is that a street lamp, more than the average object, «has a story to tell», the story or stories of what it has «witnessed», thereby providing his projected novel with a peculiar imaginary dimension which is not that of unrestricted fantasy, for his street lamps will do no more than converse while the other actors in the drama will be people. The title of this novel is *El farol número 185*, undoubtedly suggested by Xavier de Montepin's *Le Fiacre número 13*. The first chapter or preamble consists of a eulogy of street lamps and lamplighters, including passages which are diluted aphorisms («son una clase de testigos presenciales admirables, y lo que ellos saben es lo que sólo sabrá el mundo cuando esté deshabitado, en la noche ya excesiva de su experiencia», p. 63) and undiluted aphorisms («en el fondo del farol la camisa es como la niña en camisolín largo, que es lo que más se parece a un alma. Es la niña vista en su alcoba antes de saltar a su cama», p. 65). The second chapter is the actual beginning of the «novel» of a particular street lamp, employing the usual devices of narration and description, exterior and interior monologue. This transition from the preamble to the beginning of the story is particularly effective for discerning the difference between the aphoristic and the novelistic manifestations of Ramón's gregueristic style. The themes of destiny and happiness reappear. A woman is wooed by her sweetheart at the foot of the street lamp: «Nunca se la olvidaría aquella escena y el farol quedaría grabado en su memoria como un atributo de su destino» (p. 72); «El 185 echó su bendición a los que se alejaban hasta... la casa de la felicidad» (p. 73). The narrator tells us that the novelist, Castilla, must now find characters for the street lamp, thus contradicting (the paradox within the *greguería*) the object's own purported historicity, and the real connection between the street lamp and the novelist is eludicated:

> ¡Qué gran novela se puede hacer contando bien con el gran personaje sobrehumano de la noche!
> El novelista sentía pensamientos súbitos bajo la luz de ciertos faroles y sacaba su cuaderno de apuntes y apuntaba clarividencias que parecía haberle inspirado el Espíritu Santo.

With this reprise of the gregueristic image of Inspiration and an allusion to Castilla-Ramón's method of composition, the narrative switches to another story: «El novelista, cortada en ese punto la novela del farol 185, se dedicó a terminar *El barrio de Doña Benita*.» The description (Ramón's forte) of domestic, quotidian life would be marred by such an ineffectual plot were it not for the impact of the author's obvious intent: to encase a most trite situation in a most innovative form. Rosario and Rafael are married, but she does not know that he knows about her dishonor; she grows more beautiful every day; the brother returns, and brother and sister cannot deny their attraction to each other; as he had already planned, Rafael kills them both. We have a series of actions as seen by an omniscient author who is himself seen by another omniscient author. Furthermore, this is not just a novel within a novel; there is some veiled self-conscious writing involved, with the stylistic device twice removed: «'Eso... eso', decía alegremente el trapero cuando Rafael encontraba una imagen feliz, llegando a pedirle en muchas ocasiones como un gran favor cuando le gustaba mucho una frase: '¿Me la regalas? ¿Me dejas que yo la diga también?'» (p. 76). One can only guess at the possible irony present in these lines. And there is also the kind of pun on which Ramón sometimes fashions his aphorisms: «un lupanar lleno de luna»; «La flema más espesa de su vida le hacía flemático» (p. 78).

CHAPTER XII. Los días trascordados.

Ramón's whimsy is sometimes obvious in the extreme: «El novelista abría siempre las puertas con miedo, porque detrás de las puertas están los personajes de novela esperando. En toda obscuridad, en las escaleras sobre todo, hay argumentos de novela en gran número...» (p. 81). This chapter is a 'greguerization' of the absence of Inspiration (a state of mind mentioned also by Azorín in *Doña Inés*). It is not all whimsy, for it refers to the separation of the author as human being from the author as writer. «Cuando el novelista veía el día con clarividencia, ya no era novelista», says the narrator, with seeming paradox, but later explains: «Los días no novelables... eran por lo visto los días para ver todo lo superficial, los días en que las miradas no pasan de las verjas al pasar junto a los jardines» (p. 83).

CHAPTER XIII.   Polémica del hombre de la mañana
con el hombre de la noche.

Another greguerization of a whimsical notion: that Castilla's characters are the products of the afternoon and the night. The morning, according to the novelist, is a time akin to the days lacking Inspiration: «En la mañana todo se ve con una obscura simplicidad dotada de una falsa y absurda claridad» (p. 85). But an unidentified individual who has the opposite view criticizes the monotony of Castilla's works. «El novelista se quedó un poco perplejo. '¿Podría suceder que sus novelas adoleciesen de tener pocas mañanas?'» He decides to see what happens by going out and looking at the world in the morning. The results are very disappointing: «El abrir las maderas a la mañana bobalicona y agria es completamente inútil para el novelista» (p. 86). This is, of course, humorously dogmatic, but it is interesting to keep in mind that Ramón worked at night and went to sleep after dawn.

CHAPTER XIV.   Fin de *La Criada.*

Castilla has gone back to finish this novel, which ends with the death of Micaela, the servant girl, after having visited a female abortionist because of the condition in which she was put by either the son or the father of the family for whom she works. Micaela's life, like that of her equals, has been nothing but suffering in many different households. Ramón, as the narrator of this work, and his novelist-protagonist provide in this chapter a theoretic ambivalence, reality-realism. «El novelista desenlazaba la novela hedionda de los señores, las señoras y las señoritas de cada casa en que estaba Micaela, añadiendo detalles de realidad a su novela realista...» (p. 88); «¡Qué gran realidad tumefacta, innoble, esclavizada, hipócrita, sensual, tomaba la vida apoyándose en el fogón y viendo cómo Micaela cosía alrededor del huevo de la costura!» (p. 90). After reproducing the last chapter of *La criada,* the narrator tells us that Castilla, having finished the novel, «sintió que le envolvía, que estaba envuelto por la ola de la realidad, que era un náufrago del dolor que sugería su propia novela, y sin numerar las cuartillas tomó el sombrero y salió a la calle» (p. 95).

CHAPTER XV. El frío y *La moribunda.*

Another whimsical notion: cold weather as an ambience in which life is close to death. Andrés Castilla is uncomfortable in Madrid during the winter, but being a novelist decides to make the most of it by writing an appropriate novel, «una novela en que moría una mujer, la mujer que acababa por ser infiel al que la cuidaba en su invierno último» (p. 96). Often the novel has been compared to a slice of life. Here we find the gregueristic opposite: «La vida corta se alargaba en su novela. Miraba al almanaque como a la inspiración.» The heroine, Magdalena, is dying of an unknown disease; the hero, Fernando, has doctor's orders not to have intercourse with her; he respects those orders only to find that she deceives him with all the neighbors. After beautiful metaphors, such as «Abrió con una llave aplastada, como llave del silencio, y el espejo del recibimiento, roto en la sombra, le cortó la cara» and «Huyó en la sombra hacia atrás como si la resaca del mar del desengaño se le llevara hacia la noche», the novelist refers to that long part of the novel not reproduced: «Nosotros, que en cada capítulo impar hemos visto a Magdalena en brazos de otro después del capítulo de pasión con Fernando, estábamos ya hartos de que Fernando no se diese cuenta, pero ahora que se la ha dado, estamos espantados» (pp. 100-01). The narrative point of view, ironically turned back on itself, adds a dimension of unequivocal Ramonesque humor. Nevertheless, the narrator once again varies the emotional value of the chapter ending, stating that, in empathy with Fernando's experience as if it were reality, «el novelista... se lanzó a la noche fría que convertía en mendigo abandonado al que transitaba por ella». Here, as we have seen in *El Incongruente,* is a variant image of the future: *El hombre perdido.*

CHAPTER XVI. El enemigo de las novelas.

The person described by the title of this chapter is an admirer of science who comes to chastise the novelist; he wants to know «qué se propone usted al escribir esas que usted llama novelas» (p. 103). In the first part of the chapter, the narrator has already given us the answer in a sort of «ars novelistica» of Andrés Castilla (who is, of course, none other than the narrator and *ultimately* none other than Ramón):

> Siempre se había discutido la novela y se la había querido hacer gran obra de construcción como un puente que fuese al mismo tiempo escala de los cielos. El no entendía de eso. El se dejaba llevar por el más sigiloso de los guías y no se proponía ni se decía nada.
> Caminaba por la realidad supuesta como por una novela de magia en que hablan los cuadros y un plumero se convierte en un ramo de flores...
> La novela se puebla de lo inconcebible y se habla con las más dudosas palabras, las que no se esperan.

> El seguía en su barca por los subterráneos del mundo y sólo estaba
> entregado a la fidelidad de su imaginación. Lo que no tenía era técnica,
> aunque se reconociesen sus novelas por algunas repeticiones y por un aire
> arbitrario...
> El adoraba poner en pie toda la realidad...
> Si los lectores querían encontrar la vida en su verdad, sin dudas [sic]
> tenían que buscar sus novelas... Las novelas de los demás eran mazmorras
> en que daban tormento al lector por más que el cobarde lector sea eso
> lo que más apetezca. (pp. 102-03)

There is no doubt that Ramón is referring here to his own work and
it is interesting to note the way, half ironic, half sincere, in which he
disclaims any technique. This passage of self-criticism suggests how
consciously the gregueristic style is allowed to pervade Ramón's novelistic structure, as it does his aphoristic structures.

CHAPTER XVII.  Otro capítulo final.

We are back with the novel of Fernando and Magdalena, *La moribunda;* the narrator reproduces Castilla's last chapter, entitled «Día de
agonía» (p. 105). There are many gregueristic images describing the gray
melancholy of the fatal day; included are aphorisms on the theme of
melancholy days. Magdalena dies, and Fernando, who loved her so much,
is emotionally crushed yet saved from suicide by the thought of her
infidelity. Ironic humor triumphs over sentimentality.

CHAPTER XVIII.  Vuelta a la nebulosa.

> Los tipos de naturaleza sincera y noble como el del novelista tienden
> de nuevo a la nebulosa primitiva con la afinidad más franca entre los
> sentimientos humanos.
> El novelista deseaba hacer una novela en que la vida entrase sin
> tesis y sin ser sectorizada ni demasiado individualizada. (p. 110)

With these words the narrator begins this chapter in which he presents
a fragment of a novel entitled *Todos* which the novelist Castilla has had
planned for a long time but finds himself forced to give up because «la
nebulosa se traga las novelas y por el deseo de dar capacidad a la novela
la perdía en la masa cosmogónica primera, desprovista de formas, de gé-
neros, de salvedades, de excepciones, de concreción» (p. 117).
This segment of the book is the principal link with the rest of the
group which Ramón calls «novelas de la nebulosa», and it is the first
direct statement of his own «nebular hypothesis» of literature, so obviously derived from his own peculiar vision of life. The fragment of *Todos*
evinces its multitudinous, cinematic structure, the product of Ramón's

well-known talents for observation and imagination applied here to the «characteristic» activities of «all» human beings. It is made of images, either specifically or generally associated with the main theme, images stitched together with a thematic thread, tending to make the narrative primarily descriptive, without a story line of consecutive action. That is why, being the novel of «all», it is not the novel of anyone; the novelist wants a novel without a thesis (plot) and thus free of «individualization». Castilla, the narrator tells us, «rompió las cuartillas de *Todos,* novela vana, hija del deseo estéril de la universalidad y de la totalidad». Ramón himself was not ready seriously to attempt coming to terms with such an insoluble problem; later he would realize that, when put in a different way, the problem had the solution of a compromise between the inoperable plan of *Todos* and the narrative technique he had already used in *El Incongruente.*

CHAPTER XIX.  La visita de la admiradora.

We find here short fragments of «novelas posibles» (p. 118). Castilla «estaba en vena de incongruencias y comienzos», when he is visited by a young woman who admires him. She wants his autograph on a copy of his novel entitled *Dos cachorras.* Suddenly, she asks him why he does not have a child, and hiding his regret in specious philosophy, the novelist answers that he does not want one.

CHAPTER XX.  Comienza *Pueblo de Adobes.*

It would seem that, along with the views on the novel genre expressed in the sixteenth chapter, the account of attempting a «nebular novel» in the eighteenth, and other passages still to come, the beginning of this chapter constitutes a defense of Ramón's own novelistic structures. He has the narrator tell us, regarding Castilla, that

> Cada vez desconfiaban más de que fuese un novelista. Su visión sin pesadez, arbitraria como la vida y aferrada en vez de a una realidad simbólica y resabiada, a todas las realidades que pululan alrededor de un suceso, no satisfacía a los críticos que necesitaban la coordinación cortés, la fórmula urbana.
> El novelista era discutido frente a sus últimas novelas como frente a las primeras. Esta increación de la fama le hacía más el mismo. (p. 121)

Apparently, there is here a rebuttal to the criticism bestowed upon Ramón's novels up to that time in newspaper reviews to which I have no access. The position is extremely well taken, since it shields him from the critical attacks that were to continue. «Los armaschismes», the narrator says, «vivían en derredor de su corazón impenitente, siempre mozo, siempre creyendo que la literatura es la ciencia mayor.»

The novelist decides to show up those who accuse him of lack of substance in his works by writing a novel about a Castilian town entitled *Pueblo de Adobes*. The result is a delightful though naturally fragmentary greguerization of everything written before Ramón about that region and its people. We must remember the famed Castilian mystique of the Generation of 1898. Who could write the epilogue if not Andrés Castilla? After finishing the first chapter of his «novela castellana» (p. 130), he goes to seek further literary inspiration in the streets and alleys of his own town.

CHAPTER XXI.   En el pueblo seco.

An imaginative description of the *palomares* (dovecots) found in Castile and of their function in the lives of the people.

CHAPTER XXII.   Adobe tras adobe.

The narrator describes the novelist as «enamorado del detalle que hace verdad todo lo que es mentira» (p. 138). There are suggestions of *costumbrismo* and picturesqueness. Then the novelist reaches the pivotal point of his Castilian novel: «había precipitado uno sobre otro a los dos personajes principales.» These are Doña Prepedigna, who has been left an inheritance, and Clemente, the strongest of the young men of the town (both were introduced in previous chapters).

CHAPTER XXIII.   Libídine.

The spinster and Clemente are living in her house. Their life is one of passion and cruelty; in the latter she excels, thus giving the novelist an opportunity to present a brief essay on the cruelty of woman in aphoristic statements, ending with an enigmatic reference to Prepedigna's thighs, «la causa reptílica de todo, el otro secreto del hombre así como el de la mujer es el uno y el otro, la crueldad y la sensualidad» (p. 141). Clemente's strength is beginning to dwindle under Prepedigna's power.

CHAPTER XXIV.   Bajo las imprecaciones.

Doña Prepedigna's brother, Don Daniel, resents her inheritance and her conduct; his fellow numismatists agree with him. Every Saturday, Don Daniel gives alms to the poor, and such a scene is depicted in a manner worthy of Valle-Inclán (cf. *Romance de lobos*). At the end of the weekly giving, Don Daniel asks a pilgrim, whom he knows by the name of Teófilo, to put his sister back on the righteous path, and he gives him, not a penny as he has given to others at the risk of an actual protest, but a gold coin. In a simple but masterful display of authorial technique, we find the following sequence: «'Gracias, gracias...', dijo Teófilo, y salió como de la rotonda de los Templarios. Andrés Castilla también tomó su sombrero y salió a la calle como si saliese a la carretera de su novela...» (p. 147).

CHAPTER XXV. Perseverancia.

The chapter titles in *El novelista* naturally do not correspond with the chapter titles taken from Andrés Castilla's novels and presented here by the narrator. We now have «El cáncer en la lengua», Chapter XIX of *Pueblo de Adobes*. The novelist tells of Don Daniel's loss of his tongue due to cancer; even then the character insists on insulting his sister in writing. Having finished the chapter, Castilla is interrupted by «el falso novelista», and we have another incursion into the nature of the novel. The false novelist here represents a writer of conventional novels, who says to Castilla: «En su última novela el detalle perjudica al argumento» (p. 151). To which the latter replies: «la última suya tiene demasiado argumento y sobre todo se nota en ella más que en sus otras novelas que no ama usted a la literatura, que no tiene vocación literaria, que es sólo su especialidad.» (Did such a confrontation take place between Ramón and another author?) Nevertheless, after the visitor leaves, Andrés Castilla wavers in his certainty of being a novelist; yet he is sure of being «un hombre libre, porque se había fabricado la verdadera libertad suprimiendo, a su manera, problemas que no tienen solución» (p. 152). It is also interesting to note that in the same year (1923) Ramón published his *María Yarsilovna (falsa novela rusa),* which was followed by five other *falsas novelas.* However, it is only fair to add that, according to Ramón himself (see Preface to *6 falsas novelas,* Buenos Aires: Losada [1945]): «La Falsa Novela es otra cosa que la novela falsa o que la falsificada...» If Castilla-Ramón doubts himself as a novelist, he certainly does not doubt himself as a *littérateur,* and the expression or even the mere consideration of such a doubt in a book entitled *El novelista* is only further proof of his amazing control of technique which encompasses such inindulgence in self-appraisal.

CHAPTER XXVI. Nueva liberación.

The novelist is close to the end of his novel about a Castilian town: «Un pueblo castellano tiene que tener un loco, un enano y un gigante, porque si no, vive una vida precaria, incompleta, envidiando a los demás pueblos» (p. 153). There is, therefore, a giantess, whom all the townsmen are afraid to court, all, that is, except Clemente. He will find his liberation from Doña Prepedigna by making love to Engracia, the enormous daughter of Tío Bernardo, the tile maker. This he does, but Doña Prepedigna, at the climactic end of the novel, finds the lovers and kills them. Before actually reaching this *dénouement,* the novelist wonders: «El novelista estaba en ese momento de creador de destinos en que podía elegir entre vidas distintas» (p. 156). He opts accordingly and, having finished, «respiró el novelista liberado de una nueva novela»; the characters are freed from a particular situation, while the writer is freed from a particular task. «Después llamó al timbre y pidió un vaso de agua que le llevaron en seguida.» Why this particular consequence? Who brings him the glass of water? It does not matter; this is characteristic of the greguerístic narrative. The characters do not act logically because they are not supposed to; they are not «finished» characters —not even the protagonist— but images of characters appearing sporadically in the scenes that make up the open structure of the author's imagination.

CHAPTER XXVII. Al balcón.

Further play of Ramón's whimsical imagination on the relation between art and life: «Veía, a través de los visillos, el verdadero sentido de la novela de la vida, lo que nunca había alcanzado, lo que estando tan cerca resultaba indeciblemente lejos» (p. 157). In this reprise of the fifth chapter, as the novelist looks out of his balcony, there is again the autobiographical detail. Castilla sees in the evening twilight «cómo llegaban por las calles surcadas por hileras de faroles, los personajes que no llegaban nunca, y esa misma realidad tan tangible y tan admirable, se le escapaba, resultaba imposible, inasequible»; those images which he calls *personajes* (characters) are only images, and so are the «characters» of his «novels». And then the frequent paradox: «pero era como imposible concentrar en una novela la sencillez de una hora tan definitiva». Reality is precise only through its evanescence. All we actually see of it is a series of images; we have to supply the rest, the relationships and the meanings. But the essence of reality must be simple, and a novel dealing with it would only make it complex.

While at his window, Andrés Castilla is suddenly startled by the voice of a friend, Arturo, who now has relations with Rosaura, a former

51

mistress of the novelist and the protagonist (under the name Margarita; cf. Dumas's *La Dame aux Camélias*) of his novel entitled *La Encontradiza,* one of his «libros de venganza» (p. 159). The sentimental spite which Castilla feels upon remembering his past affair is, like everything else, transfused with Ramón's usual humor.

CHAPTER XXVIII. Viaje a Londres.

In search of new characters, the novelist goes to London; he is sure of meeting one at the turning of a street corner. With him he has the manuscript or *El farol 185,* which he is determined to finish during the trip. The London street lamps should inspire him, for it was there that the gaslight was invented by William Murdreh (*sic;* it is impossible to tell whether this orthographical distortion is accidental or intended; the historical model was William Murdock, who in 1802 invented a lighting process employing coal gas). However, «a lo que él iba, principalmente, era a merodear la casa del gran escritor inglés Ardith Colmer... Iba con el deseo de... oír la inspiración del maestro y de recoger los efluvios que se escapasen de su despacho...» (pp. 160-61). Castilla gazes from afar upon the silhouette of the famous Englishman seated at his desk: «Andrés, el gran novelista de las novelas con luz, tenía envidia de aquellas novelas obscuras y psicológicas que fabricaba el novelista inglés, y en las que el misterio hacía personajes de la novela hasta de los armarios de la casa.» Castilla-Ramón is the novelist who uses images; external reality is the ambience of the «novels with light». Does he really envy the writer of «dark and psychological novels» in which the characters are more consistent than images and thus contain little mysteries of human life? But this would require greater «individualization» (see synopsis of the eighteenth chapter above). At this point the narrator suggests that a writer's reputation usually colors his actual production: Castilla suddenly has reason to believe that Ardith Colmer (possibly an imperfect anagram, e.g., Carl Meredith or Richard Thomas) not only is an ordinary man but also has the same problems that he has in writing his novels, in finding Inspiration. The problems may be «the same»; it is the solutions which are different for different writers. Castilla decides to go back to his hotel and continue writing *El farol 185.*

There follow Chapters XII, XIII, and XIV of the novel whose protagonist is a street lamp. There is such a human being (Ramón himself), the novelist tells us, who is a «friend of street lamps». And street lamps tell stories like the one called *El niño perdido* in which, naturally, they take part; in this particular one, Street Lamp 77 not only talks but also takes home a little lost boy. «Después, el farol número 77 se fue como había llegado allí, dando saltitos en un juego de las esquinas en que aprovechaba para moverse la distracción de todo el público» (p. 163). It is interesting to note that Ramón strives to implement a separation between utterly fantastic behavior on the part of what is normally an inanimate object and its whimsical participation in the life of the human being which stems from an intensified use of perception and intuition as bases for imagination. To Ortega's remark concerning Ramón's part in the dehumanization of art, one might oppose an argument in favor of a humanization of things; but this humanization is twofold and inconsistent, for it sometimes tends to the fantasy of the fairy tale and more usually to the humorous metaphor of the gregueristic construct. Aphorisms on the theme of the street lamp are interspersed in the narrative structure of the chapter.

Street Lamp 185 is vandalized by thieves who were chased by policemen in response to its alarm whistle. The breakage prevents 185 from clearly seeing what happens in its surroundings, including the tryst of an eager Lothario and a reluctant young girl, whose voice it can hear but whose face it cannot see, thus undoubtedly being «la mujer de la belleza ideal» (p. 165; cf. with similar remarks in *El Incongruente*). After being repaired, the street lamp is stolen during a local religious festival (probably Midsummer Eve) and ends up lighting a cabin. This particular turn of his invention discourages the novelist, who must stop writing for the moment. In this chapter, however, we find an extremely accurate statement of the philosophy of the *greguería*: «Lo que no saben los hombres es que a cada cosa la rodea la idea de sí y en esa idea está, por comparación, la idea de todo lo demás.»

CHAPTER XXIX. El farol rojo.

Castilla has been a month in London; the proximity of the great English novelist has enabled him to make strides in composing *El farol 185*: «El farol de la calle de Ardith Colmer era el más inspirado de los que había visto» (p. 167). The tongue-in-cheek type of expression is one of the various turns the *greguería* can take in a narrative structure. There is an interesting reprise of the ending of *El Incongruente*: «El balcón de Ardith era como un telón de cinematógrafo, en el que se veían las figuras de las primeras obras de Ardith y los ensayos de las últimas» (pp. 167-68). The intermixing of narrator and character is going to advance one imaginary step further: «Como con la pluma de Ardith escribía Andrés aquellas páginas en que triunfaba su deber de hacer una novela sobre un farol» (it will be noted that the initials of the two writers' names are the same).

Street Lamp 185 had reached thirty years of service. One day the lamplighter comes to clean it and afterwards changes its glasspanes for

53

some red ones: «En la casa de las citas se había establecido una Casa de Socorro, y él resultaba el semáforo estratégico de la Casa de Socorro» (page 169). The irony of establishing an emergency hospital where there had been a hostel of ill fame leads the novelist to indulge in a literary pun: «Ahora todo lo vería dramático, porque nunca es más recordable que en este caso —no lo hubiera recordado si no— que todo es según el color del cristal con que se mira.» The final drama is supplied by another damsel involved in a tryst which ends in a double suicide. The house of love is now the house of death, and the former clear light of 185 has been extinguished forever, like the beautiful young lover, «la eterna novia de su éxtasis, la novia de su luz blanca».

CHAPTER XXX.   En casa del gran Remy Valey.

On the way back to Madrid from London, Andrés Castilla stops in Paris in order to visit Remy Valey, a famous French novelist (undoubtedly suggested by the combined names of his friends, Rémy de Gourmont and Valéry Larbaud). Castilla tells him about *Pueblo de Adobes* and admits writing twenty-five novels. «Yo soy el escritor más indígena de España», he says. «Más que clásico o imitador solapado de los clásicos, indígena, con todo lo que de añadido por el tiempo hay en eso y con la misma degeneración del tiempo que hay en ello» (pp. 170-71). The French novelist, Andrés observes, is in the last stages of his life's work; he wonders: «¿Es él el hijo de los personajes de sus libros de extraños tipos, o son ellos sus hijos? De cualquier manera, es importante y no se sabe qué es lo que le da más importancia, si ser el padre o el hijo» (page 172) —a refined conclusion to the well-known hypothesis submitted by Unamuno on the relative importance of Cervantes and his Don Quixote. How is it that Valey was able to write a novel about a woman who spoke only two words to him? «Pues porque seguí su rastro ideal hasta dar con ella aquí, en mi propia habitación, que es donde hay que dar con las cosas, no en la vida... Todo está escondido aquí en este momento, todo... Lo que es menester es encontrarlo» (p. 173). Obviously he is a «psychological» novelist, unlike Castilla-Ramón, and yet we are left with a certain doubt; in his last novel, he says, «recojo... todas las confidencias y todas las calumnias que sopla el aire... No he rechazado nada de lo que he oído a la inspiración».

CHAPTER XXXI.   Rasgando originales.

Castilla returns to his house in Madrid and destroys many works in progress, among them a «novela humorística» (p. 174) entitled *X* and, after rereading it, a love story, apparently autobiographical, entitled *Lo inolvidable*. The *dénouement* he had intended to give the latter was about how «después de momentos en que volvió a encontrarse a Pilar y pudo realizarse de nuevo lo inolvidable, nunca pudo volver a ser suya, nunca; se frustró siempre la segunda vez, y sólo *lo inolvidable* de aquel primer día de juventud pudo permanecer en su memoria» (p. 179). The way this idyllic fragment is told is very different from the rest of the book and shows the range of which Ramón is capable; the gregueristic style is «toned down» and the narrative is executed in such a way as to turn sensuality into aestheticism. It would be interesting to know how many Spanish writers, especially poets, of the so-called Generation of 1925 read this; it could be as much a model for their refined eroticism as certain passages of Juan Ramón Jiménez.

CHAPTER XXXII. Fiebre de novelador.

The novelist is hard at work on two novels at once which he must remit almost immediately to his publishers. These novels are *El adolescente,* whose protagonist is described as «injusto, antipático, inmoderado» (p. 182), and *El León de Oro,* of which a fragment is reproduced and which takes place in Venice where, according to the narrator, «se hace vivir a los personajes, se les lleva al teatro, se les enamora, se les casa y se les mata con gran facilidad».

CHAPTER XXXIII. En la ciudad novelística.

According to the narrator, Andrés Castilla thinks of Lisbon as the city particularly conducive to writing novels. So Castilla goes there to write a detective novel he has planned for some time. The title is *El inencontrable;* the plot deals with a rich Irishman who hires a Spanish-Irish investigator to find his long-lost son presumed to be in Lisbon. To find Williams, Mr. Oscar Belly chooses Rivas Ericson because he wears rubber-soled shoes, speaks Spanish, and is optimistic—«mezclaba el optimismo irlandés con el optimismo español, lo que hacía de él uno de esos pocos hombres que tienen alegres los dos lados de la cara» (p. 184). This novel-fragment has many specific traits in common with some passages of *El Incongruente,* particularly the quest and the sense of destiny.

CHAPTER XXXIV. La ciudad de los personajes
de novela.

For his part, the novelist is also searching: «paseaba por Lisboa como el que busca la pareja de un candelabro que le dejó su abuelo, es decir, lo inencontrable entre lo inencontrable» (p. 188). Once again we see the intended reflection of reiteration of images between that of the novelist-character and that of one of «his» characters. All the people seen by the novelist during his wanderings are potential characters of his novels. Indeed, Lisbon is for him the urban image of literary motivation or Inspiration: «Toda la ciudad le acosaba a esa hora para que volviese a tramar su novela. Era la ciudad emulativa de la narración. 'Corto el asueto y numerosa la imaginación', era el lema de Lisboa la novelística» (page 189). And so we are offered chapters X, XI (skip XII), and XIII of *El inencontrable,* in which Rivas Ericson follows elusive clues, experiences strange adventures, thinks several times that he has found the heir of the rich Irishman only to realize he has been mistaken.

CHAPTER XXXV.  Por las calles intrincadas.

Rivas Ericson continues his search; he goes to all lengths to find some trace of his subject. The novelist, in turn, goes on writing and when he comes to the end of this chapter, «aunque en su novela había anochecido, él se lanzó con alegría a la tarde, aun clara y primaveral, de Lisboa...» (page 199).

CHAPTER XXXVI.  Días de lluvia.

Andrés Castilla continues his detective novel, and Rivas Ericson continues his fruitless search: «se levantaba todas las mañanas como oficinista que no sabe dónde está su oficina» (p. 200). The novelist attributes unfailing humor to his protagonist. At one point the sleuth thinks he has found his man —drowned— but again it is the wrong man.

CHAPTER XXXVII.  En vísperas del embarque.

The gregueristic identification of characters is multiplied: «El novelista se había perdido en cien aventuras para encontrar a su irlandés y estaba deseoso de hallarle al fin» (p. 205). He begins the last chapter of his detective novel, in which Rivas Ericson finally accomplishes his mission, thanks to a casual display of the English flag «en el día de fiesta en que se engalana de banderas toda Lisboa» (p. 206), finding the Irish heir married to a Negress and the father of two black children. Such had been the reason for his disappearance; now the father must be willing to accept and show affection for his grandchildren, for destiny has chosen this life for Williams Belly and he has found happiness. «¡Pero qué heroico y temeroso había sido el obstinado silencio del que peca contra su raza implacablemente céltica!» (p. 208).

If nothing else, this particular story within a story proves that Ramón can invent a plot which could serve for a conventional novel; what he does with it, however, is not conventional. Depth of character is certainly something he does not produce, for reasons he himself has already given in this very novel (see synopsis of eighteenth chapter), and even the skeletal plot evaporates into humorous inconsequence as the whimsical details which are its flesh actually take over the narrative with a perfunctory action of their own.

## CHAPTER XXXVIII. *Las siamesas.*

The spirit of the *greguería,* its very principle, as told by Ramón in his *Automoribundia,* finds a parallel in the character-images of this fragmentary novel by Andrés Castilla: «Siempre le había tentado al novelista el conflicto de aquellas dos almas juntas, inseparables y, sin embargo, distintas», a phenomenon which he defines as a «paradoja de la vida con complicadas seducciones» (p. 209). A woman gives birth to female Siamese twins; the parents do their best to care for the monstrous offspring but eventually the girls are left orphan: «El pobre padre, de tanto seguir la meditación comenzada por la madre, fue decayendo, envejeciendo, disminuyendo y al fin desapareció. ¡Había sufrido mucho acariciando aquellas dos cabezas de una sola hija trágica!» (p. 211). Relatives care for the twins until they are sent away to school. Dorotea is jovial; Gracia is taciturn, but everything seems all right between them, considering the circumstances.

## CHAPTER XXXIX. En la pura teratología.

The novelist gives free rein to his pen «porque le entusiasmaba aquella doble novia de su fantasía...» (p. 215). The narrator plays with the concept of fictional character: «En el diván de enfrente de su mesa, estaban sentadas las dos hermanas en entretenida tertulia con él.» Finally fate intervenes; Dorotea is attracted to Wenceslao, a young man to whom Gracia is not attracted. The latter poisons herself, simultaneously sentencing her twin sister to death because, though emergency surgery is performed, it proves unsuccessful. Having finished the novel, Andrés Castilla finds his hands stained with blood.

## CHAPTER XL. La nueva fantasma.

After a period of rest from writing, the novelist begins another novel he had had in mind. It was to be entitled *¿De cristal?* «Largo rato estuvo mirando al rincón de la inspiración, inspiración suroeste» (p. 220); then he began to write about a disdainful woman, like one who once had smiled at him coldly at a dance. Pure imagination on the part of Andrés Castilla, after all, it was only the image of a woman that he was going to turn into a character. Her name is Beatriz; Corpus, the protagonist, meets her at a dinner party and soon becomes fascinated, particularly by her right eye, which has something odd about it and which he begins to suspect is made of glass. There are grounds for such suspicion, for as they walk together to the dinner table she smiles at him, «dejándole caer el ojo derecho en una mano, gesto por el que descubrió Corpus que aquel ojo derecho era un ojo desviado» (p. 221). This time, the whimsical emphasis on physical detail results in a variant of the gregueristic principle: «estaba rota esa mirada conjunta que arrojan los ojos normales...» (page 223). After dinner Beatriz drifts away from her chance partner, but he resorts to his friend Ernesto for more information about the mysterious woman.

CHAPTER XLI. Tras la mujer dudosa.

The narrator states that «trazando los garrapatos caídos en los abismos de las letras... aparecían notas para aquella novela...» (p. 225). The capricious manner of paralleling Andrés Castilla's method of nocturnal composition with that of the author himself reveals aspects of style as well. For the «garrapatos» are not merely calligraphic but actually in the mind of the novelist; in other words, they are the stuff *greguerías* are made of. Castilla's objective in this novel, we are told, is to portray «una mujer fría, tenaz, escurridiza pero obsedante, verdadera pareja del hombre que si no la posee, tendrá que suicidarse». Corpus is that man, «entusiasmado por aquella Beatriz que siempre se le aparecía desnuda y reidora» (p. 226). When his friend Ernesto teases him about the woman's active suitor, Corpus assures him that his only real concern is whether or not she has a glass eye: «No me caso con ella porque no sé si su ojo es de cristal, y no sabré si su ojo es de cristal porque no me casaré con ella... Pero ya sabes que es la cuestión más delicada que te he consultado y que nadie debe saber nuestra duda» (p. 227). Corpus sees Beatriz at different social functions and tries to discover the truth but finds only how awkward it is to talk to her when he is more interested in her right eye than in her left eye: «Todo en la conversación se ladea hacia ese ojo y la mujer parpadea entuertecida» (p. 228). And yet that very conversation fascinates Corpus, since it reveals to him that Beatriz is what he considers an «interesting woman» inasmuch as he wishes to court her, but her dubious eye inhibits his desire.

CHAPTER XLII. Enredos.

A friend tells Corpus that Beatriz had met the king at the Countess of Capuleto's house and for a time had been his mistress. Knowing the countess, Corpus goes there but finds out nothing. He remembers hearing, however, that the king always gave his favorites a diamond bracelet, and Beatriz faithfully wears one. Now there are two things that intrigue him: her right eye and her diamond bracelet. Meanwhile, a foreign diplomat is courting Beatriz. The novelist goes on writing about his characters until a climax is inevitable; it must take place in the nineteenth and last chapter, entitled «En el sanatorio» (p. 233), at the beginning of which the gregueristic emphasis is given to the description of a hospital environment. Word comes to Corpus that Beatriz has entered that hospital. The first time he goes to inquire about her, he is told that she is gravely ill and about to undergo surgery; the second time, that she has died: «Corpus se quedó anonadado como si la tierra se fuese a llevar varias incógnitas, la de su ojo de cristal, la de si le hubiera llegado a querer o no y la de quién le había regalado su pulsera» (p. 234). After a terrible night, he plans to attend the funeral: «parecía uno de aquellos amigos, que como hubieran asistido a su boda, asistía a su entierro.» Suddenly he thinks of making a few more inquiries at the hospital; he approaches the nurse in charge of the room where Beatriz had been and asks her outright whether the lady had a glass eye. Her reluctant answer is the epitome of gregueristic invention, the climax of the whole narrative: «Sí, se escapó a su órbita contraída con tal fuerza, que se rompió contra su propia imagen en el espejo del cuarto.» Corpus decides not to attend the burial: «Tenía en el fondo de su alma un quimo repugnante, mezcla de toda la insinuación de aquella aventura, que por ser el hombre tímido había sido la única aventura de su vida» (pp. 234-35).

As Andrés Castilla is about to reward himself with a cigar for having finished his latest novel, the doorbell rings. To the novelist's surprise (but not much), it is the protagonist of a past and nameless novel, Dr. Witerman, who used one of his own twin daughters while still a baby to experiment with a heart transplant unsuccessfully. The frequent use of chemicals has turned his eyes, described in the «original» novel as green, to the black color of a living reality. Castilla's relative suspicion of his character's visit is met with the rejoinder: «No se dan ustedes cuenta los novelistas de que la imaginación del mundo es un todo compacto al que atraviesan recuerdos y concepciones que están en alguna parte... Estoy seguro que, como yo, ha habido muchos doctores que han tenido que soportar las gratuidades de las novelas.» In this novel Ramón visualizes a future development of science, as he would also prefigure the atom bomb in *El dueño del átomo,* published in 1928. Having «invented»

59

Dr. Witerman, Andrés Castilla feels that «entre los dos habían cometido un crimen por amor a fantasmagorías tan parecidas como el arte y la ciencia» (p. 236), a variation on the Unamuno-Augusto Pérez relationship.

CHAPTER XLIII. Nuevos avatares.

The title of this chapter is extremely suggestive of much that Ramón does with his playful yet serious intermingling of his characters' identities. The narrator is a manifestation of the author Ramón. To what extent is Andrés Castilla, the novelist, another manifestation? And here in the new «novel», entitled *El biombo,* begun in this chapter, the narrative in the first person allows for still another unfolding of the series of authorial superpositions. Furthermore, we find in this story the notion of the «otherness» pertinent to every entity; not necessarily the *Doppelgänger* suggested in *El Incongruente,* but the basis of metaphysical duality.

The vague, fragmentary history of the protagonist's family revolves around an Oriental screen whose origin is intentionally kept secret. There is a Valle-Inclanesque air of hallucinatory mystery full of erotic and superstitious implications, to which are added various ontological notions associated in the *greguería.* For example, the protagonist confesses close to the start that «a través de las rendijas del biombo reconocí que mi padre era otro. Mi padre era un 'señor', esa cosa vaga que expresamos cuando decimos 'un señor'» (p. 238). The uncertain, sometimes ambiguous nature of reality is expressed by the effect of the screen in the protagonist's household and in his life: «El biombo se oponía entre un lado y otro de la vida, dividiéndola. Volvía del colegio decidido y alegre, pero hasta que no volvía la esquina del biombo no lo estaba completamente.» Of the screen's six panels, «the third from the right» (arbitrary detail characteristic of gregueristic thinking) is the one «belonging» to the protagonist; it is a kind of dark mirror of an ultimate reality: «lo que yo buscaba en su lago negro era la comprobación de que 'estaba allí'; pues de niños nos acoge la congoja de lo vago, la congoja de la inexistencia.» There is a digression in the first chapter in which aphoristic and quasi-aphoristic sentences are used to describe the qualities of a screen; used to hide from sight, a screen has to do with vision and image, which are Ramón's primary preoccupation and his instrument of knowledge of the world. In effect, from the point of view assumed by Ramón in this story, screens are «imprescindibles porque hacen percatarse de muchas cosas y gracias a su rendija permiten que se cojan infragranti [*sic*] muchos gestos de las cosas...» (p. 240). The screen in this story is capriciously depicted as a determining factor in the protagonist's life according to his own belief, as part of the sort of mythology invented by children, including allusions to the screen as a cover for the presence of evil. The protagonist's mother

60

dies in the first chapter and his father in the second; he has three brothers left, and among the four the estate is divided. The protagonist is
allowed to keep the screen intact, with the stipulation that if he quarrels
with any of the others, he will have to forfeit a panel of the screen: «me
lo llevé a mi nueva casa... Ya comenzaba el biombo a crear esa dualidad
adversaria que crea de un lado la luz y del otro la sombra, de un lado
la vida y del otro la muerte» (p. 244). As the novelist finishes this chapter,
he gets up and walks around the room, looking at his own screen.

CHAPTER XLIV. Detrás del parapeto.

The novelist is now working on the thirteenth chapter of *El biombo,*
the novel whose «other» protagonist, the screen, «avanzaba mantenién-
dose erguido, insensible, como lo que posee un misterio fiero que no es
que se invente sino que existe» (p. 245). Castilla's obsession with the
object and its idea stems from the ambiguity of their reality: «hasta que
no resuelva el desenlace... no podré ocuparme de otra novela... El día
que acabe regalaré mi biombo.» The protagonist feels compelled by the
presence of the screen in his study to engage in a farce; he will act as if
he were a painter just to have a model come and undress behind the
screen: «Iba a poner del otro lado del biombo algo verdadero, algo con
lo que soñaba el biombo. Iba a satisfacer de algún modo su instinto»
(page 246). And then the novelist launches into the unnumbered «next»
chapter, «el nuevo capítulo de la pura obsesión», which gives us a taste
of another aspect of the nebular narratives which Ramón was later to
write. «Nada» and «nadie» are the key words of this passage; the *greguería* has reached its metaphysical apex: «Hago yo la excursión por la
noche con el pie forzado de buscar la nada, con el afán de que me encuentre» (p. 247). Whimsical and hence undeveloped as this concern for
nothingness may be, it antedates much that has later become significant
in literature. Absurdity and illogicality become cornerstones of poten-
tially serious thought, such as the protagonist's dialogue with himself,
anticipating such existentialistic literary behavior as that which appears
in Octavio Paz's *¿Aguila o sol?* The notion of marginal space, like that
of the stairwell in *El Incongruente,* acquires a temporal dimension which
brings it closer to a total conception of the 'para-real': «En la caja del
reloj podrá darse por ejemplo la presentación de eso que no es nada,
que no es nadie y que estoy deseando ver... 'Nada', 'Nadie', no hay que
darle vueltas, eso es lo que hay fuera de nuestra vida, la vida que nos
ha tocado transportar por el mundo, conservar por instinto y lucir por
vanidad.» In the human complex of chance, consciousness, and will
there are cracks like those in a screen through which Ramón visualizes
«something else»: «¿Sería 'eso' —nada, nadie— lo que dejó encendida

61

la luz del comedor la noche aquella? / Yo estoy seguro de que la apagué, y, sin embargo, amaneció encendida. ¿Denunció su mala intención con ese rasgo, 'eso' que no se me ha descubierto nunca? No. Me dediqué a perseguir la verdad, me estudié, indagué, me anduve en el fondo de la americana. Y por fin di con el momento medio sonambúlico en que encendí la luz...: Nunca 'Nada' ni 'Nadie', porque el ladrón o el asesino que se me apareciesen serían alguien. / Siempre detrás del biombo 'nada' 'nadie'» (pp. 247-48; slashes represent paragraph breaks). The simple device of capitalization is used here to distinguish between ontological categories; Ramón will develop these notions in subsequent novels. How many outstanding Hispanic contemporary writers have been influenced by those works without the recognition of the critics?

(Chapter XV) A friend asks the protagonist to let him use the study (turned studio) to take a woman there. When the friend and his girl leave, the protagonist cannot work; he is overcome by the playful sensuousness left behind by the woman. «Desde aquel día busqué a aquella seducida y busqué las vueltas al amigo, y no paré hasta que di con ella, que, como toda seducida en casa ajena había quedado corrompida para la fidelidad y por eso logré que volviese al sitio de su bautismo galante» (page 249). The love affair ends on a tragic note, as the woman takes arsenic, thereby suggesting a play on words between *seducida* and *suicida;* the erotic and morbid aspects of *ramonismo* are present here. (Chapter XVI) The narrative takes up again the device of autodialogue; cynicism creeps in: «Como la maldad es la patrona del mundo, la da vergüenza conceder la felicidad y tiene que alargar la mano con el regalo feliz desde detrás de un biombo.» And the notion of «otherness» pervades the whole atmosphere: «Cada vez tenía más una cosa de espejo de otra casa, de la casa de enfrente, por ejemplo, de espejo intrincado y lejano.» The «otherness» of the *greguería,* modulated by a narrative context, develops into something mysterious and dramatic with the expectancy of future revelations. The protagonist now fears the screen; he is advised to get rid of it but refuses, turns his words to it in challenge. «El biombo litúrgico y mitrado, realiza con esa especie de gran cartera mágica que es, todos los actos de prestidigitación» (p. 250); in effect, it makes people appear and disappear. Moreover, without being totally aware, the protagonist has been forced into a strange relationship with the screen: «¿Qué ser que no soy yo es este que acaba de salir de detrás del biombo con una sonrisa tan osada? —me he dicho varias ocasiones a mí mismo». (Chapter XVII) The protagonist's fear extends to all screens. The necessity arises for the brothers to sell a valuable pearl bequeathed to them; the protagonist goes to Paris to sell it to a famous collector, but this woman tricks him by substituting another pearl behind a screen of her own. (Chapter XVIII) Without explanation, the protagonist is suddenly given a wife by the novelist. The protagonist, however, has peculiar designs on her sister («la cuñada que me reservaba para caso de viudez», page 253), and when his brother Paco attempts to seduce the sister-in-law, the protagonist evicts him from the house even though he will have to forfeit a panel of the screen. The wife comes upon the scene: «tropezó con el biombo haciéndose sangre en la frente. El quinto personaje, el biombo, se ofrecía como interposición entre todas las cosas» (p. 254). Without apparent reason, unless it is to change the point of view to the screen itself, the narrative switches to the third person in one paragraph: «En eso entró el primo Carlos, que veía a la esposa inclinada sobre el hombro del marido, y a éste recriminando al hermano.» Equally interesting is the following self-conscious remark: «La escena, al convertirse en comedia de enredo perdió toda su fuerza.» (Chapter XIX) The screen now has suffered the loss of a panel, and professional writer yo-Castilla-Ramón cannot resist this simile: «Era como un libro al que le faltase el final. El final no, porque para que no se viesen las bisagras le había dado la hoja del centro, la que tenía impresos mis sufrimientos de hijo solo en el mundo, y mis preparativos de boda» (p. 255). In the dark mirror of the diminished screen, the protagonist sees a prognostication of his diminished life represented by the image of his wife, Esperanza, dressed in mourning.

CHAPTER XLV. El empujón libertador.

Castilla continues his novel; by the twenty-second chapter he has given the protagonist a son. His wife has become fond of the screen and wishes to keep it. The protagonist (in whom certain habits of Ramón are perhaps unconsciously reproduced) likes to sit in a particular armchair to read; there, a baroque sense of time is evident: «Del brazo salía el atril en que colocaba la lectura y junto al balcón me pasaba la tarde, oyendo el ritmo del tiempo, cómo se desmenuza, cómo transcurre matando el mundo» (p. 258). Suddenly he hears the wife screaming; the son, who had been making burnt-sugar candy, has burned his face. As the boy appears before his parents, there is an imagistic relationship between his caramel-colored face and the dark lacquer of the screen; the incident can only be defined as part of a narrative based on gregueristic imagination: «¡Qué minuto de talón de la tragedia cuyo procedimiento se ignora, tuvo el negro biombo!... Hubo un momento que fue cuando el niño estuvo en la alcoba, un momento antes de presentárseme, atravesando el telón del biombo, que el biombo lo agravó todo como no puede tenerse idea, pues vi a mi hijo con el dardo clavado en el corazón.» The complaint that some critics have lodged against Ramón's frequent solecisms is puerile; the strange syntax is part of the necessary linguistic mechanism used to express his complex though capricious vision. (Chapter XXIII) The narrative continuity is unbroken; despite the unfortunate incident, the wife refuses to part with the screen, and the protagonist does not really want to lose it, because he reasons paradoxically that if they got rid of it «nos tomaría el destino por débiles y miedosos». She looks upon it sentimentally («¡Ha figurado tanto en nuestro amor!»), while he is still apprehensive: «lo veía enlazado a la fatalidad de la vida» (page 259). One day, he sees a seductive woman in the house across the street; he gets up to take a better look and finds he can no longer see her, for she is an illusion created by the screen: «Me di cuenta que era una visión de las rendijas del biombo, algo que en realidad quizá no existía, una estampa que sólo aparecía cuando nadie la contemplaba.» We are on the way to discovering the texture of the 'para-real'. But in this story of mystery and suspense, the dramatic impulse requires an ethical springboard: «En el jardín de la vecindad, en un laboratorio de otra vida, en la casa deshabitada de más allá, es donde se fragua el atentado contra nuestra vida.» Though evil auguries are in the air, the protagonist delights for a time in the contemplation of «that pure and incomprehensible woman» through the cracks between the panels of the screen. On several occasions his wife asks him what he is doing, finally slipping up on him and seeing what he sees, the beautiful, tousled-haired woman just having awakened from her sleep. What happens then can only be defined as a daring fictional device, almost a trick played by the author on himself or on his own concept of fiction. Actually it is a humorous forerunner of the kind of «consummate experimentation» practiced by writers like Borges, Cortázar, and Fuentes: the kind of game that deals with the possibilities of reality and the limits of fiction, in which realities of different ontological nature are merged or transposed (a cornerstone of this sort of fiction can be seen in Cortázar's «Continuidad de los parques», *Final de juego*). What takes place is that the wife pushes the screen forward, exposing the protagonist «a la vista de la vecina en aquella actitud de fisgón, mientras mi esposa me recriminaba» (p. 260). The upshot, of course, is that «la hermosa vecina se metió corriendo y no se volvió a asomar nunca». (Chapter XXIV) In this last chapter of *El biombo,* there is the unexpected mention of the protagonist's having «gone to his job». On this occasion he returns home early and he is about to go into his room, when he hears his wife pleading with him not to come in. The protagonist is suddenly beset by suspicions of adultery; through the screen he seems to detect strange motions. He gets his gun and kicks the screen, smashing it against the fireplace. The wife was simply engaged in her toilette and was embarrassed at being thus surprised. This somehow turns out to be a lesson to the protagonist; he gets rid of the broken screen and thus begins a more tranquil period of his life.

CHAPTER XLVI. Las obras completas.

Andrés Castilla has aged. He is at home, expecting a publisher who will buy his collected works and pay him enough to buy a small hotel by the sea, «under the threat of Vesuvius». Castilla feels that the purpose of his life has been achieved, though he hears the voices of unwritten novels clamoring for existence. So far, his works classified as «novelas grandes» (a favorite denomination of Ramón's) number thirty-eight; the titles (p. 262) include some of those reproduced in this book, some merely mentioned, and some of which we have never heard before. As he dreams of the «little hotel» he has wanted for so long «en el recodo lejano del mundo», Castilla sees himself among all his literary paraphernalia adding to each of his published works «un capítulo que mezclará mi nueva sensatez a mi antigua insensatez» (p. 263). Ramón himself lived in Naples, where he constantly worked late into the night, searching for «the ideal novel» (see *Automoribundia*, pp. 450-58, and Luis S. Granjel, *Retrato de Ramón*, p. 31). In preparation, Castilla goes about visiting the characters of his novels and decides to take some of the females to live with him in his «asilo final» (p. 264); they agree.

CHAPTER XLVII. En el retiro.

The novelist is settled in his hotel «que ya iba a ser suyo hasta la muerte» (p. 265). He is old but he is happy; he is afraid of catching cold (another autobiographical trait of Ramón) but he is enthusiastic about his life, to the extent of producing new works: «No se había libertado de la muerte, pero sí del altercado del mal tiempo con el buen tiempo...» He indulges in meditation and this, not surprisingly, results in a series of gregueristic aphorisms of intermediate length, about which there is an interesting statement on the part of the narrator: «Y Andrés Castilla, que pensaba inundar las habitaciones del hotel con las cuartillas de numerosas novelas futuras se desleía en la luz y no se atrevía a aprovechar nada de aquello como elemento novelesco» (p. 268). An abrupt transition gives way to the reflective passage that ends the book: «Y en este último momento es cuando puede preguntarse: ¿Qué clase de novelista ha sido éste? ¿Es el tipo de novelista ideal?» Further parallels with the true author and his literary theory and practice follow: «hay mil aspectos de lo real en sus mareas movidas por lo fantástico que hay que perpetuar. Todas las combinaciones del mundo son necesarias para que éste acabe bien desenlazado...» And finally: «Hay que decir todas las frases, hay que fantasear todas las fantasías, hay que apuntar todas las realidades, hay que cruzar cuantas veces se pueda la carta del vano mundo...»

Is Andrés Castilla at first a synthetic parody of the Generation of 1898 (the novels of Azorín, Baroja, Unamuno, Valle-Inclán) that gradually becomes an autobiographical image of Ramón? Quite possibly.

*El novelista* can be described as a cluster of novels. It has some affinities with Boccaccio's *Decameron*. Actually, it is a series of fragmentary stories within a story (which itself is not a novel in the conventional sense of the word) with the narrator assuming the role of protagonist and, in turn, the protagonist assuming that of narrator. The result is an unfolding of character and theme in a constantly shifting plot suggestive of a kaleidoscope. Ramón has found one way of developing an open novelistic structure, but it is a segmented one, obviously the result of his special method of composition. As a novelistic structure, *El novelista* gives the impression of a tapestry, with its basic pattern conveying the grotesquerie of Ramonesque humor and all the fill-in decorations fashioned of whimsical imagery. It is, however, more than that; in his own theoretic way, Ramón has given us in this work a gregueristic reflection on the art of writing novels; it is, in a sense, the «laboratory record» of his experiments with the kind of narrative he was really interested in writing, that is, the kind he was to call «novels of the nebula».

# IV

## ¡REBECA!, OR THE IMAGE OF ILLUSION

The title of this section might give the impression of a redundancy. Actually, it is meant to follow the form of the preceding section titles while conveying the idea of the third nebular novel, which is the account of a man's quest for the signs of reality and the personal meaning of life.

According to Ramón himself[1] and to Gaspar Gómez de la Serna,[2] this novel was first published in 1936[3]; I have not been able to find a copy of this edition. It was published again in 1947[4] (the same year *El hombre perdido* appeared for the first time). My lack of access to a copy of the 1936 version is unfortunate indeed, because it is quite probable, for reasons which will be pointed out presently, that there is revision in the «primera edición, marzo 1947» thus captioned by its publisher Janés. There are also some curious sidelights, only one of which I will mention at this point, and that is that, halfway through the book, the narrator says about the protagonist that «sólo él tenía que encontrar la cifra de la posible llegada de la escondida» (p. 102), while among the «novelas grandes» attributed to Andrés Castilla in *El novelista* there is one entitled *La escondida,* about which nothing further is written in that book. The obvious question is whether at the time *El Incongruente* and *El novelista* were published (1922-1923) Ramón was contemplating or indeed writing another novel on the search for reality in life.

*¡Rebeca!* can best be analyzed by summarizing what happens externally or dynamically, so to speak, in the story, that is, what actions take place, and concomitantly pointing out the repeated themes and reiterated images which represent what there is internally or statically

---

[1] *Obras selectas* (Madrid: Editorial Plenitud [1947]), p. 1090 (in the bibliography which appears in that anthology, the date given to *¡Rebeca!* is 1937; see p. 1316). *El hombre perdido,* «Prólogo a las novelas de la nebulosa» (Madrid, Espasa Calpe, Colección Austral [1947], p. 12).

[2] *Ramón (Obra y vida)* (Madrid, Taurus [1963]), p. 281 (bibliography).

[3] Santiago de Chile, Editorial Ercilla.

[4] Barcelona, José Janés, Editor; all quotations are from this edition.

in the narrative. This is, in essence, what I have done with the earlier novels.

The novel revolves almost exclusively around one character, whose name is simply Luis. As in the cases of Gustavo in *El Incongruente* and Andrés Castilla in *El novelista,* Luis is a member of a privileged social class, a fact that needs no explanation. He knows that life is an enigma but he wishes to find whatever would represent to him its solution, and he thinks that the joy of true love should be the most likely source of such a solution. «Entre sus pocos muebles, entre diván y librería, tenía un armario con tipo de puerta, opaco, pintado de negro, donde guardaba recuerdos inconexos, lo que traía de los días de busca y captura y todo lo mezclaba sin arreglo» (p. 8). From that cabinet or wardrobe he expects that someday the dream of his life will appear: «Le satisfacía tener una sombra secreta como incubadora de lo que no se acaba de encontrar, como nido de los pájaros secretos, como guarida de los triángulos y otras formas geométricas de la geometría de lo escondido» (p. 9). It is interesting to compare the function of this cabinet in Luis' life with that of Gustavo's oneiric wardrobe in *El Incongruente,* Chapter XXVII. He hardly opens the cabinet except to put things in it, but once he briefly shows the inside to his brother and sister; when she tries to prod deeper she can not, because there is something of herself in it.

Somehow there is a vague consistency in the accumulation of old things that seems to suggest the consistency of life. That mixture, that disorder (reminiscent of Ramón's theory of the *greguería* and of his very style of writing) constitutes Luis' hope and expectation of finding what he seeks, which he has unconsciously baptized with the name of Rebeca. The name had to be that of a woman because «sólo parejas de alma —una masculina y otra femenina— sorben un poco de inmortalidad en la vida si se comprendieron y se amaron...» (p. 10). And so Luis looks everywhere for his Rebeca: «sabía que aquella mujer o pátera o tazón estaba en la vida, iba a encontrarla en cuerpo y alma o en sustitutivo de quinqué o jarrón...» So far, it would seem that the name and its femininity can apply to something other than a real woman; it can apply even to an inanimate object, though such an application provides a fulfillment much too brief, and Luis goes on looking for a woman to whom he can justifiably give the name of Rebeca. Thus the quest for a definite reality results in the frequent deception of illusion: «Muchas mujeres se habían indignado con él al llamarlas Rebeca y muchas cosas se le habían caído de la mano... porque en ellas creyó encontrar el indicio de Rebeca, la ideal catalizadora nebulosa...»

How did he choose the name? His female cousins once asked him who his girl friend was, and he replied Rebeca. «Entonces notó que había lanzado el nombre más pecaminoso y femenino que se le podía haber ocurrido» (p. 11). When they asked him who she was, he answered: «¡Ah, eso sólo lo sé yo! Nadie sabrá nunca nada de ella» (p. 12). His cousin Asunción opined that he and Rebeca would someday get married; this worried Luis because of Rebeca's insubstantiality: «Esa tarde fue cuando se dio cuenta de que todo el mundo podía encerrarse en una caja de cerillas y que sólo Rebeca quedaba fuera» (pp. 12-13). The most amazing thing is that a chance name would become his one obsession, and yet there are conflicts within him, for he is afraid of actually finding her. She is not an ideal; he is sure that she is somewhere among all the things and all the people: «¡No hay más que Rebeca, primer premio de realidad...!» Is Rebeca, then, life itself? «Le repugnaba esa idea como cualquier otro simbolismo más espiritual. Rebeca era sólo Rebeca» (p. 14).

Luis' sensuality makes all kinds of things attractive to him, for anything could be Rebeca and Rebeca could be anywhere, but the magnetic preponderance is toward women (in this we have a clear resemblance to Gustavo the Misfit and to many of the *greguerías:* «no perdía esa obsesión por la mujer que era lo único que vencía la muerte, la hipocresía de todos, lo que animaba al profesor a hablar a sus alumnas a las que veía en traje de baño...» (p. 16). Thus increases the number of relationships with different women. Though there is no mention of what is happening to any other character except when in the presence of Luis, there are vague references to an impending social conflict: «Le atraían más aquellas vidas fallecidas de los que fueron más viejos y más pobres que él, que las vidas que se prometían los insurgentes de su alrededor» (p. 18). We get the impression of a man obsessed and unable or unwilling to entertain certain kinds of ideas, as well as a man who prefers to subordinate ideas as such to the images provided by the senses: «Tenía cada vez más amor a aquel sofá heredado en cuyo pelote se guarecía la nebulosa.» The narrative rises dramatically as Rebeca takes the form of a blue teapot and Luis converses with her. She says: «Vuestro defecto es creer en la prioridad del tiempo...» (p. 19). When Luis inquires if, after all, one o'clock does not come before two o'clock, she says no, expressing a thought which Luis characterizes as one typical of a teapot. Nevertheless, he is impressed; she explains that this is so only because he never listened before to his teapot, «la sustituta de sus días sin contagio de mujer...». The teapot is ceramic: «Del barro con agua brota la única idea superior a la muerte...» He is willing to listen indefinitely; he has no appointment. To which she replies: «Siempre se está citado con una idea... No aceptes la que ibas a tener... No me oigas más que a mí.» What about love, he asks; love me, Rebeca, she says. What about woman; that comes later. What about the soul; it remains in a teapot as it previously remained in an amphora. Imagination turns the teapot into an erotic object: «Representa el seno y la cadera» (p. 21). He is convinced: «Desde luego eres la realidad embarrancada al nivel del corazón... Eres quinqué y mujer... contéstame a las preguntas más insolubles de mi vida: ¿Con qué dar interés a la novela de la existencia?» She answers: «Suponte cambiado en la cuna y que eres otro que el que crees ser. Obra como otro y siempre supón que el malo está entre los gitanos y los agitadores.» The concept of «otherness» found in El novelista reappears here, as does that of the novel as an imaginative recreation of historical facts.

From the dialogue with the teapot the story moves quickly and without transition to a public park where Luis indulges in lovemaking with a young girl: «Obrerilla de la erotología, el destino la lanzaba a pimentar el jardín...» (p. 24). The theme of destiny, so prevalent in El Incongruente, reappears here. Then we find Luis in a heated argument with an uncle, Don Alejandrito; the latter contends that «la cuestión social es lo más importante» (p. 25); the former holds that the most important thing is more personal, and not merely an animalistic desire for the female. When Don Alejandrito finally asks him what is Rebeca in the abstract, Luis replies: «es lo que evidencia la vida sin rencor ni violencia, lo que encanta de nitidez del vivir, la que no nos hace olvidar la muerte». It is interesting to note that within the sentence he shifts from the abstract to the feminine concrete when faced with the prospect of death; anything can delight, but only the right woman can make a man forget his mortality. Luis declares that Rebeca is the only woman who can be his alone. Don Alejandrito tells him that he has seen such a woman; Luis at first denies the possibility; then, giving in to wishful thinking, agrees to meet her at his uncle's place of employment. In the following chapter of the novel (VII), joined by perfect narrative continuity, we find the protagonist at the Ministry where his uncle is a minor functionary. He meets the promised widow: «la saludó y siguió buscando en ella los rasgos que tenía su figura de la mujer buscada. Poseía algunos, pero en un grado mortecino...» (p. 29). They leave the office together and go to a café. Luis is aware that he is in command and asks her name: «Rosa...» (p. 31). She invites him to her apartment, where first he notices a screen (see the story of that name in El novelista), then the picture of a navy captain of whom she is the sponsor; Luis advises her to sever the relationship. As he is about to seduce her, she knocks over the screen, an accident which has the strange effect of rendering him powerless. The next chapter begins with an unexpected visit by Rosa to his quarters: the captain has shown up and has shown bad manners. «Los militares le habían quitado a Rebeca, pero, sin embargo, él no tenía que vengarse en ellos, sino en ella», Rosa (p. 34). Luis seduces her. She tells him that she has given away the screen. «¿Tú me querrás siempre?» she asks, just like the women Gustavo seduces in El Incongruente. Luis tells her that she might have been Rebeca, except that Rebeca is to be found «más metida en armarios de luna... más invisible, sin haber usado nunca ese cuellecito de martas...» (p. 35). Luis is actually the opposite of Gustavo: «Luis creaba el destino, aunque pareciese que el destino le creaba a él.» The immense difference is that Gustavo is looking for the right woman, without knowing who she is, while Luis knows who the right woman is and therefore is looking for her. Rosa starts to leave; Luis helps her out: «Se despedía de una mujer que pudo ser suya, pero que él no quiso recoger» (p. 36).

Don Alejandrito asks if the girl was Rebeca; Luis answers negatively, though he must admit there was a slight resemblance. «¿No será que das vuelta alrededor de otra mujer de la que estuviste enamorado?» The name of the girl in question is Elisa. Luis goes home, calls his brother on the telephone, and asks him to come over. While he waits, he tears up Elisa's love letters and those of another girl named Carmen. When the brother arrives, he is surprised that Luis still has the old cabinet. «Un día saldrá de él la reconstrucción del ser que espero», answers the protagonist (p. 39). The dialogue that follows is a polemic on the validity of conventions; Luis rejects it; he even rejects the proposition that two plus two make four on the grounds that every individual's twos are different. Despite the total disagreement, the brothers part amicably.

Luis finds himself seated at a desk in an agency for message delivery: «nadie puede escoger su presente» (p. 42). He is going to write a letter, but to whom? «A Rebeca, la no encontrada... / En el almanaque para todas las consultas de los ojos estaba la fecha actual. Pero esa realidad iba contra la irrealidad de Rebeca. / No puso la fecha que hubiese querido... porque tampoco convenía contravenir la verdadera...» The letter expresses Luis' resignation toward his constant yet hopeless search: «Eres la que desenmascara la luz y revela que la evidencia no es evidente...» (p. 43; again, the slashes used throughout represent paragraph breaks). He closes by describing the letter as «llena de golondrinas que alguna vez vendrán...». It is interesting to note, in passing, that in 1949 Ramón published his *Cartas a las golondrinas;* in the preface to the 1962 edition (Madrid: Espasa-Calpe [Colección Austral]), he states: «Este libro nació de una carta que fue como una declaración de amor...» How will Luis' letter reach Rebeca? On the envelope he writes an arbitrary address: «El jefe apuntó sus señas en el libro y el chico corrió no se sabe dónde.» Luis goes to a café; he is not satisfied with the letter he has written, so he decides to write another there: «te escribo por un conducto mejor y con más seguridad en encontrarte en lo inhallado... / Es más veloz tu nombre que todos los automóviles. Eres la marca del futuro y no dejas de ser como todo el pasado...» (p. 44). Luis' resignation is now shot through with eroticism: «No me vas a dar una función de 'soirée' nunca ni me vas a dejar frío de alta tensión con tus senos.» He tells Rebeca that, in effect, neither she nor her immediate ancestor has been born, and yet she has «una antepasada de medallón». Such a letter serves to show that Rebeca exists among the nonexistent, and thus she is not «el arquetipo de mujer sino su nombre esquelético e inconsútil» (p. 45).

Luis thinks he sees Rebeca in the most unlikely places, in the nooks and crannies of his imagination. Though he reprimands himself, he cannot blot out his erotic desire for Rebeca, yet he knows that such desire is, in this case, the carnal aspect of true love: «no era un aventurero sino un enamorado, un voluptuoso más que un acometedor» (p. 47). A dialogue on future love between Luis and the nonexistent woman follows an extremely significant statement: «El secreto de todo es que el silencio tiene voz de mujer» (p. 48). This is an excellent example of how this novel is structured. Narrative statements can be attributed to the narrator, just as the dialogue can be attributed to the character or characters. But aphoristic statements such as the one just quoted must be attributed to both the narrator and the protagonist. The same goes for the asseverations which follow it on the same page and the next: «—No te preocupa el problema social. / —El problema social es la declaración de los unos contra los otros...» (p. 49), where interior monologue and authorial commentary blend in a single statement.

Luis is visited by a friend named Aníbal: «Tenían que vencer a aquel día impar con uno de aquellos diálogos en que procuraban hacer laboratorio» (p. 50). The «conversation», in effect, consists of aphorisms and fragmentary phrases which complement one another to make up other aphorisms: «La muestra de una guantería nos enseñó el camino de la realidad» (p. 52) and «La oreja de la llave es la única que oye la voz del futuro» (p. 53). Suddenly out of patience, they decide to seek distraction in the public bar downstairs. This sort of narrative subterfuge used for transition is frequent in Ramón's works.

Luis «necesitaba verse en el espejo, acercarse a su imagen, consolar su frente con su propia frente» (p. 54). The gregueristic duality of the mirror effect is operative here, and it is interesting to find mention of the protagonist's image, for that is precisely all we have in the whole novelistic structure. Luis is now in the company of Alicia, who looks at him «como sospechando en sus palabras broma y verdad». The description is very much a parallel of Ramón's definition of the greguería, as humor and metaphor. The author's whimsy soars once again as we learn that Alicia, when suffering from one of her chronic headaches, resembles Rebeca: «La otra que hubiera podido ser se revela en mis dolores de cabeza... No buscas siempre una Rebeca, pues esa quiere salir de mí cuando me pongo así» (p. 55). Things are not what they seem and any deviance is potency for changing anything. Luis at first is prone to believe Alicia's statement because «un sentimiento extraño de comprobación le hacía buscar su pasión precisamente cuando ella se quejaba de sus sienes». She, in turn, takes advantage of her discomfort «para ser otra del otro lado del respaldo manicomial». (The motif of the headache will reappear on pp. 77, 174). But is Luis crazy? We have to proceed on the assumption that this is not so, for we have been told: «Él no estaba loco, pero quería vivir la locura de la vida con todos sus trastornos y sus esquizofrenias» (p. 7). Is Alicia the one who is crazy? Luis knows that she is just a substitute for what he really wants and feels that she is trying to get revenge for that, so he leaves: «iba a perderse en la madrugada como un perro... / Rebeca cada vez estaba más lejos, sin guía posible, detrás de todas las mentiras» (p. 56).

Luis' desire of the impossible becomes manifest in further ways: «Quería leer los libros que no se habían escrito...» This opens a literary passage: «Debía de haber una novela en que la protagonista estuviese vestida de cortina y llevase a la cintura el cíngulo de los pasamanos. Sólo en ese traje representaría a la espía que... quiere... decirnos: 'Todo es mentira menos la llave del gas» (p. 57). The suggestion of suicide as an easy way out of the frustrating labyrinth of life is obvious. What is more interesting for my purpose is the manner in which Ramón evidently thinks of fictional characters, that is, as images, perhaps as moving images in a motion picture; his frequent mention of cinematography encourages such a conclusion. His references to the whole atmosphere of novels, on the other hand, is also interesting: «Novelas que oliesen a claraboyas grises llenas de polvo antiguo, esas claraboyas de patio sobre las que se está al otro lado del mundo, del lado de los ratones y de los abortos» (pp. 57-58). From a gregueristic point of view, this is as close as we can get in real life to the 'para-real' which Ramón is trying to explore and of which Luis' Rebeca would constitute a much more desirable facet. «'La claraboya' se podría titular esa novela, y mujeres inequívocas vendrían a visitar al personaje principal...» (p. 58) —the images and situations do not vary even in hypothetical versions of the same novel in which they appear. Here is the quid of this unexpected critique: «Estaba cansado de lecturas vanas con canarios de los que no se dice la verdad, que 'cantan con una alegría de cucharillas' y en que si pasan trenes nunca dice el autor que 'sonaban a tinajas asmáticas' y si se ve una red no dice que 'es el suspensorio íntimo del mar'.» In other words, Luis-Ramón is attacking conventional realism in literature and advocating the use of gregueristic images, even at the expense of «character development», because what people do does not matter as long as they do it «on this side of the world» without suspecting that there is another side. Realism is «esperar lo que suceda», and that does not interest him; «se necesitan nuevas asociaciones de ideas, algo que salve el momento...» Another conversation with himself leaves

Luis «en el limbo de lo que no se ha dicho nunca y es necesario que alguien diga para que el hombre pueda agarrarse mejor en la incertidumbre del mundo» (p. 59). Again the narrator overcomes the thoughts of the protagonist: «las paredes son el sostén del pensamiento... / Las paredes y los techos crean la inspiración... / Las frases nacen de las paredes o de la nada». There follows a group of statements, introduced by the adverb *como,* regarding what is not to be found in books. In the end, «le dolía la cabeza ya a Luis por haber hecho el esfuerzo de leer lo no escrito...» (p. 60).

Luis goes to an art museum (cf. Chapter XXXVI of *El Incongruente)* and comes across the portrait of a woman whom he likes. He asks the woman in the picture what her name is, and she answers Rebeca. The portrait is, of course, not for sale: «¡Rebeca otra vez perdida después de habérsele mostrado con ese sigilo y con esa imposibilidad con que sólo una Rebeca de cuadro podía haber jugado con su corazón insaciado!» (p. 62). Out of sorts, Luis takes to the street one night looking for Rebeca. He comes across a girl and, under the pressure of his obstinate desire, is deluded into saying: «Tiene usted la belleza por la que siempre he suspirado» (p. 63). The desire is mutual but, after a brief dalliance, Luis realizes that she is what he does not want. And so thirty minutes later he is on his way to visit a former mistress. She lets him in and he begins to recognize the premises: «El armario, el baúl, la cómoda de aquella mujer eran lo interesante. / Conquistar esa arca de recuerdos y trivialidades era el éxito para un hombre que odiaba la repetición de la vida» (p. 65). Critics who have remarked on the role of the trivial in Ramón's vision and work can add to it the role of memory and come closer to the origin of the *greguería,* its purpose here explained paradoxically by Luis-Ramón as the transcendence of everyday living. The woman, who had lavished her breasts over all of Spanish America, once again leaves Luis with the impression that «quizás una posible Rebeca se había dejado pedazos desgarrados en todas las repúblicas...» (p. 68).

Having received some unexpected money, Luis wishes to purchase «un objeto comparativo... algo para esperar». In a draper's shop he sees an inexpensive tapestry depicting five women who look alike, each bracketed by columns. He buys it, because «por poco dinero había encontrado un reposorio para su busca de novia...» and because «el misterio de las cinco mujeres que eran la misma le angustiaba como si perpetuase alguno de sus amores pasados» (p. 70). It should be pointed out that under the pseudonymn Tristán, Ramón had published in 1913 a volume entitled *Tapices,* comprised mostly of rather sensual sketches. In *¡Rebeca!* the aesthetic value which the tapestry holds for the narrator-protagonist is significant and evident, as he states: «En el tapiz está incinerada la imagen, como curada en el recuerdo. Está hecho para que apoye en él la cabeza la impaciencia y tenga ventana la desidia.» To what extent does the tapestry fill in for Rebeca? Within the gregueristic disquisition on the textile object, this paragraph suddenly confronts the reader: «Decoración de perspectiva de nichos: La sencillez de Rebeca es posible que se asombre cuando lo vea y sea el fondo adecuado a la fotografía del beso.» The strangely important tapestry is, in effect, a preparation for the ultimate discovery. Luis «se sentía feliz con su tapiz de ocasión... y sentía que la novela de su vida ya tenía una ilustración digna entre las muchas páginas de peregrinación, buscando por todas las ferias la señorita que se desmaya de pie» (p. 71). A new reference to the social conflict: «Prefería ser ese adolescente de malos tapices económicos a ser ese tembladeral de los rumores de revolución...» He goes to sleep and dreams about the «mujer de túnica y sandalias que completaban las cinco mujeres en el cinematógrafo rancio del tapiz» —a touching variation on the last scene of *El Incongruente*.

Luis and a nameless friend engage in debate. «¡No hay que abolir el azar!» says Luis (p. 72), in a parody of Mallarmé's great innovative poem. The what is one to do, asks the friend. Luis replies: «No querer arreglar todos los destinos para arreglar el nuestro, porque la vida carecería de interés si se suprime en ella la libre competencia para vivir o morir.» Through his protagonist, Ramón gives us here a sample of what some critics (see Chabás, *op. cit.*, for example) have labeled as his conservatism; and in truth he was conservative and unpolitical simultaneously. Luis-Ramón puts it this way: «Mientras no tengan los más su palabra pacífica, su Rebeca íntima, se matarán por mantener la paz, serán fratricidas en nombre de la fraternidad... La fe en las ideas generales no lleva más que a la destrucción...» And, again characteristically mixing the practical with the poetic, he says: «Esos que no saben lo que quieren saquearán o aplastarán la novela de la vida... La vida sin novela no tiene ningún interés...» (p. 73). When his friend chides him for having a weak theory, Luis is undaunted and naively continues: «Sólo se sostuvo tranquilo el mundo cuando todos vivieron de sus detalles... Cuando se ha dejado de mirar todo eso la vida es una porquería en discusión...» And what about beliefs, asks the friend. A Romantic element rises above both religion and social justice in Luis' approach to life; as far as he is concerned, the thing that keeps man from being completely savage is «la afinidad de la materia del espíritu con las demás materias». His friend accuses him of having an indefinite attitude; Luis replies that he is equally perplexed by such a definite one: «Dios no está más que en la fe y en las observaciones que se vayan haciendo por los caminos» (p. 74). They could never agree, but Luis assures his friend that he could never resort to the use of a gun to force the issue. They part; Luis feels that «en su lengua saburrosa estaban las playas de lo indecible y lo incontestable... / necesitaba la calle y se metió en su laberinto». The social concern evinced by the early *Entrando en fuego* and the passage entitled «La criada» in *El novelista* has given way to aesthetic aloofness. Luis comes upon a book bindery, and his whimsy cannot keep away from its bookish inclination. «Hay que saber encuadernar la vida de uno» (p. 75), he thinks to himself, a notion which for Ramón could have autobiographical implications. Then, a store which sells bell jars suggests to Luis the possibility of protecting Rebeca with one if she turned out to be something small; after all bell jars are «incubadoras de sueños, ... confinamientos que purifican el espacio y que podían dar albergue al corazón herido o al alma sin mansión». Instead he goes to the apartment of Candelaria, «mujer vulgar aunque bondadosa, la maestra del piso bajo, la de la llamada sigilosa en las maderas cerradas...». As on other occasions, the narrator takes the opportunity of indulging in word-plays (puns and alliterations); at the street corner there is a «vieja vendedora de cacahuetes que parecía una alcahueta», and Luis is on his way toward «los muebles modestos de la maestra...» (p. 76). Longing for Rebeca, disillusioned by other women, Luis finds respite in the abode of that «obrera de la pedagogía» who receives him without rancor.

A thunderstorm wakes Luis up during the night in an atmosphere of hallucination: «Rebeca, como una imagen de la electricidad, triste de no tener sombrero, le pedía aspirina» (p. 77). The schoolteacher does not have even an aspirin. Why did he remember Rebeca, she asks Luis; he answers: «Porque dejé un libro con las páginas dobladas como si quisiera acordarme de algo y no sé de qué quisiera acordarme.» Amid the noise of the thunderstorm, Luis «quería encontrar la razón de la vida, la verdadera razón de esperar a esa cómica de la tregua que debía ser Rebeca, despreciadora de sortijas». An apparently gratuitous foreshadowing, which actually serves the purpose of increasing the dimensions of the gregueristic imagery, appears in the statement: «Acorde de tormenta es haber dicho ¡Basta! su tío Jorge que había de morir al año siguiente...» (p. 78). A peremptory remark —«¿Y ahora quiero bergamotas?»— and suddenly the illusion of Rebeca is there, turned into a momentary reality, asking the right questions, giving the right answers, understanding him, and then it disappears; Luis knows this when the words are contradicted by the memory of his cousin who had typhus during stormy days. How can he hold on to reality? The answer lies implicit in gregueristic images: «Un sable entrando del revés —curva contra curva— en su vaina... la extraña asociación de violín y guillotina, el grito de la gallina a la que han cortado el pescuezo...» (p. 80). Luis is not a true Romantic, for he has always suffered during thunderstorms, but his quest is just as tenacious: «Su crisis de buscador de Rebeca le hacía buscar aún el coágulo que fuese la señal de haber vivido, el sello en relieve y en seco del certificado indudable.» Is he looking for an object or for a relation between objects? The fictional quest in this narrative seems such a parallel of Ramón's objective as a writer of aphorisms. Luis is not mad, but «pensaba todas las locuras posibles para ver de encontrar la señal verdadera...» (p. 81). He is about to cry out in anguish the title of his novel, when the rain diminishes, erasing what was «written on his mind».

The daughter of a former mistress goes to see Luis. (One is reminded of Campoamor's «Las hijas de las madres que yo amé...».) The narrator notes that «fue a verle con la idea homicida de la seducción aquella noche». What if Rebeca were to emerge from María, daughter of Elisa? «Nunca creyó que pudiese sonreír al aceptar a aquella criatura... junto a la conciencia palpitante de su armario negro, pero sonrió con bastante felicidad» (p. 82). With a Cuban accent she murmurs: «Esperé siempre este momento» (p. 84). It is not love they find but passion: «Si a alguien se iba a parecer Rebeca al ser hallada era a esta mujer que hundía al cisne al echarse hacia atrás» (p. 85). But he reconsiders; something could be wrong: «Sospechaba que algo funcionaba mal en él y que el gusto de aquella mujer le había hecho olvidar lo único que le servía para salvarse de la mujer, su ilusión de Rebeca.» The reality he seeks is unattainable; the reality he possesses is insufficient; the illusion he can continue to perceive is the only thing on which he can predicate his existence. And yet Luis cannot deny his pleasure in this girl, in her antics, and in the illusion provided by carnal love. María seems to eclipse Rebeca; she is a Salomé who «traía cabezas de hombres con barba que tiraba en la carbonera» (p. 86). Luis is confident that the situation will not last; her own excess of desire will free him of her.

As a reaction to his recent experience, Luis begins to find traces of Rebeca in other domestic objects. And yet María «era la única mujer a la que había dado el nombre de Rebeca...» (p. 90). Something which she had in common with the inanimate was her barrenness. He cannot help feeling disconsolate, though he knows that other men will follow him into the abyss. After mourning the loss of such deep love, he turns for consolation to his renewed loneliness. Later, at the expense of the electric service, Luis goes out and buys a *bibelot;* we are never told what the «object» is (Ramón had so many, and Mallarmé abolished one of resonant inanity), but when he asks the question «¿Eres Rebeca?» (p. 93), the object replies: «Soy Rebeca.»

One morning the girl who picks up the trash comes calling. The encounter has a peculiar effect on Luis; he opens his mysterious cabinet for her to look: «Nunca había abierto de par en par el armario de la gestación, y cuando ella estuvo cerca abrió sus dos compuertas para que ella viese que él también tenía un basurero confuso» (p. 94). From such a reminder of Luis' whimsical magic-box, the narrator goes back to the crude realities of human desire. Luis and the garbage girl participate in a humorous and joyful love-affair. As for him, «ni su memoria se atrevía a decir Rebeca y celebraba como una venganza por la espera a que le tenía sometido» (p. 97). After a while the chance lovers part cordially. He promises to call her again, and she leaves as she had entered, «sin dar importancia al umbral de la puerta» (p. 98).

Luis becomes more and more aware of other people in his environment who are in favor of violence and death; «querían apagar el mundo», says the narrator (p. 98) in a way reminiscent of the last line of *El novelista:* «el mundo que morirá de un apagón» (p. 268). However, «el personaje de novela de esas épocas —que no es el héroe que va a parar a la ilegible poesía épica— vive su vida casera de un modo supremo, escapándose a la destrucción, sin que pueda hacer tabla rasa con él la tontería criminal» (p. 99). The narrator has referred already to Luis's novel-like life; evidently Luis is here the fictional character who, not being heroic, will manage to escape the degeneracy of violence. Luis is totally unpolitical, which is to say that for him society is a fact but the social question is a threat. His only reply to this sort of thing is Rebeca, for she «sustituiría a la muerte en vida y sería el fantasma que es necesario para que la casa no se pueble de fantasmas» (p. 100). This thought is followed by a dialogue between Luis and a conjuration of his longed-for woman. He tells the illusion: «No creas que soy de los que creen que la mujer es la escanciadora... / Sólo aspiraré a saber que me quieres...» How will he ever find her in reality? «Sólo podría dar con ella llevando el santo y seña cazado en el crepúsculo matutino como un talismán, como un pez del cielo aún vivo en la mano de esa hora del otro crepúsculo» (p. 102). There is an infinite number of possible passwords. «La madrugada que él encontrase las palabras 'Embarcadero' o 'Carey' combinadas con otras o quizás solitarias, encontraría a la mujer con qué viajar y morir cuando el mismo cristal roto les degollase a los dos» (pp. 102-03). As one could have predicted, Luis is said to rely on the words, the traditional units of language (and passwords are traditionally magic units), ultimately to unlock the secret of his life. Actually he already has the password: Rebeca. What he is seeking is the woman whom he can effectively address with that name. This whimsical situation is, by the way, a novelistic counterpart of an aspect of the aphorism already discussed with respect to Ramón, namely, his use of language as an instrument of 'precognition'.

Luis feels progressively more alienated. «Perdido, cada vez más perdido en este tiempo de perdición en que parece como si en la tierra no hubiese ni caminos ni pueblos» (p. 103). Thus the narrator describes the protagonist, in a way which anticipates the title and theme of the fourth and last of Ramón's nebular novels. The answer he gives is the answer he seeks: «Su empeño de loco era Rebeca como única solución al abandono, como posibilidad de oír la voz que le secundase, el reloj paralelo que da la hora al mismo tiempo que el de la casa» (p. 103). The Platonic doctrine of the halves searching for each other reappears, as in *El Incongruente*. Luis is absorbed in thought: «Hay que volver a inventar el lío de la vida, el laberinto, el préstamo del calor de las alfombras y la sorpresa de las ternuras» (p. 104). Suddenly, his «diálogo íntimo» is interrupted by the ringing of the telephone; it is «su espía», a man appointed perhaps by fate to watch his movements, and the spy wants to see him. Luis agrees; maybe the spy can tell him where to find the real Rebeca, «la solución de su vida». The spy admits being aware of Luis' search for a woman who is forbidden. Why forbidden? Luis inquires. «Porque no sabe usted el daño que haría a la vida el que hubiese una mujer como la que usted busca, desinteresada y capaz de fomentar la independencia de usted que roba ya los objetos de las tiendas con sólo mirarlos...» (p. 105). No doubt that Luis-Ramón subsists on the visual (and to a great extent physical) acquisition of material objects; Rebeca would complete his gregueristic cosmos and help him exhaust the universe. Luis denies being «un erótico»; the fact that he is looking for Rebeca has nothing to do with eroticism (?). Rebeca is not an ideal; she is a real woman who exists somewhere. She is expected, however, to be ideally perfect. And yet Luis does not say that (there is only the implication); he barely knows her name which, surprisingly, the spy did not already know: «Rebeca es inencontrable porque las que se llaman Rebeca no son Rebeca.» This is a very important detail on which I shall comment later. Finding Rebeca is truly a world-shaking event; the spy asks: «¿No comprende que puede variar la estabilidad del mundo el que un ser como usted encuentre lo que busca?» (p. 106). The emphasis has been shifted from the object sought to the seeker, Luis-Ramón, from the *greguería* to the maker of *greguerías*, the exhauster of worlds. The protagonist smiles to himself after furtively glancing at his secret cabinet. But the spy notices the gesture and inquires accordingly. Luis confesses: «Es el secreto de mi vida... Ahí se está organizando Rebeca...» (p. 107). As the spy sticks his head into the cabinet to see what is there, Luis closes the doors on him sharply «guillotinando el ¡ay! de aquel hombre». After a while the corpse flattens out all by itself until there is nothing left but a suit of clothes on the floor, with a white balloon for a head and two rubber gloves for hands. «Así se puede cometer un crimen», comments the narrator, undoubtedly meaning that one can «kill» figments of one's imagination, not people (again the parody of Unamuno and Augusto Pérez). The telephone rings once more; it is his brother. They set a date for getting together. Luis is left with the gregueristic thought that a man always spies on his brother.

Another reprise of *El Incongruente:* «Siempre estaba esperando Luis que sucediesen en la vida fenómenos extraños y caprichosos» (p. 108). At a café he perceives that the couples present are mismatched: «La mujer de larga toca debía estar con el muchacho rubio y la mujer del jersey blanco con senos puntiagudos debía estar con el moreno.» *Gregueria* is not so much plain association as it is dissociation followed by a new association; the preceding is a good narrative example. A woman approaches him: «Luis la aceptó. Probaba la voluptuosidad casual, que es la más pura de las voluptuosidades. / Rebeca podía ser la mujer más impensada. Bastaba que le dijese la palabra de la dedicación.» She wishes to tell him all about her, and again Luis does not refuse because «también podía ser Rebeca la verdadera voluptuosidad, no la palabra» (p. 109). Her name is Concepción; she is a «poor little rich girl», who, having been deceived by a gypsy lover, has now left the convent where she took refuge in the hope of rejoining her family. She is obviously very much attracted to him: «le miró como si le hubiese dicho lo que después querrá volver a oír y por lo que pedirá clemencia en las cartas de llamada» (p. 110). He is attracted to her also: «En su mirada se notaba cada vez más que era la voluptuosa, la que se atraganta de palabras y de cera» (p. 111). Does this refer to the words of literature and the wax of dolls like those mentioned in *El Incongruente?* Gustavo was said to have lost «the most beautiful woman in the world».

The amorous adventures in *¡Rebeca!* resemble those of *El Incongruente* because of a basic need on the part of both protagonists. But, as I have pointed out, Gustavo is looking for the right woman blindly, as it were, while Luis knows that the woman he is looking for is, in effect, a concrete manifestation of an abstraction. This is an obstinate quest; Luis is drawn to women in order to discover their potentialities as that manifestation. At this point in the narrative, he notices a woman in whose turquoise ring «copulaban el rosa y el azul» (p. 111), but before he can approach her, he remembers that he has an appointment, for he is now regularly meeting the gypsy's love-victim on Fridays. This time her flesh incites painful caresses, and her protest elicits sarcasm. «Búscate otra Rebeca», she tells him (p. 113) and leaves him forever.

There is a unique and gratuitous commentary on the nature of business: «la realidad del vacío de lo que es el comercio, el gran engaño de la vida». Beyond its own significance, the unexpected character of the allusion technically helps to point out the unity of narration and interior monologue, a product of the inextricable, «nebulous» cross-identity of author, narrator, and protagonist in this work. This is followed by plays on words: «cuando falla la vida es cuando no hay opción a entrar en el Bar y al bajar al metro se es barómetro y no varón» (p. 114). The need of finding Rebeca has many strange effects; there is even an imaginary dialogue with the object of this need, at the end of which Luis states: «reconoceré que eres Rebeca, la mujer que no guarda sus sueños... La que aún no pude encontrar...» (p. 115). His family (brothers and sister) are of no help; his sister acts as if she were his widow: «pues la hermana siempre es la viuda del hermano mayor.» This is indeed a suggestive yet abstruse notion. Luis is deep in thought; he knows that, if he ever finds her, Rebeca will be a martyr and, «en la posibilidad del hijo casual iba a ir todo eso mezclado y sólo gracias a eso tendría alma ese hijo...» (p. 117). This is an emphatic moment for Luis psychologically, encapsulating his whole life: «Estaba bajo el en- sañamiento del deseo de capturar la muestra del cosmos, lo que pudiera servir de reclamo en el escaparate de haber vivido» (pp. 117-18). He is desperate; nothing seems to abate his loneliness. Then, «tropezó de pronto con un pisapapeles de ágata y comenzó a jugar como un gigante con una pirámide. / Ágata le pareció un nombre como el de Rebeca». Once again an inanimate object comes to the rescue of Luis-Ramón; the world has many compensations for a man who lives from illusion.

In a «Winter tavern» filled with smoke, the smell of liquor, and Galician words (?), Luis is confronted with a situation he did not know he would experience. He feels the cold wind through the door left open by someone who must be an *agent provocateur*. Luis asks that the door be properly closed and an altercation follows. «¡Maldita sea Rebeca!» Luis hears the man shout and immediately throws a glass at him. The man shoots him in the hand and flees. Luis is accompanied by someone to get first aid and then to the police station; he is in good spirits because the incident has reanimated his faith in Rebeca. The testimony varies; some say the man shouted «¡Maldita sea su madre!» but Luis insists on what he heard, and when asked how that could have offended him, he explains: «Para mí, Rebeca es el más alto ideal» (p. 120). When subsequently asked who is Rebeca and he is unable to answer to the policeman's satisfaction, Luis is sent before a magistrate. There he de- clares: «hay una clave de nuestra vida que lleva un nombre... Para mí es Rebeca... Está entre las páginas de un libro, es la imagen que triunfa de una revista que hemos tirado, está en el vaso de agua que bebimos con más sed...» (p. 121). The judge realizes that Luis' apparent madness contains a fundamental truth: «Todo el que dispara sin motivo dispara contra el ideal sagrado que llevamos en el corazón...» (p. 122). Luis is set free; he feels that what happened «añadía realidad a la inmacu- lada de sus sueños, a la nunca habida». He goes to sleep that night wondering if the criminal has been caught. When he awakes to the «clay» of living humanity, Luis wonders if Rebeca has ever had a lover. Between the night of the altercation and the new day, the process of sleep has added reality to his hope of finding Rebeca. Somehow the quest has developed a structure of its own within the mind of the protagonist: «La novela de Rebeca que no tenía el asunto de audiencia de todas las novelas, parecía entrar en una fase eslabonada» (p. 123).

Luis reads the morning newspaper; the tavern incident is treated inconsequentially. He concludes that he will have to carry on the search for the culprit in order to discover why he cursed Rebeca, «ya que sólo se maldice lo que se adora». He begins frequenting taverns; his sister criticizes his behavior: «Todos conspiraban contra la felicidad, contra el encuentro con Rebeca...» (p. 124). Life itself seems to shout that Rebeca does not exist. One night he sits at a table beside a young woman with the appearance of a typist about to be accosted by a revolutionary. Luis challenges the man's comradeship with the typist and leaves the tavern with her. «Hubiera querido dictarle una carta para que la hubiese escrito en la noche con las teclas de su seno: una carta a Rebeca que le disculpase de haber improvisado aquella rivalidad» (p. 126). Actually, Luis feels that the girl he has treated so gallantly is almost the opposite of his «ideal»; hence he is quite surprised to find out that her name is Rebeca Gracián. He has been the butt of a practical joke played on him by destiny (cf. *El Incongruente)* and decides not to allow himself to get into anything «que tuviese argumento», thus desisting from looking for the man who shot him. Too many names and conventional relations would undoubtedly lead to the plot of an unsophisticated novelistic structure: «El folletín llevaba a Rebeca, pero a la falsa Rebeca, nombrada así por el mal novelista que conduce los capítulos falsos según el deber del verdadero destinatario de ideales» (p. 127). Ramón indulges in a complex game: the narrator was about to become a «mal novelista» who would allow the novel of Rebeca to degenerate into a *folletín* by introducing a character whose «real» name is Rebeca and who thus could be only a false Rebeca.

Women are all around Luis, beckoning to him, tempting him, yet he has not found the one he needs. Once again, life is the touchstone: «Quería demostrar con todo eso que conocía la vida y hacer méritos para que viniese la que oculta una belleza que hace volver la cabeza a los que aún no la han visto...» (p. 129). And illusion is the consequence: «Siempre al pasar por las calles en persecución de Rebeca —la del corsé de plata— le quedaba la confusión del que entra en una farmacia y le dan una medicina equivocada» (p. 130). The novelistic structure of the *greguería* depends to a great extent on interior monologue. The reader is not at all surprised to find an interrogative reference to Luis' state of mind, bracketed by paragraphs telling of what he does: «¿Se perdía cada vez más?» The foreshadowing of *El hombre perdido* is evident.

At home, Luis is told by the maid that a gentleman wants to see him. Is he really looking for him or his double, Luis wonders, telling the girl to show in the man. The effeminate visitor is a casual acquaintance. In reply to a question about the magical cabinet, Luis states: «En ese armario se está vistiendo de novia la mujer de mis sueños... Es como esas casetas... que sacan los ilusionistas...» (p. 132). Luis explains that he is in love with Rebeca, who does not look like any movie star, whereupon the man suggests that perhaps she looks like his sister. Could it be that this chance acquaintance would lead to his finding «la clave de su vida?» (p. 133). They agree to go, all three together, to the movies. The girl, it turns out, considers Luis' pining for Rebeca something out of a pastoral novel. In the darkness of the movie house, Luis becomes convinced that «el hermano le había quitado media feminidad sin habérsela sustituido con nada» (p. 135). Suddenly he notices that «había aparecido la mitad de Rebeca en el bisel del espejo de la pantalla» (p. 136; cf. last chapter of *El Incongruente*). Could the other half be the «half-woman» he is sitting next to? That would only make her good company for the movies but not for the theater. «Al llegar a casa abrió una sola puerta del armario y echó el programa de la sesión de cine.» The following day he receives an anonymous letter warning him of the deceit of which Rebeca is capable; she might even show up in Buenos Aires (!). The letter gives added reality to Rebeca in Luis' mind. He takes to the street in renewed search, but soon he begins to suspect that the letter was sent by his movie-going acquaintances out of malice, because the sister was jealous of Rebeca and wanted to thwart his hope, thus becoming the «tapón de su destino» (p. 138; cf. *El Incongruente*). Luis wishes to chastise the culprit: «salió en busca de la infiel Rebeca —¡pobre Rebeca!— y de aquella media novia entrometida... / Entre la Rebeca no existente y él, se había introducido la Señorita que pone la fecha de la moda... a la vida que de otro modo puede quedarse sólo en esperadora» (p. 139). He finds the girl, as he expected, looking into a jewelry store window, putting the theory of her anonymous letter into practice, ready to give all of herself provided she succeeds in supplanting the «real» Rebeca. Luis would be lost if he succumbed to that sinuous creature that sought to change his destiny. He goes into a café and eats three bowls of ice cream, one right after another: «Al final estaba otra vez soltero y dueño de nuevo de su ensueño a largo plazo» (p. 141). The only defense against such a conventional temptation is ice cream.

One night when the telephone rings, Luis inquires who is calling and hears a woman's voice reply «Rebeca». Which of the many women he has called Rebeca at one time or another could it be? Because Rebeca is the name of love in Luis' vocabulary of love. The narrator tells us that «si todos creyesen en la vida como creía Luis habría más arraigo y se podrían quebrar las guerras» (p. 142) and that «entendía el amor como una autopsia en que robaba su secreto a los cementerios que sigilosamente va formando la vida» (p. 143). Platitudinous as it may seem, life and love, when freely attainable, are the sources of the protagonist's illusion. The telephone rings again; Luis tells the woman to come over: «No era la mejor de las que podían haber sido pero venía convertida en Rebeca de broma y quizás sólo por eso con realidad de la no encontrada.» When she arrives, the woman turns out to be María; a bedroom scene follows. Suddenly the doorbell rings; it is his sister Teresa, a possible threat to their love-making but not for long; Teresa is sent back to her husband Alberto.

Walking through a cemetery one day, Luis comes upon the inscription: «¡Rebeca! 18 de noviembre de 1914» (p. 146). Could it be that the girl he has been looking for has died already? «Sentía su realidad muerta, su posibilidad malgastada. Se le había adelantado la muerte» (p. 147). Did she at least utter the name «¡Luis!» before dying? As Luis has been living with María, she complains to him for leaving her alone all afternoon. She asks him if he has found Rebeca, and afraid of her demanding marriage if she learns of the assumed death of Rebeca, he calls her Rebeca more vehemently than ever before: «ya podía ser dadivoso y falso con aquella mujer puesto que había perdido la esperanza de Rebeca. El fondo que tocase en la vida era el fondo de María» (p. 149).

The grand deception of love is now hardly a deception or illusion. María has become the admitted substitute of Rebeca in Luis' life. They accept an invitation to a party at the house of a friend named Iride. Given the fatalistic element in gregueristic narratives, it is not surprising to find the narrator forewarning that the characters should not have attended that party. In the course of the evening, María disappears in the company of the hostess. Minutes pass; Luis grows inexplicably jealous and screams for her. When she reappears, the scene is one of mutual embarrassment and anger. Luis leaves María there and goes home; he cannot even go to visit his sympathetic friend, the schoolteacher, because he had come to believe that María could fill the emptiness inside him without increasing the resentment. His cabinet seems to ask if he has brought something to put in it. The answer is no, but before falling asleep Luis thinks it timely for the cabinet to come through with his ideal woman.

Perhaps in his sleep Luis undertakes with his illusory woman a dialogue of possibilities. The ideal woman is naturally gregueristic: «El caso es tenerte por vecina cuando no ibas a ser nunca mi vecina, cuando no me tocaba encontrarte al salir de ninguna puerta, cuando naciste en la calle que más ignoro» (p. 155). The dialogue acquires highly erotic overtones, as well as poetic manifestations of existentialism: «Sin ti no puedo comprobar si merece la pena morir y si el hablar por teléfono puede tener abrazos» (p. 157). When the illusory woman admits that she might be a sleepwalking companion to his insomnia, Luis explains: «Eso es lo único que es como el símbolo de la locura de vivir juntos, lo que merece la pena y deja a la alcoba bien contagiada de muerte, de muerte viva.» Such a chapter of the novel as this one in which the dialogue unfolds in almost complete authorial thinking is utterly static and very much akin to the technique of the aphoristic structure: «No hay amor porque nadie evita la revolución por el amor. Por el amor se trasladan a muy remoto tiempo las utopías» (p. 158). The topical references are evident. In his somnolent condition Luis calls to Rebeca and she is heard to answer that she is on her way. Is she really? Luis subsequently has many other relationships only to find that the women with whom he gets involved are not Rebeca even when something about them makes him think of her. One day an elegant young woman with long brown hair calls on him; her reason is that she is a stenographer who might be useful to him. Somewhat perplexed, Luis decides to test her by dictating a letter intended for his friend Aníbal. When they finish, Luis reads the letter and finds that it is not the same letter; it does not say what he said and it is addressed to a woman —perhaps the stenographer. They look at each other and laugh, a new insignificant love-affair is about to take place. Now the city is filled with unrest. Interior monologue makes gregueristic allusions to the situation: «La grieta impensada que se hace al mueble, ¿a qué grutas quiere dar?» (p. 167). Everything conventional, whether politics or literature, is detestable: «Las novelas de crímenes son fáciles y sus líos de familia larguísimos, ¿pero por qué está reñida la hoja del almanaque de hoy con la ventana del retrete? / Rebeca lo aclararía todo...» Luis-Ramón, obviously, insists on trying to look behind the phenomena: «Quería tropezar con la escalera no secreta de la realidad, esa escalera que puede estar en una frase y en un pensamiento iluminado por otro pensamiento distante, en el recuerdo de uno que se asomaba a la ventana y en la caída de un hilo muerto de teléfono» (p. 168). The power of gregueristic language makes «precognition» possible; it is a capability analogous to the mnemotic scaffoldings of intuition. Another dialogue with the illusory Rebeca follows; she is his unfailing hope for seizing reality. «Soy la antimuerte», she declares (p. 169); «Eres la anti-funeraria», he agrees. Her illusion is the fiction that goes before the revelation of reality. That is why Luis-Ramón «indagaba, que indagar en estas cosas crea la novela». But only at the cafés of railroad stations «estuvo alguna vez a pique de saber lo que sólo se entrevé entre los desgarrones de la toquilla de la vida...» (cf. *El Incongruente* and *El hombre perdido*). What is human life all about? How can there be unity in the natural unfolding of things? Luis is not satisfied with the pleasures of nostalgia; he wants the truth: «El alma de Luis no quería recuerdos de niño sino recuerdos de lo que no se pudo ver nunca, una veta blanca corriendo una pared como un gusano caligrafista de signos» (p. 170). Luis did not want to go off «on the tangent» of substituting a child for his quest of the meaning of life, «la clave de lo que es estar en la vida». He must rely on the eventual appearance of Rebeca. «El secreto que buscaba era una mezcla de cosas al correr de su pensamiento... todo lo que inventariar así por lo menudo» (p. 171). Like the poet of Mallarmé's sonnet («Je suis hanté!»), Luis finally cries out: «¡Rebeca! ¡Rebeca!»

85

That sensuous and suggestive bloom, the tuberose, seems to materialize some aspects of the protagonist's obsession: «Los nardos componían con su carnosidad —de la que brotaba un flujo angelical cuando se separaba una flor—, el nombre de Rebeca» (p. 172). Even the quest seems to become reversed: «Esos días estaba Rebeca como buscando algo en la noche...» Is it part of the complex illusion or is it the other half seeking its earthly companion? There follows a series of aphorisms on spikenards, adapted to the narrative, and another dialogue with Rebeca. Her voice is familiar to Luis, something out of tradition. She explains the enigma of the man-woman duality in their relationship; her voice, she says, «es femenina para que no sea tu propia voz la que te responde... / Algún día sabrás que el diálogo es verdad y la vida mentira» (p. 173). More than ever, Luis must find the real Rebeca: «no valía ninguna mujer del pasado, tenía que encontrar la venidera» (p. 174). And so, following her own admonition not to reject any possibility, he again throws himself in the arms of fate and takes up with another woman, whom he meets at a funeral. She is graceful and willing, but that night in his rooms, the spikenards remind him of the fact that she is not Rebeca.

While reading the newspaper, Luis comes across the story of a murder. A beautiful young woman, whose name was Rebeca Asor, has been stabbed to death. The information includes this detail: the girl received an income from Cuba. At the morgue, «admirado del silencio con que le había recibido aquella pura imagen de mujer» (p. 178), Luis can only say to himself that it «might have been» Rebeca, but «lo que pudiera tener de Rebeca se había ido a los jardines públicos...». How could anyone have killed her? The narrator, obviously thinking beyond this fiction, indulges in unprecedented preachment: «Es preferible tener paciencia y no matar. Se puede esperar toda la vida antes de matar una vez. Hay que dejar a la Providencia que ella se atreva a cometer el acto fatal de suprimir una vida» (pp. 178-79). The link between Luis and the dead girl, according to the narrator, is simply that she had answered to the name Rebeca and she no longer would, even if he were to cry out to her (like the poet of Rilke's *Duino Elegies*). When questioned by the authorities, Luis says that he went to see the body out of simple curiosity; he is told to be on hand for further questioning. And yet one must remember that the narrator has described the character named María as having a Cuban pronunciation (her mother, Elisa, would not have been described in the newspaper as a «joven bellísima» (p. 177). At the time of their love-affair, Luis had rented an apartment for her and then, having suffered from her infidelity, had thought of killing her, though presumably not in earnest: «si hubiese encontrado aquel gancho de cocina... la hubiera matado. / No merecía otra arma sino aquélla... como vehículo el entonces del hoy, necesitaba con hartura de razón» (p. 89). Are these some sort of prefigurements? Also, the fictional surname Asor is an anagram of Rosa, another character who, Luis thinks early in the novel, will turn out to be Rebeca. In any case, Luis is accosted by news photographers. Always apprehensive of cameras (cf. incident at photographer's in *El Incongruente*), he tries to get away: «Ahora esas máquinas caminaban hacia él como catafalcos de una ilusión» (p. 180). Luis has no alternative but to resort to his uncle Don Alejandrito, who has friends among the judiciary, although he knows that the uncle regards his quest for Rebeca as a symptom of neurosis. Don Alejandrito, in effect, has him go to see a psychiatrist friend, Dr. Azcot. «Luis no quiso pagarle con una desatención el haberle salvado del peor lío de su vida...» (p. 181). Of course, Luis is secretly contemptuous of the psychiatrist and decides to play with him by acceding to his method of hearing the patient tell all about his childhood. Luis' reminiscences are told in a style quite ungreguristic (just as the quotations from the newspaper story are completely conventional), which is extremely interesting when considering the basic facts of a writer's preference in employing a particular narrative technique. Certainly, one cannot say that Ramón was not able to tell a story in an ordinary way, for there is evidence here that he could (as there is also in his early writings); the inevitable conclusion is, however, that he did not want to. With respect to the psychiatric diagnosis of Luis' malady, the doctor tells him that it all began on the day he found a lost little lamb when he was a boy in the country estate of his father's friends. What about the woman's qualities that he has bestowed upon the ideal? The doctor replies: «Más superposiciones a la primera ilusión de estar sólo con una niña que usted experimentó en la propicia soledad de la siesta» (p. 182). Better to forget the whole thing, says the psychiatrist, for Luis could never find the ideal woman. Doctor and patient bid each other goodbye, having practiced mutual deceit. As he walks down the mystic stairs, Luis congratulates himself on having baited the psychiatrist by telling him about the lamb as he could have told him so many other recollections, and yet he begins to doubt: «¿no será que yo la he elegido involuntariamente?» (p. 183). But he immediately regains his confidence in himself and in Rebeca. As for psychiatry, «suprime una inquietud que supremiza la vida..., va contra las 'sublimaciones', los únicos conceptos que sobrepasan la vida y que a veces son hallados en la misma realidad». The narrator is speaking here in almost the same terms in which Ramón speaks of the *greguería* in the preface to his *Total de greguerías*. But the element of femininity implicit in the illusory woman and the love which Luis reserves for her divert the purely theoretical aspects of greguristic definition: «Junto a la oveja sentimental aparecía Rebeca como en un retrato del romanticismo, con pamela de recoger amapolas, sonriendo de la farsa cursi que había armado en su galería de fotógrafo el doctor escabroso» (pp. 183-84; cf. *El Incongruente*). In honor of the event, Luis ironically goes to a restaurant and orders roast lamb, which he eats while «en una mujer vuelta de espaldas en una mesa lejana veía la nuca de Rebeca, la mujer que habla y festeja la vida diciendo la consigna que no está ni en el reloj, ni en el almanaque, ni en el amigo» (p. 184).

The visit to the psychiatrist makes an impression on him; as a consequence, he sees sheep and women in his dreams. His wakeful hours are spent in meditation, interspersed with the imaginary dialogue between him and the illusory woman. A metaphorical synthesis of his life crosses his mind like a motion picture, but there is nothing to hold on to: «Quería haber vivido pero no sabía que eso nadie lo iba a saber porque iban a morir todos los que podían haberlo sabido» (pp. 185-86). Despite the undercurrent of futility, Luis is bent on finding the only thing that he thinks can help him; he is convinced that «sólo en coro con la mujer» (page 186) can one meaningfully say anything about life, especially everyday life. But it must be «the woman», for casual women he has had many. And in their dialogue, what does she say about herself? «Soy sólo el maniquí azul», she says; to which he responds: «Tengo velocidad de anillo cósmico alrededor de tu maniquí azul.» The narrator's voice, suggesting more than a simple interior monologue, interweaves around the hallucinatory exclamations; in a manner reminiscent of Azorín's *Doña Inés* he says: «¿Vivir, qué era?» only to become the typical Ramón of the *greguería*: «Ver caer los zapatos del cajón en que se guardan...» (p. 187). For Luis-Ramón, Rebeca is the shield of loving peace and reason. When he complains that «al ver que no te tengo me querrán llevar al servicio obligatorio por cualquier fanatismo», she replies: «Diles que yo tengo razones de medias de seda y así te dejarán por loco.» The defense against demagoguery, he feels, is to be found in the kind of fear that harbors love and humor. In his solitude and apprehension, Luis clings to the hope that his «sombra amada» (p. 188; cf. similar notions of the ideal in Bécquer) will eventually be there to comfort him, having emerged from his mysterious cabinet. The allusions to politics and war have been leading to a statement of self-justification when confronted by Revolution in a dialogue which amounts to allegory. Revolution says to Luis-Ramón: «sabía que buscabas una mujer y he venido a ser su sustituta» (p. 190). And he replies: «Tú no eres sustitutivo de nada... Tú eres el acabóse y entre acabóses prefiero el suicidio a tu intemperancia.» Revolución: «Soy lo único que hace variar la vida.» Luis-Ramón: «Mentira... Eres como un enterramiento de todo...» But neither does the author-protagonist condone capitalism unconditionally; it is his opinion that «puede haber capitalistas, pero dadivosos, inteligentes, artistas», who will protect «la bohemia de la vida...» (p. 193). The narrative attains in these last stages what seems to be a more confessional tone. Therefore it is not surprising to find statements that refer to aspects of Ramón's work which the reader has already been able to discover for himself, such as the following: «Nunca hizo trascendentes las ideas que los demás quieren que sean trascendentes puesto que él no creía en su trascendencia.» And then the metaphorical exaggeration: «Había matado en él a su madre y llevaba las manos azules de aquel crimen. Así se había librado de lo arbitrario, de lo gangoso, de la mayor convención de la vida» (p. 194). It should be remembered that Luis threw the liquor glass at the agitator, insisting that he had heard him curse Rebeca, not his mother, as some of the bystanders had thought. «Por eso era tan ansioso y tan libre en la busca de la mujer que no invalidase su vida. No quería otro absoluto que el del amor...» Everything else is confused in Luis' mind, and one should remember that the Ramón who glosses his own aphorisms states that he has disarranged, upset or disturbed everything on purpose. Yet there seem to be some tricky rules to the game of the *greguería* as exemplified in this novel; the narrator generalizes Luis' sensitivity after using a dinner knife instead of the misplaced letter-opener: «Cuchillo de comedor en mesa de despacho lo involucra todo... 'Dónde está cuchillo?', se preguntaban las cucharas» (p. 196). Such a state of mind is not unusual for Luis-Ramón: «Aquel día se sentía más hiperestésico de la realidad que nunca porque había notado que la luz de la mañana olía a cristales recién lavados» (p. 197). Luis' bachelor life is finally about to come to an end. There are ominous indications. One of them is a brief synthesis of the conclusion of *El Incongruente* and of the adventure in the novel involving the «half Rebeca»: «Había echado muchas cosas al armario aquellos días, los guantes blancos que le había dejado la mujer del cinematógrafo a la que había conquistado...» Another is the evident feeling of expectation on the part of the protagonist: «Se sentía en vísperas de algo y por eso había aceptado la reunión en casa del anticuario para pasar el último del año.» The antique shop full of old furniture, paintings and statues, closed to the public for a private party, would be the ideal place for something unusual to happen, and the last day of the year would be the right time to find the ideal woman. Every man, whether he admits it or not, is susceptible to the wiles of woman; Luis at least knows this and does not deceive himself. His obsession continues to grow: «Abría un libro y le salía la misma estampa. Repasaba el Diccionario Enciclopédico y le salía Salomé con la cabeza del profeta en la jofaina» (p. 198). Illusion, yes; reality, no: «Rebeca no aparecía por ningún lado y eso que encontró seres extraordinarios como la mujer metida en la jaula del canario...» (page 200). Is he reading the signs correctly, the protagonist wonders. «La vida le trataba ya con una sinceridad suprema pero no llegaba a ese momento del azar que está perdido entre todos los momentos» (p. 201). Is the plot of the narrative following the same direction as *El Incongruente,* with the chance-fate complex as the sole force? How much is the author bringing together the elements of fiction and those of history? In his desperate loneliness the protagonist has even wondered if perhaps it is the daughter of the manicurist in the apartment above who, like an angel descending, could resolve his ultimate concern (the last phrase here is used advisedly).

At the party given by the antique dealer, Luis meets a pale woman of Jewish descent: «Ya no supo ni vio más. No tenía nombre bíblico, pero ya estaba en camino de ser Rebeca... / Era una imagen más que un ser humano y daba las miradas como la diosa de la vía láctea apretando su seno pone las estrellas en el cielo» (p. 200). Love has brought out the lyrical potential of the *greguería*. The woman's name is Leonor. Luis is obvious in his courtship, and the dialogue between the characters reflects the dialogues previously realized between Luis and his imagination. There are also reprises of other incidents and expressions. When she refers to his lyrical stammerings as «gitanerías» (p. 204), he recalls the former nun who had been deceived by the gypsy. Now that he has met Leonor, the «mujer ideal» becomes the «judía ideal». Luis is apprehensive of destroying the possible illusion which he hopes is a reality. He hardly speaks; words of endearment he finally says in her ear «como un hombre perdido... en la primera frase de un delirio mortal» (p. 205). The narrator puts it plainly; Luis is in love. Leonor is a widow faithful to the memory of her husband (?) but, as far as Luis is concerned, she must terminate with such a memory and widowhood. The new relationship elicits in Luis a new vocation; he begins a diary. A world once empty acquires meaning. A chivalric kind of devotion is invoked: «Hay un encono sobrenatural en el amor, un velar las armas que no tiene fin» (p. 207). The new dialogue must go on. The praise of woman is now effusive and the man-woman relationship is not unlike the principle of the greguería: «Morirse, desesperarse por eso que mira desde la mujer, por esa otra cosa que tiene que no es de hombre. La mujer es el otro lado de la cuestión, lo pronunciado de otra manera...» And then a rather amazing conviction which one cannot help relating to the Christian faith: «En el futuro lo más grande que sucederá es que una lección pavorosa del amor llenará el mundo» (p. 208). Luis is unable to proceed with his diary that first day; he resigns himself instead to writing his first letter to the «real» Rebeca, whom he addresses as «Tú de mi vida», the future sleepwalker that «reduces the world to her shape». While away, asleep, she is like a cloistered nun afraid to come to the jalousie, but Luis tells her: «mis palabras encontrarán el revés de la rejilla entrecruzada que te oculta» (page 210). Luis will guard her innocence; the nonsense of the world he will reveal to her as marvelous (the objective of the *greguería*). In turn, she transfigures human existence and makes time bearable: «Pones orla de violetas a lo que miras y prometes hacer sentir que no sentiremos el peso de la existencia. Si ilusionamos al tiempo tendremos esa holgura que el tiempo nunca logra tener.» Illusion has become reality, and reality, illusion. The halves are about to be united: «Contra la avalancha de todos está el círculo que sólo cierra la pareja enamorada...» (p. 211). The narrator indulges in lyrical word-plays of rhyme and paronomasia on beauty («veo en el filamento de tu figura algo que baila como una bailarina en miniatura detrás de tu belleza») and love («tengo que decirte que te adoro—, que es dorar a fuego el amor...»). Time must stand still, locked in the tenses of verbs: «Siempre nos despediremos cuando comenzábamos a hablar» (p. 212). The letter is a definite proposal, a proposal of marriage for life. Luis stops all calls and engagements; he mysteriously gets rid of the mysterious cabinet, now useless. Together at last, Luis and Leonor assay their compatibility. «Su diálogo revelaba que había logrado la Rebeca posible...» (p. 213). The dialogue is at once playful and profound. «El amor es como haber muerto y vivir», he says. «Sentirse resucitado de toda la vida que pasó.» She replies: «Morir de nuevo sin haber muerto nunca.» Her background, foreign to him, is somewhat frightening at times, materialized in her strange fingers. Is it once again a threat of destiny? So be it; the narrator conveys the thought of the protagonist: «Al escoger mujer hay que acertar con que sea la verduga» (p. 214).

If *El Incongruente* is an innovative approach to the novel genre, a manner peculiar to Ramón of injecting his style into a more or less sustained piece of prose fiction, and if *El novelista* is a novelized series of examples of Ramón's *métier, ¡Rebeca!* represents a deeper and more consistent «greguerization» of its author's life-experience. It is deeper, more because of its confessional tone than because of its insight into personality. It is more consistent because the novelistic structure is tighter, the seams of the pattern not so visible, thus producing a greater unity of vision composed of the gregueristic imagery. The psychic events are more homogeneous, thus preventing such imagery from its natural tendency to fragment and even dissolve. The tone is more solid. This is perhaps all the more amazing when one considers that the historical content of this work is greater than that of the preceding nebular novels. There is little doubt that the protagonist's attitudes are those of Ramón, that many of the events actually happened, that some of the «characters» are taken from life, making the novel, at least partially, a sort of *roman à clef*. One of these in particular, Leonor, the «ideal» woman found, bears comment. It has been supposed (and privately confirmed by the subject) that this figure represents Ramón's wife Luisa Sofovich. Reference is made in the story to her Jewish ancestry. She is the reality that fulfills the illusory Rebeca, whose name in Hebrew means something like a troth or peacemaker. The treatment given in a Spanish dictionary of names perhaps explains further Ramón's choice:

> REBECA. Hebreo, *Rivká,* «lazo», literalmente «nudo corredizo», de *rabak,* «atar». El nombre se refiere tal vez a la firmeza del lazo matrimonial; pero su valor, en sentido figurado, de hermosa, voluptuosa, deseable, se

debe a una imagen menos poética: la de los animales cebados y *atados* para sacrificarlos...[5]

At the risk of oversimplifying matters, I suggest that the ultimate key to the characters' symbolic identity is to be found in the shift of nominality from the historical Luisa to the fictional Luis. Thus the two Platonic halves come together.

[5] GUTIERRE TIBÓN, *Diccionario etimológico comparado de nombres propios* (México, Unión Tipográfica Editorial Hispano Americana [1956]), p. 456.

## EL HOMBRE PERDIDO, OR THE IMAGE
## OF VACUITY

The techniques employed by Ramón in his previous works, especially the other nebular novels, are found here in a more intense and harmonious blend. The novelistic structure is developed from a first person singular point of view, something not so openly practiced before, except in some sections of *El novelista,* although the first person intent has been constant.

This book represents the culmination of Ramón's total literary vision and inventiveness. As in *¡Rebeca!* the familiar imagery of the *greguería,* based on whimsical association, is «supervised» by subtle symbolism. For example, the first line of the book reads: «Papeles azules corrían detrás de papeles rosas.»[1] The seemingly detached statement, predicated on a verb in the imperfect tense, is strangely related to the story through a mixture of description and narration. The novelistic structure is clearly developed from a first person singular point of view («yo iba saltando por encima de los supuestos loros poniendo un pie desigualmente lejos de otro, con temor a tropezar con los contagiosos animales...»), which of course does not preclude the use of the third person as either a conventional or an unconventional associative device («Como se sabe la epidemia más fuerte de psitacosis sucedió en Milán... / ¡Cuántos loros muertos...!»), as well as the use of the first person plural with either personal or impersonal references. More than in any other work by Ramón, the aphoristic modality which lurks behind the prose is absorbed here by the narrative impetus of the novel.

The image of a lost man, already pointed out in the preceding works included in this analysis, is soon advanced:

> No tiene forma la vida, no es libre, no es el primer camino del tiempo
> y del mundo. No le deja al hombre actual gozar del camino mural que

---

[1] *El hombre perdido* (Madrid, Espasa-Calpe, Colección Austral [1962]), p. 19; all quotations are from this edition. The first edition is that of Editorial Poseidón (Buenos Aires, 1947). I have collated the two and found them essentially alike, except for incidental punctuation (see p. 111 below).

ya no existe con la grandeza del primer palacio junto al zócalo, cuando pasaban los hombres pequeñitos y perdidos junto al polvo blanco, lo más rico de lo comestible cuando la aplastante grandeza gravitaba sobre el caminante. (p. 21)

At this very point in the narrative, the nameless narrator-protagonist, out for a walk at dawn, is approached by a bum who asks him for a light. Dialogue follows. The bum explains that he is «la radiografía que salió mal» and (doffing his hair like a hat) «el sillón que ya no sirve para el imposibilitado y la peluca del cómico viejo...». The narrator-protagonist thinks of this as «lo más inesperado entre lo inesperado». When asked what he does with his time, the bum replies: «... abrir la lata de sardinas del alba y después durante todo el día tengo que estar perdido e inadvertido en los lugares que yo me sé...» (p. 22). The narrator-protagonist inquires if he can spend the day with him, and the bum agrees, but only until two o'clock in the afternoon. For a while they walk together silently («pasamos el primer puente como en victoria mágica sobre los abismos, vencido el suicidio, ganadas las lavanderas»; hence a eulogy on bridges), and then an amazing synthesis takes place: «Los dos hombres perdidos íbamos pensando lo mismo...» (p. 23). Where are they going? «Pronto lo sabrás», says the mysterious man of dawn with sudden familiarity. The bum leads the narrator-protagonist to a small neglected house by the river, which must have been used by Goya as a studio no one knows about —«la casilla perdida y miserable que adora el artista» (p. 25; cf. similar situations in El novelista). The bum, having now removed his hairpiece, says that after two o'clock he finds other refuge because the night is overpowering in that house. The narrator-protagonist marvels at the unknown works of Goya existing there but soon wishes to get away. «Aquí está uno perdido como en galería de fotógrafo muerto», he says to the other man (p. 24; the photographic image is evidently of considerable concern to Ramón), and finally: «temí incurrir en una inexplicable complicidad» (p. 25). The house by the river is left as «el refugio ideal de los miserables futuros».

Somehow the experience with the man of dawn and the unknown works of Goya drives the narrator-protagonist to «hacer pesquisas del crimen que sospechaba». The crime in question is one committed by him: «mi crimen estaba detrás de mí.» Was it something he did when he was a child? Out of a dim past comes the image of a little man who played the cello and lusted after his nursemaid. The recollection stops with his rescue of the girl from the strange villain, whom he stabs to death, subsequently stuffing the body in the cello. But even if that had been a reality and not a dream, it was not «el crimen que yo mismo indagaba para saber bien cuál había sido» (p. 26). This seems to suggest a gregueristic version of at least some aspects of existentialism. The individual human being here represented by the nameless protagonist telling the story (more about him later) is launched on the unavoidable quest of his own identity. The result is a quasi-metaphysical detective adventure in which subject and object merge, a veritable «whodunit» in which all the elements are either unknown or questionable. Furthermore, the quest is endless: «ya sé que voy a pasar toda la vida buscando las huellas de mi crimen, con deseo de reconstruirlo, con ansias de saber en qué generación anterior a la mía lo cometió un antepasado ya muerto.» Does this imply something having to do with the doctrine of reincarnation or with the Biblical notion that the sins of the fathers are visited upon the sons? The protagonist tells of an incident involving *déjà vu:* he calls at a house and asks the lady if he has been there before; she answers negatively but he describes and identifies things and people accurately. He might have been there but without committing a crime. Thus he confesses that «seguía buscando mi crimen, lo único que me amenizaba el recuerdo de haber vivido ya treinta y cinco años como un hombre perdido» (p. 27). This particular reference to the age of the protagonist-author is extremely interesting and bears comment which I will reserve, however, for the last section of the present chapter.

Again in a manner reminiscent of Azorín's in *Doña Inés,* the narrator refers to the all-important topic of human life: «¿Se vive la vida que estamos viviendo?» (p. 29). At this point the narrative takes new whimsical turns as the protagonist finds an affirmative answer to his question in the discovery of a ship secretly stranded in mid-city: «Comprendí que aquello sucedía porque lo que volvería verdaderamente supuesto a un barco encallado en una calle es que estuviese cerrado a la posibilidad de visitarlo, es que pudiese parecer una fortaleza» (pp. 29-30). He boards the ship and eventually finds the mysterious woman (see preceding chapters): «En efecto apareció ella... / la miré como a la mujer que me pertenecía...» (p. 31). She tells him to pretend that he has known her always, but feeling that she looks upon him as a gigolo, the protagonist rejects her and the whole make-believe pleasure cruise, accusing all those around him of indulging in collective deceit. He gets off the stranded ship, which he regards as a perfidious device to corrupt free souls, in other words, to conventionalize eccentrics («perdernos a los perdidos», p. 32). The foregoing experience actually proves to be a disappointment conducive to boredom. The protagonist needs more than ever to have some proof of his existence. The notion of speed so often found in Ramón's imagery has a bearing even in this context: «La vida no es cierta en ningún momento y lo único cierto que hay es que hay algo que nos empuja como un torrente a una velocidad inconcebible» (p. 32). The immediacy of the word-image complex precludes the refinement of conventional syntax; the repetition of words and the peculiar use of subordinate clauses are colloquial. In this sense, Ramón represents the antithesis of literary polish such as that practiced by Azorín. The fatality of death, the narrator tells us, operates swiftly upon us, while there is hardly anything we can do about life: «Lo único que puede ir un poco de prisa es la aventura intelectual, la aceptación de lo que se nos ocurra» (p. 33). The familiar capriciousness of the *greguería* spreads from the imagistic to the grammatical plane, as an impromptu dialogue between the protagonist and an unidentified speaker reveals the following arrangement:

—Sí, siéntese en cualquier sitio.
—Aquí estoy bien.
—¿Y?
—Eso digo yo. ¿Y?
—Lo último que sepa.
—Lo último que sé es que las locomotoras se han reunido y quieren irse por lo subterráneo.

This kind of sudden exchange, subsequently so common in the theater of the absurd, is also characteristic of Ramón's own dramatic works. The reference to locomotives here is extremely significant; it develops enigmatically in the novel for two pages and holds the key to the final conclusion.

The thematic or scenic transitions in the book are usually quick and unexpected. The protagonist-narrator continues in his search for evidence of his identity: «¿Es una prueba decir un nombre cuando se sale del cloroformo después de la operación? / Pues ella, según las monjas, pronunció mi nombre después de salir de la nada ambigua» (p. 35). Once again the mysterious woman that represents love; once again dialogue leads to dialect: «¿Qué hace la cariño?» (p. 36). Just as there is use of the concept of nothingness (p. 35) and of the image of the screen (page 28) that hides reality, there is a scene reminiscent of the story entitled «El biombo» which appears in *El novelista*: «Nos asomábamos juntos al balcón y veíamos cosas inmortales como el baile de los visillos en la casa lejana...» This apparent repetition could be significant merely as indicative of Ramón's imagistic repertory, but it could also reflect a particular stage of his production.

The erotic motif returns: «Extendida sobre el lecho a la media luz era como un cielo abierto y desparramado.» At this point we encounter the first mention of God: «El placer es un secreto que nos dio Dios y por el que pierden la cabeza los seres humanos al no saber lo que sienten» (p. 37). The mysterious woman is a manifestation of the protagonist-narrator's capacity to love and feel pleasure: «¡Adoración! ¡Adoración! Tu crimen no es de este mundo.» The only way that love can end is «con el afán de venganza o con el desatino de desorientación que llena al hombre». Love is such an important emotion in the life of the protagonist-narrator that everything else seems to be predicated on it and its disillusionment: «Lo único que vale la pena en la vida es pillar a la mujer *in fraganti* y si se es valiente y digno librarse de esa mujer para toda la vida» (p. 38). This and other statements follow the protagonist's confession that he broke up with a girl named Rosa (see previous chapter dealing with ¡Rebeca!); nevertheless, their essayistic form betrays their latent affiliation with the aphorism and the fundamental disposition of Ramón's aphoristic and novelistic structures as stemming from his gregueristic vision. The protagonist's dreams give way to wakeful meditations on his actions being repeated by someone else, «como si hubiese un actor que repitiese la obra de su vida, sin término...» (p. 39); thus Ramón's idea of the Other or *Doppelgänger,* first introduced in *El Incongruente,* is found here also. A variant approach to the central quest is given as: «Antes de no ser quiero saber lo que es no ser y así saber qué es haber sido» (p. 41, which suggests further cribbing from Unamuno; cf. preface to *Tres novelas ejemplares y un prólogo*). If the lost man introduced in the first chapter was characterized as a badly developed X-ray, the protagonist-narrator turns out to be «el hombre que se tragó un rosario...» (p. 40), whose religion is thus a part of his organism. But as in ¡Rebeca!, the inner metaphysical quest is often externalized in the form of an affectionate interest in things: «Hay que encontrar la taza del que bebió más tranquilo» (p. 41). Hence the antique bibelot can be the «metaphysical object». The result of such a discovery or of its image is utter surprise: «Lo inesperado. Esas palabras que hacen temblar a la vida.» Such is the essence of the *greguería,* here encountered in its most startling novelistic uses:

> Entonces podemos ver el mundo de otra manera y llegar a comprender que los tranvías andan al revés tirados por añanas amarillas y todos los que van dentro con los pies cortados aunque crean que los llevan enteros...
>
> Todo esto quiere decir que me pierdo más cada día que pasa y que sin depravarme lo que hay que hacer es acabar por perderse en absoluto. (p. 42)

Such imagistic content gives way to work invention, as the protagonist-narrator resorts to familiar narrative mechanisms: «Sonaba el reloj a que sonase una llave mecida en la espiral de alambre de la sonería. / La llave que sonaba entrechocándose con la sonería era la llave de mi casa. / Eso me atomizó de caserismo y me eché a la calle» (p. 44; the slashes represent paragraph breaks). Nothing could better prepare the reader for the narrator's notions of the «para-real» than such «para-language»: «Yo no pretendía nada sino saber a qué atenerme, y que por un juego de cajas de cartón vacías se me revelase el hiperespacio, el recinto ese en que se es muñeco y maletín, libro tirado y alfiler» (p. 15). The metaphysical preoccupations of the author, which have been encountered and discussed earlier in this study, are more clearly developed in this novel. And yet all the habitual themes are still present, themes which have been significant and constant since *El Incongruente,* such

as the amorous adventure and the disguises of reality: «Todos los enga-
ños están preparados y todos se lavan la cara y las manos como Pilatos
se lavó una vez las manos en agua de plata» (p. 49). It is probably not
surprising that the reference to Pilate should lead to the loftier though
somewhat conventional considerations of the Almighty: «No se puede
olvidar a Dios, porque está en todo lo que va sucediendo y es lo único
que lo salva, que lo lleva adelante y hace que pase...» A mathematical
term holds the quid of this key work of Ramón's: «Yo conocía la ecua-
ción de vivir y eso era lo único que me hacía seguir viviendo» (p. 50).
Critics such as Ilie, who remark on the lack of the novelist's interest
in the problem of time in a work like *El Incongruente,* should consider the works later confected by Ramón in which the notion of
time, though certainly not consistent with the linear movement of
conventional narrative, shares with the notion of space the central importance in the development of the novelistic imagery. Anatole France's
maxim to the effect that memory is man's only reality gives way to this
«greguerization»: «La identidad del tiempo es de lo más desconcertante
porque vivimos lo que ya está muerto» (p. 51). Here one can visualize
the ideology behind the title of Ramón's magnificently imaginative autobiography, *Automoribundia.* The inward voyage into one's own life is
a novelistic form of introspection often used by Ramón, and corresponding images are gregueristically fitting. At one point the protagonist-
narrator, tired of going about aimlessly, makes a sudden decision: «Entonces se me ocurrió lo salvador. Hacía tiempo quería comprar un sillón
de mimbre...» (p. 52). This he does, after coming to the conclusion that
the gist of the world is purely commercial. «Aquello había arreglado la
situación insostenible de mi frenético andar y ahora me podía meter en
casa a esperar de rodillas la llegada del sillón del reposo y de la peniten-
cia, el andador mimbresco de la infancia que creció con el tiempo y volvía
a ser mi mueble favorito» (p. 54).

An impending storm seems to set the scene of an important event:
«¿Para la llegada de qué personaje se preparaba la escena?... Yo había
presentido siempre que en la hora de la tormenta nuestro destino va por
otro sitio y es otro completamente distinto» (pp. 54-55). A brief dialogue
suggests the presence of a woman in the narrative. The level of being is
that of the «para-real»: «Sin embargo, nunca había comprobado la realidad del acoplamiento de la otra realidad como esta tarde... Presentía
que la aventura de la otra dimensión se podría dar aquella tarde, pero
tardaban en traer el reloj de ménsula» (p. 55). Who is the woman? Is it
the one whose telephone number does not exist? At the end of the
passage her image vanishes as the storm abates, leaving behind a huge
metaphor of sensuality and loneliness.

There is, as in the novels previously discussed, a varying degree of
continuity. Sometimes the straight narrative sketch will occupy more

than one chapter. In the next passage, the erotic theme is continued and heightened. The protagonist's encounter with another woman is thrust upon the reader by means of a gratuitous dialogue. The topics of conversation are multiple and mixed, but their center is erotic: «Ya ves», she says familiarly, «Yo tenía una entrada para la Opera esta noche y he venido a verte... Pero antes de continuar, ¿me quieres quitar las medias?» (p. 58). The old gregueristic theme of romance on the staircase found in *El Incongruente* reappears: «Yo no busco sino la sorpresa. ¡Qué sublime un idilio en la escalera sin entrar en casa, mientras la otra mujer duerme!» The more subjective intimacy of an embrace infuriates the woman, who discards her familiarity: «Póngame las medias...» (p. 59). The protagonist trembles in the face of such unrealness in reality, but an unexpected medical interest which they share brings him and the woman to happier terms. Their second conversation includes an insight into the «para-real»: «Sólo en la inconsciencia se hace pie, se puede tocar con la mano la pared de fondo.» The woman asks the protagonist to speak to her about the truth of the crime of living («el crimen de vivir», page 60); he is not very successful and the time comes for her to leave: «Me dejó amargado, más perdido que nunca...» (p. 61). But on the following day, the protagonist-narrator is paid a visit by his new paramour's husband, who is a psychiatrist and claims that her mind wanders («tiene extraviado el espíritu»). The woman, too, shows up, and a three-way conversation takes place. The protagonist-narrator asserts that «La epilepsia de la vida de cada uno no tiene respuesta... La mujer es lo que contesta algo al enigma» (p. 62). But what he and the woman impart to each other is not enough for him to take her away from the doctor; after all, the doctor knows about madness thanks to her: «La extraña mujer se levantó..., se despidió de mí y vi cómo se iba, como si no hubiese venido» (page 63).

There are marked transitions in the narrative, both in the action and in the tone. In a passage which deals with a salesman who tries to sell the protagonist-narrator a coin-operated clock, one finds the kind of dialogue that strengthens the work as a novel, helping to hold it together with the humor (not comedy) so characteristic of the gregueristic spirit. The protagonist relates the goings-on to the seriousness of his plight: «Usted quiere aumentar mi miseria y mi perdición» (p. 64). The imagistic reprise is to be found here, acknowledging the eccentricity of the situation: «Me miró como quien mira a un loco, con mirada de loco...» (page 65; cf. *¡Rebeca!*, p. 121). The salesman happens to notice a photograph on the table and declares that he has sold an identical clock to the woman in the picture. The protagonist-narrator is inwardly crushed: «Despedí al hombre del reloj usurario y me dispuse a salir en busca de X. No podía perdonar aquella secreta compra de un reloj, que revelaba su afán de sisa y lucro» (p. 66). And then, further betraying this novel's kinship with the other «Novels of the Nebula», especially *¡Rebeca!,* he exclaims: «Ella, la ideal, pidiéndome todas las noches una moneda para que anduviese el reloj de sus sueños.» In the next breath he reconsiders and decides to write her a letter, the kind of letter Luis had written to Rebeca: «Llamé para que llevaran la carta y me quedé mareado viendo grandes cantidades de relojes con ruido de tragar monedas, despertadores atragantados que me despertaban para ir a la fábrica de hacer alpargatas.» The segment of narrative experienced is thus resolved in what would be the most ineffectual of greguerístic possibilities, the pun, were it not for the fact that the structure already established admits such periodic resolutions, in which neither the association nor dissociation of sounds, images, or meanings makes too much difference.

Chapter XIII of this book is included in Ramón's *Obras selectas,* under the designation of XII. It tells of the protagonist-narrator's visit to an amusement ground called Luna Park and, as might be expected, lends itself to imagistic pyrotechnics; however, if Ramón's *El circo* (1917) presents an optimistic picture, the description of this other, more mechanistic amusement is ultimately pessimistic. Luna Park is, like so many other things in Ramón's novels, allegorical: «Es el sitio en que somos emigrantes aun en nuestra propia patria... Es donde los hombres perdidos están menos perdidos y toman apariencias de hacer algo e interesarse por algo» (p. 67). Humor belies the actual intent as the ever possible pun appears: «Nada era allí simbólico o irreal porque se sentían muy cansadas nuestras piernas al recorrer el planisferio de la feria» (p. 68). A large caption which announces «PALACIO DEL PSICOANALISIS» (page 69), reiterates Ramón's concern with the new science, though naturally in the same context as the whole greguerístic *mélange.* This visit to Luna Park is highly significant for the overall meaning of the work: «Yo comprobaba allí hasta dónde es inútil vivir la vida y cómo lo que se deja detrás no es más que un Luna Park con diversiones aburridas y con locura atontada» (p. 71). Nevertheless, the protagonist as usual is in search of «la gran liosa —morena y guapa— entre las mujeres que se cruzan y entrecruzan en el Luna Park y siempre creía haberla encontrado cuando en el segundo convite me convencía que era como caballito de cartón». Ramón's purported method of composition (already described in another of my studies) is partially verified by what is undoubtedly an oversight. A paragraph composed of metaphors characterizing Luna Park ends with the following: «campo de aviación con hangares que sirven para otras cosas...» (p. 72). On the next page there is a series of isolated images depicting the amusement ground; one of them is the same metaphor as the one just quoted. The protagonist-narrator falls prey to the beguiling effects of inane diversion: «el Luna Park me empujaba a seguir viviendo y a no seguir buscando, ya que allí se encontraba vital como en ningún sitio todo el anonidismo [sic] humano» (p. 74). Paul

Ilie's remarks on Ramón's «awareness of the whimsical foundation of modern society» (*op. cit.,* p. 153) in *El Incongruente* are quite perceptive, even when extended to *El hombre perdido,* except that here we find such awareness to be overwhelmed by pessimism: «allí, en el gran Luna Park con los últimos adelantos, estaba la triste y verdadera parodia del progreso humano.» The author's humor enables the protagonist-narrator to throw off the spell of illusion: «En mi desolación aprendía a tener cuidado con los apresamientos del mundo y prefería seguir siendo un hombre perdido a ser un hombre mal hallado...» (p. 75). Hence, when finally, not a brunette but a blonde makes herself available to him, he is careful to maintain the most inconsequential relations, which fortunately for him, are the only kind the place is conducive to: «Se arrasaba la pretensión individual en aquel sitio y uno se perdía en el gran todo, convertido en una alpargata» (p. 76). Despite the narrative first person, the whole passage is geared in the timeless immobility of the aphorism. But there is one image that suggests a time of composition subsequent to 1941: «Entonces vi el subsuelo y revés del gran campo de aviación con los aparatos en estertor, como después de una traición japonesa.» How does this fit with the protagonist-narrator's assertion that he has already «lived» thirty-five years as a «lost man»? His fictional age?

Returning from a funeral, the protagonist-narrator ponders his habitual question about the meaning of life. Three strange men of different ages and all with their heads turned backwards are waiting for him to elucidate; they represent past, present, and future time, three stages of a cycle: «el presente es el porvenir y el pasado con una identidad abrumadora» (p. 78). The protagonist tries to recall the last particular formulation given to his question in the car while returning from the funeral; finally he says: «¿Qué cosa... es la que debió abstraer más a los que se fueron?» (p. 79). The answer comes as a half pun: «Toda abstracción es muerte... No debieron abstraerse... Debieron distraerse más...» Awareness, not attention, is the key to the secrets of things: «ese no querer estar el plumero en el vasar o en la cornisa en que se le remete... o ese querer caer la escoba resbalando su mango en el rincón... Porque la escoba no es sólo un objeto para barrer...» (p. 80). Abstraction makes out of things only what is expected, while distraction makes possible the discovery of their unexpected images or *greguerías.* The meaning of life is thus the awareness of the constant flux of its parts, of the 'split-second objects'.

Reminiscent of Gustavo el Incongruente, the protagonist-narrator finds himself on a train and besieged once more by the call of an amorous adventure with a beautiful woman, whom he espies while looking for the dining car. Her name is Desdémona and she invites him into her private car, luxurious like everything else about her, which «acaba cerrado en sus dos polos por biombos misteriosos» (p. 81). The allegorical and symbolic

101

penchants of the previous narrative segments disappear in favor of a more simple and familiar technique, namely, the fantastic. But the relevance to the structure of the novel as a whole does not diminish. The protagonist-narrator recounts that the woman «me miró con extrañeza, como si recelase que yo la metía en una aventura más novelesca que la que ella me había ofrecido a mí» (p. 82), for somehow he has identified her as the «sister» of another woman whom he knew. The prospects seem excellent for a night of love, but suddenly the protagonist-narrator becomes intimidated by these words: «Nada nos debe importar... En cierto momento de la madrugada desengancharán mi vagón y lo dejarán en una vía muerta... ¡He vivido tantas vías muertas ideales!» (p. 83). Allegory again looms. Although he admits that «era aquella una aventura esperada, en la que la realidad se superaba» (p. 84), that is, a most desirable experience of the 'para-real', the protagonist-narrator feels recalled to his usual «lostness» and thus finds an excuse to quarrel with and leave the beautiful woman of mystery.

The narrator-protagonist goes to an elegant dinner party. A taxi takes him to a mansion where aristocrats have gathered. The passage is not totally devoid of «surrealistic» events; a young man complains about the newspaper taste of the whiskey being served and, with the hostess's permission, flies out the window. After the meal, the guests repair to the drawing room. The protagonist-narrator takes the opportunity of commenting critically on the various types, especially the women; among them only the hostess's daughter is attractive to him. The parlor conversation offers isolated *greguerías,* which the narrator purportedly transcribes. Of these, the following is of particular interest: «La vida es beberse una copa en la cantina de una estación mientras se cambia de tren» (p. 88).

A modern parable emerges from Ramón's pen as the protagonist-narrator, feeling himself followed by a cold city-square fountain, buys some magazines and takes refuge in one of his favorite places, a café. Familiar themes appear —happiness, destiny, loneliness: «Aquello que veía no me iba a servir para nada sino un rato, un rato corto e inútil» (p. 91). He remembers seeing, in one of the magazines he has thrown under the table, the photograph of a certain Señora de Aviñón: «Era guapísima y buscaba a alguien detrás del fotógrafo.» Suddenly he hears a voice from the floor complaining of being badly treated. As he looks under his seat, he becomes aware of a pair of feminine legs covered in black taffeta standing by his table. As usual, the amorous theme leads to fantasy; the lady in the magazine photograph has materialized before his very eyes. But such fantasy is infused with the metaphysical spirit of the novel: «Yo sabía la verdad y esperaba comprobar un nuevo sentimiento incomprobado: la relación entre el lector, la fotografiada y el retrato que se vio y que por una casualidad se acaba de tirar. / Es lo más que el hombre arrojado de cualquier modo al mundo puede esperar una noche sin sentido, llena sólo de pasteles iluminados» (p. 92). Plus and minus, the beautiful woman and the husband who accompanies her, prey upon the protagonist-narrator's emotions. As with the woman on the train, retreat seems the best course to take: «Esa mujer que se iba a arropar con el olvido al salir del café, me había revelado que admirar revistas es lo más vano del mundo» (p. 93).

The image of railroads, already employed suggestively in the novel, acquires further impact: «El estar vivo llenaba mi vida y buscaba estaciones en que comprender a los trenes, el acto de marcharse, el acto de morir.» The implications of the image, so important to the whole work, are developed on multiple levels; there is in the consciousness of the protagonist-narrator-author a necessity of expansion: «Lo que tenemos a nuestro alrededor repite demasiado nuestro nombre de un modo consabido y así no salimos de dudas y no sabemos si somos guerreros o sedentarios.» Life is apparently not so much a transit in itself as a station from which one departs on a voyage to the unknown and final proof: «En la antesala de la fría noche y la fría muerte del gran anteandén me parecía que iba a presentir lo que buscaba, ese algo anclado en la vida que he buscado por tantos caminos» (pp. 93-94). The protagonist-narrator-author prefers his own deceitful adventures to those told by novelists, because his have more potential. Anything, no matter how whimsical (the 'split-second object') can contain the ultimate explanation: «¿No me daría toda la realidad de los trajes viejos sobre carnes nuevas el encontrarme un nabo con su rabo de ratón en la limpia vaciedad de la gran antesala de los trenes?» (p. 94). Inevitably, there is a fleeting presence of woman; this time it will turn out to be a happy one. Again reminiscent of *El Incongruente* (ending), the protagonist-narrator has the following certainty: «La gracia había de tenerla la que aprovechando el brazo mío en jarras, aprovechase el asa que formaba así para enhebrarme y llevarme a la casa con fríos ladrillos, que pisaría como con los pies desnudos por causa de la extrañeza de visitarla» (p. 95). There seems to be little doubt of the genealogical ties existing between Gustavo the Misfit and the protagonist-narrator-author of *El hombre perdido,* who makes the following confession: «Toda mi vida ha sido suerte de la casualidad, que me ha hecho encontrar lo que no es ni lo vago y soporífico que se llama lo soñado ni lo grasiento y fofo que se llama lo real.» Neither reality nor unreality but 'para-reality'; perhaps the way to that sought-after world of imagination is out of the expected emptiness of life through the unexpected emptiness of whimsy: «¡A lo mejor esa jaula vacía de un loro que tiene la mujer del traje rojo me daría el contacto con la realidad que busco para no morir en vano!» Here we have another good example of an image of the 'split-second object' which is the essence of the *greguería.* A woman does indeed beckon to the protagonist-narrator, at the other end of a loose thread he wonderingly has stepped on. (Is there a subtle use of the Ariadne-Theseus myth here?) He catches up with her and they board a train for Villapolis. After a pleasant ride, full of conversation, they arrive and go directly to her house, and there the protagonist-narrator muses on his prospects: «Si esta noche no agarraba el secreto por el que vivimos no sé cuándo iba a arramblar con él» (p. 98).

The following day (if we dare believe the apparent sequence of the narrative) the protagonist-narrator finds that «me había llegado la hora de vivir sin casa... El frío y el cristal del balcón preparaban una guillotina de afilada hoja» (pp. 98-99). The omens are bad. He consoles himself with the conviction that «el secreto de la vida no está en las ambiciones de la vida, en las vanidades, en las abstracciones» (p. 99). Where, then, is it to be found? At this point there is a most unexpected and curious dialogue between the protagonist-narrator-author (henceforth called the Lost Man) and an eggplant. Justifications: «La berenjena es más sostenedora de la vida que la tecnocracia» (p. 100); «soy una verdad y me nutrí de verdad... basta que me tengan en la mano para que todo quede comprobado»; «Contra tintero, berenjena... Contra idea, berenjena... Contra conflicto de amor, berenjena» (p. 102; cf. similar function of Rebeca in my Chapter IV). Does the eggplant somehow epitomize the natural manifestation of the metaphysical object? What is important is not to have any preconceptions. For example, if one considers crystal goblets merely as objects to be used during solemn occasions, one will not be intimate with them and thus will lack sufficient clarity (p. 103).

The Lost Man has read an essay on termites and is eager to expound on it to someone. Conveniently, he is visited by Herreros, first identified as «aquel muchacho que había conocido en un bar y que tan gran aire de conspiración tenía» (p. 105). The situation and the description both are reminiscent of ¡Rebeca! The gist of the conversation is the notion that termites are superior in their life style to ants which, like men, sometimes succumb to anarchy and subversion thereby bringing about the destruction of their society. But toward the end of the dialogue the identifies become confused. «Yo soy de los marginales ya que hay margen para nosotros... Por eso me empleo en todas las cosas que voy inventando, por absurdas que parezcan», says Herreros. «Quiero un mundo más divertido que el que me quieren hacer tragar... Por eso tengo mis museos secretos y mis museos públicos» (p. 107). To which the Lost Man replies: «Yo también pretendo lo mismo, y aunque tú has logrado penetrar más en el misterio de otra dimensión, no deja de preocuparme encontrar una explicación al lío de vivir.» When at last the Lost Man refers to the other character as «el vagabundo del primer día, cuando comencé a buscar gracias a él la novela de detrás de las cosas», we surmise that this is nothing more than another unfolding of the author himself (cf. beginning

104

of novel) used here as a pretext for voicing some of his feelings about society.

In an episode seemingly inspired by New York City, the Lost Man visits a millionaire financier. He asks the financier questions like «What is the formula for combining time and water?» (p. 108) and «What is the composition of the dawn?» (p. 109). Would he give anything in exchange for such a phenomenon? The financier answers negatively, though he has recognized in the Lost Man the kindred spirit of a different kind of speculator. They part and, as he leaves, the Lost Man is convinced that there is a vast difference between them, for the millionaire lives in a devitalized world of lies and promises. Ironically, the Lost Man goes into a bar and drinks Coca-Cola.

An elaborate complaint on the part of the Lost Man about the pro- liferation of medical nurses and the likes of them gives way to a vision which he shared with a bald «philosopher»; while in the park they see that «unos dirigibles-tranvía adornados con colores alegres y con jardi- neras abiertas paseaban su grupo de turistas, volando muy bajo» (p. 112). The Lost Man has an idea: he shoves the other man's hat halfway down his head and hails a taxi which rushes them to his photographer. If only the unlikely vision could be captured on the man's bald head as on a photographic plate! Unfortunately such has not happened; the skeptical photographer does his client's bidding by trying to «develop» the philosopher's scalp. In the end, the two visionaries console them- selves drinking wine and exchanging impressions in a tavern. This episode preserves the lighter side of Ramón's gregueristic humor, and the echo of El Incongruente is clear: «No esperaba que aquello se repitiese porque eso sería una persecución de la Providencia...» (p. 115). It is not surpris- ing that the Lost Man should have a gregueristic vision of life: «En mi sabida desorientación aquello me había hecho pensar que se vive entre telones que pueden levantarse en un momento dado y mostrar lo inde- cible.» But it is surprising, especially at this point, that there should be a reference, however vague, to earning a living: «Por la mañana cumplía con mi clientela, lo suficiente para ir viviendo...» Still in the company of the vagabond philosopher, the Lost Man suspects that the latter knew of «algún vericueto por aquellos sitios orilleros del río; donde había algo digno de verse y que aclarase el fondo de la vida entreabriendo una ven- tana que pudiese dar al vivir siempre». Such possibility had nothing to do with politics, the Lost Man feels compelled to explain, because po- litics is what most eclipses life. The vagabond philosopher offers some- thing rather unexpected: the chance to attend a witches' Sabbath at half past three on a Tuesday morning. The Goyaesque element of the gathering constitutes a reprise of the first chapter of the novel and its fantastic qualities. It is interesting to note the reiteration of the image of the «man of dawn» in that of the vagabond philosopher. The Lost Man cannot seem to take such an event too seriously; even there he is on the lookout for his ideal woman: «¿No estaría allí la que no quiere amar? ¿La morena que siendo pálida no se conforme con su palidez?» (p. 117).

One of the Lost Man's great desires is to spend the night in the storage of the Opera. He makes friends with the watchman, a character by the name of Minoni, whose secret is having allowed important gentlemen to meet professional dancers in the privacy of the cloak rooms, for a fee. Minoni agrees to let the Lost Man among the stage sets and numerous decorations. Why does he want to do this? To find the truth among so much make-believe, but it proves futile: «Nada. Todo cartón piedra, todo molde de nebulosidades, todo cajas de cartón sin zapatos siquiera dentro» (p. 120). Subjectively, at least, everything that passes for reality is nothing but an empty form.

It is evident that the whole environment of the novel emanates from the arch-images of voids and railroads. The Lost Man wanders about aimlessly like a locomotive, in the etymological sense. Futhermore, the web of human activity can be looked upon as a network of railroads. Hence, it is not surprising to hear the Lost Man narrate as follows: «La mayor emoción de la vida, mezcla de viaje, noche y reexpedición estuvo en aquella sala de facturación de no sé qué punto del globo, pero ella fue la verdadera capilla en que se me aclaró la base del vivir, lo que es estar sobre la faz de la tierra, lo que es ser invitado por la corriente de aire frío al viaje vagabundo» (p. 121). Ramón's familiar penchant for duality or plurality, so basic to his gregueristic vision, is given further novelistic impetus in the Lost Man's life, torn between his errant soul and the rest of his existence: «Ese es el misterio de la vida, el de la incierta ubicuidad que nos tocó en suerte porque nuestro destino no ha estado sólo en su sitio, sino en varios.» The Lost Man has been musing about all this, when there is an urgent knock at the door. A housekeeper goes to say that he is not in (a frequent narrative subterfuge in Ramón), but the caller insists. The Lost Man finally lets him enter; he is from a small town called Tejerina and is looking for an aunt. The Lost Man surmises that he is none other than his spiritual brother, for the soul he has been missing was dispatched from the train station to Tejerina in the space left empty at the top of a sack of grain. The following day the Lost Man helps his country double named Tiburcio find his aunt, who sells eggs in the city. Amid the conversation, a remarkable gregueristic idea is put forth, that of eggs being produced by the sun and the moon: «El sol pone la yema y la luna, la clara» (p. 124). Before terminating his visit to that woman who seemed to penetrate him with her eyes accustomed to looking at eggs against a light globe, the Lost Man elaborates to the reader on his relationship with Tiburcio. Included is a very interesting statement; on the way to Tejerina his soul made all the stops and waited «en algunas vías muertas mientras llegaban los vagones vacíos... (p. 125). As an anticipation of the conclusion to the novel, this is significant.

The Lost Man goes for a ride in a streetcar, thereby providing a pretext for a eulogy of such a vehicle. In the streetcar, the Lost Man comes across Herreros, the «vagabundo de aquel día... personaje de la casa misteriosa de Goya...» (p. 126). They joke about being constantly at loose ends, for they seem to have no choice in the matter. Says the Lost Man (Ramón), injecting a social comment: «Por eso es bárbaro querer igualitar la vida, que ni en su azar llega a tener sentido» (p. 127). The bum offers to take him to meet «el hombre que se salvó a la muerte» (p. 129), a convict who had escaped being hanged in the prison close to which the streetcar left them and who now lives in an underground abode. After the convict tells his own story (he does not go farther away because he has prescribed his own sentence), the Lost Man is strangely elated to be once again outdoors.

In the next episode, we are informed, much to our surprise, that the Lost Man is married. What brings about such unexpected information is his assertion that «la disputa con la mujer es eterna» (p. 130), a circumstance with which he copes in part by means of his «risa de suicidio y de escapada de ese mundo estrecho de la vida marital» and of his ability to invent words and phrases to use as insults: «mujer macabróntica... trapajundia... guitarra de carne... mirazapatos...» (p. 132). The dialogue ends with this accusation by the Lost Man: «tú sólo eres nada y quien viene de la nada a mí no me importa nada» (p. 133). It is, of course, an ambiguous charge, because it suggests the material non-existence of the ideal woman (cf. Rebeca) to whom the Lost Man feels in some way married. Those quarrels are very likely nothing more than metaphysical frustrations. And he confesses: «Acabadas las disputas siempre vi en el suelo un tigre pisoteado y sólo pude salir de ellas por saber que entre occipucio y nuca tiene la mujer la caricia de gato que lo arregla todo.»

Flowers, the Lost Man tells us, are important in and for his life, but so are women, as he has stated much earlier («La mujer es lo que contesta algo al enigma», p. 62). The apparent equivalence between women and flowers arises in Chapter XXIX, where the rhetoric is actually baffling. It is impossible to say with certainty what the referent of «las» is when the Lost Man says: «Yo las contemplo caídas en el vacío de los que merecen el vacío y me parece menos engañoso el balance de vacíos que el balance de llenazones que atora al que las mira o las conlleva. / Nada, nada, este ligero vacío...» (p. 134). Is this arcanum a gregueristic image or a flaw in the method of composition resulting in a copy error? The pages that follow encourage the reader to opt for the first explanation. «Mientras voy yo por en medio de esas preocupaciones que no tienen tregua», continues the Lost Man, «miro como entre cañaverales el cielo azul y la flor morada, poniendo esa distancia entre pensamiento y objeto que no me he de llevar, que es la distancia del vivir, la separación del gozar, el trayecto entre pila bautismal y entierro» (pp. 134-35). The hallucinatory images are not complete hallucinations, for obviously there is a consistent ideology behind them. The brevity of life is the flower around which human beings hover like insects; does Ramón wish for an ideal flower (cf. Mallarmé) as he wishes for an ideal woman? The Lost Man muses: «Vale la pena vagabundear y ser viudo de todo como yo lo soy si se busca lo que no hay, lo que no es una de esas cosas miserables que los demás tienen acaparadas, sino la ausencia de la corbata y del bastón» (p. 135).

The Lost Man and his younger brother (another surprise!) become obsessed with the mourning clothes of three women whose father died ten years before. When the Lost Man makes a pun by saying that «vivir después de todo es carbonizarse» (p. 136), his brother is so impressed that he begins to turn black. The humorous situation is enhanced by the existence of the Spanish expression *ponerse negro,* which means «to become livid»; and so going from *lívido* to *pálido* through fright, the brother is returned to his original white complexion. A further play on words sends the brother home: «Mi hermano como devuelto a su libertad de irse se despidió y se fue» (p. 138). The end of the episode is as enigmatic as any yet encountered: «Sólo se fue alguien aquella mañana después de haber cobrado un cheque, comprando cosas bajo un sol veraniego, llegando tarde a la corbatería del lazo azul...» (p. 139). Who is that someone? Perhaps the Lost Man himself who, changing from the third person above to the first in the same line, says: «Debí aprovechar más aquella mañana...»

The literary manifestation of Ramón's concept of the ideal woman is that of an aesthetic (not necessarily a sexual) object: «Tenía una hermosura que saciaba todos los afanes y me agarré a ella como el náufrago a la roca» (p. 140). But the natural conflict between two entities is always there, the metaphysical conflict between subject and object: «La lucha entre la bella y el hombre estaba armada entre aquella mujer y yo...» (p. 140). The aesthetic and the erotic ultimately fuse in a sort of fetichism: «Esa lucha sorda detrás de cuyo biombo estaba la modelo que servía para crear en la intimidad la escultura femenina de la vida...» (cf. similar situation in *El novelista,* Chapter XLIV, «Detrás del parapeto»). The conversation between the Lost Man and this woman figment turns to the topic of love. «Contempla la felicidad porque la felicidad no es más que contemplación y así se la fija y se la logra gozar y que no se evapore», the Lost Man counsels rather mystically. «No creas que es riqueza material... Es algo que se va si se la pierde de vista... Se te escapará como el agua cuando se deja mal cerrado el baño» (p. 140). The woman is not convinced; she complains about not having greater comforts. The Lost Man is disappointed in his companion; he realizes that she is not different from the great majority of women, whose mercenariness comes from a desire for exhibitionism: «Si no hay relación entre amor, banco público y figón pobre, el amor no existe. La mujer tiene que entrar en el arrebato vagabundo...» (p. 142).

The next episode initially partakes of the peculiar density characteristic of Madrilenian *costumbrismo*, a technique certainly not unfamiliar to Ramón (see, for example, *El novelista*, Chapter V, «La novela de la calle del Árbol»). But the reader must not be misled into expecting such a simple tradition, even for a change. A favorite narrative device of Ramón is present from the start: «En aquella esquina había un secreto y me puse a observarlo con tenacidad.» A fat man looks out of the window and invites the Lost Man to come in and have a cup of coffee. The new personage seems like a figure from Baroja, but what he says sounds more like Azorín: «Vivo aquí hace cuarenta años y sé cómo se parece la tarde de hace tres años a la tarde de hoy... No vivo más que para hacer esa estadística de lo que se repite...» (p. 143). This man's son wants to be an airplane pilot; the Lost Man expresses his opposition to such an occupation on humanitarian grounds but abandons the discussion pessimistically saying: «¡A mí qué me importa! Después de todo todos los destinos son iguales...» (p. 144). Once out of the house, the Lost Man looks at a nearby convent and thinks into the narrative: «¡Cómo se burlaba el convento de la intranquilidad de los que quieren arrasar conventos...! / Yo creía en el Dios que no quiere saber nada de la tierra y al que no le importan ni oraciones ni blasfemias, pero comprendía que era mejor vida... aquella vida respetable, que de cualquier manera elevaba al hombre» (pp. 144-45). How much does this passing comment on religion reflect Ramón's true feelings and belief? The Lost Man's meditation is interrupted by Herreros, the vagabond, who in this episode acquires a first name (Gonzalo) and invites him on another jaunt. They go to a strange, inconspicuous building, hidden in some part of town. There, on the second story, the Lost Man is introduced to a certain Don Homobono, the clothes-designer of an establishment known as «El Atrezo Civil», to which go «muchos hombres sin destino que necesitan un traje que les conduzca a donde las palabras no sirven» (p. 146). Who are those men? «Todos los arribistas y los intrigantes... Los que precisamente llegan a ser algo» (p. 147). Thus the *greguería* at the service of satire. Gonzalo Herreros has a proposition for Don Homobono, namely, the making of a suit of clothes corresponding to that of city manager.

The Lost Man's conscience sketches a trajectory along the interstices of reality: «Yo iba por los aleros de la vida, los aleros bajos cuando me malhirió un saliente con la palabra 'afán'.» For the Lost Man, the solution to the problem of life is to find his «destiny», the consistency which will radiate its meaning throughout the emptiness around him:

«me daba prisa para encontrar mi destino, ansia de llegar a él antes de que los descomponedores del mundo hubiesen logrado su propósito». The mood is set for this passage by the feeling of metaphysical solitude; the late-working Ramón could say from personal experience that «cuando se viven en la alta noche las horas solitarias se ve cómo las cuatro de la mañana son de otro mundo que las diez de la mañana o las seis y media de la tarde» (cf. *El alba y otras cosas* —1918—, in which are found the origins of *El hombre perdido;* more will be said about this at the end of the present chapter). The idea of suicide subtly crosses the mind of the Lost Man, but an impromptu meeting with a drunk distracts him. The Lost Man hails a taxi and gets away. Under the light of street-lamps, his morbid thoughts return: «En la noche había ecos de estación vacía y desconsolada, con pitidos de verdadera estación lejana que marcan la discusión de ultratumba que hay entre la noche y el más allá» (p. 148). He wishes for the sort of priest who might absolve him from his nocturnal sin (here one must remember his criminal self-investigation earlier narrated). But there is also something by which he feels victimized: «Muchos no se dan cuenta de lo que pasa en la noche, de lo que hace con ellos el trecho vacío que tiene personalidad de lavanderas y furias» (p. 149). And further: «... en busca de mi perdición me han puesto traje a rayas de cambalache y una máquina fotográfica también de casa de empeño en la cabeza.» In the night of the city he has been besieged by the objects lying in wait for him in the storewindows. Peremptory dialogue makes use of the pseudo-humanization of inanimate objects so frequently found in Ramón's aphorisms and in other novelistic passages. Such greguerístic humor, when closely examined, is found to border on metaphysical terror. Not so much hope as perseverance is inferred from the Lost Man's words: «Sigo mi rumbo y espero encontrar la clave en los días que me quedan por vivir entrando en las farmacias de turno para pedir farmacia esfervescente [*sic*] con lentes azules» (p. 151).

The Lost Man and an unidentified woman are out walking and come across a bagnio. Without realizing what he is doing, the Lost Man suggests that they go in and take a scented bath. The woman agrees, but once inside, the Lost Man has second thoughts. Instead of being seduced by the perfumes that float through the corridors like frantic harem girls, he is moved by righteous indignation. (If any of this were by chance autobiographical of Ramón, it could be explained by his well-known jealousy; see *¡Rebeca!*). A sudden puritanical change of heart makes him consider the sensuous establishment as a veritable den of iniquity. As the woman-symbol of sensuality disappears through a pink door, awaited by an unknown fate, the Lost Man decides to leave, though momentarily embarrassed by his formal dress in the presence of other bathers. He remembers with disgust his nameless older brother, who had incurred his lasting animosity by going to just such an establishment in the company of an actress. The memory is all he needs to send him running to the front door, where he waits for fewer people to pass along the street so that he can turn the corner and join them without attracting too much attention. One nagging question remains in his mind: did he invite the woman into the bagnio to get rid of her or did he let her down once they were inside?

Waking up at two in the afternoon, having gone to sleep at ten in the morning, the Lost Man reasons as follows: «quito horas al sueño como despojando a la muerte antes de que ella me despoje definitivamente... Es lo único que le queda como resarcimiento y venganza, al hombre perdido del presente» (p. 154). He goes to see a friend named Manuel Casas and finds him trying to learn English by means of phonograph records. Disappointed in his friend's gullibility, the Lost Man describes the result of such a method as linguistic onanism. As Casas suddenly experiences an asthmatic seizure of the kind he says have been frequent lately, the Lost Man, in a manner reminiscent of Dr. Vivar (see *El doctor inverosímil*), asks him if they come before or after the English lessons. The answer is, of course, «after»; and the only remedy seems to be for Casas to *write* several times the word «sunset» (p. 156). Reaching into the past for novelistic purposes, the Lost Man arbitrarily injects into the narrative the following perplexing information regarding his friend: «La mujer que en aquellos momentos era mi mujer, le tomó un gran asco.» The two friends are in agreement on social issues. They are not revolutionaries; they are conservatives because they know how to conserve what is worthwhile. People, they say, «no sabrán evitar ninguna catástrofe porque no provocan la distracción inmensa que hay que provocar en estos momentos el enredo ideal que cohoneste el enredo material» (p. 157). The anacoluthon occurring with «momentos el enredo», instead of being part of the gregueristic rhetoric, disappears when a comma found in the first edition is restored after «momentos». It would not be difficult to find Ramón's literary credo in these words of the Lost Man, childish as they might seem: «No creo más que en el juego de las cosas y que me salga en el azar la cosa entretenida» (p. 158).

There seems to be a functional time factor in this novel after all, though one can never be sure either of the kind of time or of its function. What does it mean to have a paragraph consisting of the words «Un año nuevo más»? There are, however, narrative supports. The Lost Man begins another episode thus: «Había llegado cansado, pero sin carpeta, cuando me encerré en mi habitación de la casa de huéspedes.» As much a wanderer as he might be, he is *apparently* not, like Gonzalo Herreros, a bum. We have not been able to ascertain his means of livelihood, and we cannot be sure whether or not this is where he has been living all along. Ultimately we will come to the realization that such details have neither validity nor importance; they are mere concessions to the reader's

111

habit in following a novelistic structure. Equally intriguing and of the same internal, fluctuating nature is this other statement: «yo sentía la misma incertidumbre de siempre, aunque la belleza de mi mujer había aumentado.» Thereupon follows a disquisition on hats and their attendant superstitions. Then comes the night-table —first cousin to the coffin, with its drawer for wills and farewell notes— and a somnolent dialogue ensues. It is similar to the autodialogues found in ¡Rebeca!; proof of this is that one cannot be sure of which speaker says what. The first line is: «¿Y si hoy fuese ayer muerto por el otro día?» (p. 161). Further on we find: «En la falta de lógica todo dependería de que la poesía creadora presidiese o no el alborozo del mundo... La lógica llena de miedo la vida...» Awake or asleep, the Lost Man visualizes a flaking spot on the ceiling caused by dampness, a sign of decomposition or necrosis to which there is a parallel in human life. «Confieso», he says, «que ése era mi punto de referencia cotidiano y por eso pensé que en los cines sucios de barrio está el refugio de los muertos.»

The narrative still develops in the rooming house. The Lost Man continues his self-analysis: «no había nacido para la guerra ni para entrar en un partido político... Mi destino seguía siendo independiente y libre... capaz de entrar en todas las combinaciones de la vida, las más imprevisibles, las más fantásticas» (p. 162). If nothing else, this and the following statement of purpose clearly identify the Lost Man with the historical Ramón: «Gracias a reunir todo lo imaginable podré vivir un minuto de superrealidad y tocar las orillas del sobrevivir.» The accumulation of gregueristic images comes as close as anything to being all that is imaginable. A tangent on the subject of water starts with what could be an aphorism («sólo al beber agua sabemos algo de la verdad de lo que miramos») and evolves into a childhood recollection of drinking a glass of cold water given to him by an aunt: «Aunque no tenía más que once años, reaccioné al mimo y engaño de aquella tía pálida y bolsona.» Despite the unavoidably humorous emphasis, the temporal shift enhances the novelistic intent of the narrative. «Siempre al beber un vaso de agua miro en torno de mí como hombre que avizora el peligro», he says, tightly compressing chronological and psychic time by going from the past to the present through a constant («siempre») that governs an action as well as an emotion («miro... como hombre que avizora el peligro» = hombre perdido). «Hoy», he continues, «al beber un vaso repleto, he visto que lo que estoy buscando, la señal fehaciente de vivir, está en reconocer las cuñadas de las paredes.» The passage that then follows for a page and a half, and which I quote in toto for reasons which will be obvious, is one of the outstanding examples of ramonismo within a novelistic structure. After the allusion to the Lost Man's quest, the passage includes personification or humanization of the inanimate, in the peremptory dialogue, and the all-important notions of the 'para-real' and the 'split-

112

second object'. It is easy to detect here the elements that associate *ramonismo* with surrealism and existentialism, respectively.

Las cuñadas de las paredes son algo así como nuestras hermanastras, si hubiéramos tenido hermanastras.

Ellas responden con contradicción a lo que quisiéramos y nos hacen suponer lo que no somos ni suponemos que podríamos ser.

Con el delantal abandonado en la cocina por la asistenta que no vendrá hoy, ellas se ponen a guisar cosas en las sartenes al revés.

—Yo creo que hay demasiada seguridad en la vida para saber lo que es la vida.

—No tendrías ninguna si los demás no quisieran vivir... Por ti solo no tendrías más que muerte.

—Realmente se está tan cerca a una desolación de terremoto que lo mejor es imitar al jilguero.

—¿Y no temes al peluquero que te busca con sus tijeras y su toalla de fuerza como los chalecos para los locos?

—¿Y qué he de hacer para salvarme?

—Confiésate con el aparador... Dile tu ingratitud de hombre que cree que sólo va a tener cuchillos para no partir nada.

Noté que la cuñada de la pared tenía un aire de enfermera oficiosa a la que nadie ha llamado.

—¿Qué te dedicas a curar?

—Curo el cáncer antes de que aparezca... Yo sé el grano de polvo que sería cáncer en tu garganta y lo retengo... Todas las ventanas tienen paloma amilanada de bronquitis y yo mato esas palomas. ¿Es que crees que si estuvieras completamente solo, sin los seres suplementarios que te rodean, seguirías viviendo? ¡Infeliz!

—Yo creí que había compañías de tazas y de bandejas, pero no de vosotras, enfermeras lisas como un cartón de amianto.

—Evitamos el bocio de las habitaciones y curamos la cara de muerte que da el insomnio.

—¿Qué es lo que os pone más nerviosas?

—El ruido de los portazos... Os mataríamos... Gracias a que alguien los para y cierra la puerta. ¿Pero no notaste al levantarte y hacer eso, que lo hacías por alguien que ya estaba desesperado de impaciencia?

—Sí, es verdad... No me hubiera levantado por mí ni por mi mujer... Me levantaba por alguien que no podía más y me salvaba de los mosquitos de la muerte. ¿Y lo sabéis todo?

—Todo... Quiénes han estado a veros y andado por vuestra casa en vuestra ausencia.

—¿Fantasmas?

—Nada de fantasmas... Las amigas que no visitan ya a vuestras mujeres y que fueron y siguen siendo las que os engañan con ellas..., las sacudimos con los trapos de la cocina... Entonces se van, pero son una vergüenza.

De pronto la cuñada de la pared desapareció como cuando se cae un retrato detrás de una librería y me encontré hallado por lo supuesto y sin poder suponer con verdadera evidencia si era entera verdad lo sucedido o si era que yo había ligado a mi soledad la practicanta del médico que había visto en las escaleras.

La verdad era que mi viejo paraguas de niño, el que me daban para ir al colegio los días de lluvia, me hacía señas de que sí, de que las cuñadas

113

de las paredes eran reales como lo que empuja a la silla que estaba sos-
teniendo a la puerta de muelle para que no se cerrase y, sin embargo, se
cierra. (pp. 163-64)

It is useless to indulge in philological speculations about Ramón's
image «cuñadas de las paredes»; a cursory examination of the most
dependable lexica (e.g., María Moliner, *Diccionario de uso del español*
[Madrid: Gredos, 1966], which includes a condensation of Corominas's
article on the subject «cuñadas») will persuade one of the author's
«higher» aim to suggest his notions of the 'split-second object' and the
'para-real', rather than indulging merely in a play on words.

Once again deprived of the «other» walls, those that are a demarcation
of the «other» reality, the Lost Man is momentarily left with another
illusion, namely, some love letters written on the actual walls of the
room. The letter which he reads and transcribes is signed «Livina»
(pp. 164-65). After he reads the letter, it too disappears and the insipid
wallpaper returns.

The Lost Man is thankful for the opportunities he has of experienc-
ing the 'para-real': «Mi gratitud más profunda es por esa mano misteriosa que me ha abierto a veces puertas entre los dos mundos» (p. 165).
This leads into what I will now call anecdote. The Lost Man once lived
above a fabric shop in town and yet he knew of an estate on the
outskirts which displayed a beautiful magnolia tree, whose flowers
disappeared as soon as they bloomed. The house was inhabited by some
women, who were known simply as the Magnolias. One day the Lost
Man walked into the grounds of the estate and asked the first girl he
saw if they sold flowers there. She answered negatively to his question
but invited him to visit the house. The humor and pun injected into
the dialogue are admissible only because of the absurd nature of the
scene itself (question and answer, without definite indication of speaker):
—«¿Así es que usted es víctima de las flechas del dios Cupido y de su
carcaj? / —A mí el carcaj de Cupido sólo me produce carcajadas»
(p. 166). The girl introduced the Lost Man to five other women, who
were her three sisters, mother, and grandmother, the last being, strangely,
the youngest. The six beautiful and interrelated women, surrounded by
the sumptuous and dreamy atmosphere, create a scene that is reminiscent of the episode in *¡Rebeca!* in which the protagonist, Luis, comes
across a tapestry depicting five women who look alike: «Aquel hallaz-
go fortuito era la reborondez de un deseo y no veía el momento de
escaparme al compromiso de deseo que se iba adensando en el comedor
de los espejos» (p. 169). (Part of the technique of gregueristic narrative,
by the way, is a sort of shorthand of imagery, by means of which segments of allusion and suggestion are skipped in favor of new ones, a
practice similar to that of omitting full vowel signs between consonants

114

in Arabic writing.) At the end of the anecdote, the Lost Man took the carriage offered to him by the Magnolias and was driven to the very center of town.

We have encountered successively two kinds of narrative segment in *El hombre perdido*, the one represented by the experience of the «cuñadas de las paredes» and the other exemplified by the meeting with the Magnolias. Are they different modalities of essentially the same fiction, namely, that of the 'para-real'? I believe so; the first tends more toward the aphorism, the second tends more toward the anecdote.

Much as in *El Incongruente*, the Lost Man is unexpectedly called by a lady, who was so stylishly clothed that her dress showed no fabric, only buttons. Arriving at her apartment, he finds her in bed with nothing but gloves on, while a pipsqueak of an artist is painting landscapes on her body. The woman thinks that the Lost Man should be disconcerted by her behavior, but he simply states: «ya sabe que yo vivo de estar extraviado» (p. 170). When she asks if he has anything in particular to say, he makes this interesting observation: «somos unos caracoles desnudos que después de unos días de asueto acaban por meterse en el caracol que habían abandonado.» The shell to which he refers is, as he puts it, «el nicho o el panteón, según el tamaño de la fortuna». The lady in the episode represents the aristocracy. If we have seen Ramón make some snide remarks about socialists, here we find a different line of attack: «ya me estaba volviendo loco la aristocracia, que si bien debe existir, no orienta nada en sus conversaciones. Cuando se llega a ella, se llega al laboratorio vacío» (p. 172). The vacuity of human life is even more evident to the Lost Man in this environment; he can possess the woman's body, but that is a fleeting matter. His quest goes on, only to be alternately encouraged by illusions and discouraged by the emptiness he finally discovers: «Lo que yo no sabía es cómo podía componer el nombre que me faltaba hallar y que en los bostezos del alba reflejada en los charcos, parece que va a aparecer.»

How does the Lost Man earn a living? He is some kind of agent, an «honrado comisionista sin porvenir» (p. 173). Apparently, Gonzalo Herreros is *also* au undetermined sort of agent *after all*, though perhaps less honest. The Lost Man is paid a visit by the «siempre extraño vagabundo...». They are now very familiar and employ the *tú* form of address. Gonzalo is in a particularly generous mood and invites the Lost Man to dinner and a play. After eating at a place appropriately called the Posada del Trajinante, where the two whimsical vagabonds observe and eavesdrop on the common working folk, lamenting a little snobbishly that those precisely are the people who least recognize the important things of life («Creen que no sólo no puede desaparecer esto, sino que tiene que venir una cosa mejor», p. 175), they go to the «teatro de la venganza privada». The dramatic presentation takes place in a private home and is limited to a scene in which a husband surprises his wife in the arms of another man. For a moment the husband threatens to shoot the lovers, but seeing that they are willing to die for their love, he forgives them and welcomes them to live together with him. The amazing thing about the situation is that the performance is the reproduction of an incident that happened in real life and which the crazed husband insists on repeating over and over. «Muy bien... Mejor que la última vez que se lo vi representar», Gonzalo tells the husband, indulging in the most subtle absurdity (p. 176). The latter replies candidly: «Yo no vivo más que para la llegada de esta hora, a las once en punto, la hora en que hace tres años les pillé *in fraganti*» (pp. 176-77). It will be remembered that, toward the beginning of this novel, the Lost Man says: «Lo único que vale la pena en la vida es pillar a la mujer *in fraganti...*» (p. 38). Such repetition of the theme might be interpreted as some sort of pathological obsession. And yet in *El novelista* (p. 240), Ramón employs the same Latin phrase when referring to the peculiarity of screens that enable one to surprise or catch in the act the «gestures» of things which otherwise would pass unperceived. Almost anything, any suggestion is possible in Ramón. It could be that the idea of surprising one's mate in the act of adultery is a manifestation of Ramón's capacity for jealousy, but it also could be that such a surprise is a novelistic (and dramatic) manifestation of the principle of the *greguería:* no more and no less, after all, than an association of the unexpected.

Ramón's old theme, that of happiness, so persistent in his youthful and optimistic works, makes its appearance in a negative manner. Where is happiness to be found? The Lost Man reveals his utter lack of hope: «La vida es un carro de mudanza que ha pasado lleno y que vuelve vacío» (p. 178). Literary self-awareness, which is the whole of *El novelista,* also reappears negatively, along with some important images: «Me iba convirtiendo en el hombre al que exigen los demás que escriba, pero yo sólo quería lograr un destino fijo y meditar, ver venir a la que se esconde detrás de los biombos...» A telling paragraph which already puts into common perspective the four «Novels of the Nebula». Other images follow, incongruous images that shatter the surface of anything which would be logically supposed; in other words, gregueristic images which are «todas esas cosas que entretienen el día vacío...». But the Lost Man's quest for proof of having lived goes on: «Yo voy buscando la última piedad de la herencia —de no acabo de saber qué herencia—, una herencia que quizá me deje en el porvenir alguien que no ha nacido aún» (p. 179). The ultimate consequence of time seems reversible. If reversion does not depend upon one's will, diversion does, and crime (the preoccupation with which the novel begins) is ambivalent in the consciousness of the Lost Man: «es lo que me hace ser el pesquisa interminable... ¿Qué es Dios sino el mayor pesquisa de lo que sucede? / Busco mi destino y me

116

empeño en saber por qué quieren asesinarme y cuándo en definitiva me asesinarán.» There is a slight possibility that the gregueristic style of narrative permits here an allusion to things political, but the context is really more one of metaphysics. Has the Lost Man turned in on himself the image of a criminal act? And is the crime first mentioned in the novel as a clue to the Lost Man's existence a variant of what Calderón called «el delito mayor del hombre», that is, «haber nacido» (a notion Calderón himself borrowed from the Roman soldier and writer Silenus)? The Lost Man would like at least to find the evidence of his reality in a sort of evolutionary reiteration (here again the image of the snail, the opposite of Ramón's frequent use of the idea of velocity): «¡Si encontrase por lo menos lo que tengo de caracol con kilómetros de baba!... He dado tantas vueltas para saber a qué atenerme.» The Lost Man confronts the problems of reality and time which are, of course, two aspects of the same: «¿Vivimos o no vivimos? ¿Viviremos o no viviremos?» Metaphoric elaboration: «Nos hemos lavado la cara con la luz de alrededor de palacio y hemos estado viendo a un relojero trabajar esperando que soltase su monóculo y que con el ojo espantado hiciese el aspaviento de haber encontrado la verdad del tiempo» (p. 180). The change to the first person plural is significant; what is usually commentary in the conventional novel again takes on here an aphoristic quality. The theme of vacuity acquires the variant forms of loneliness and orphanhood, in other words, the estrangement of more orthodox Existentialism: «La soledad es absoluta. Nadie se ocupa de nadie... Toda la orfandad del mundo está en este retardo del hombre con alas de blusa» (pp. 180-81). A faint hope looms in the spiritual horizon of the Lost Man: «Por lo menos me consoló la aparición de la mujer plástica toda vestida desde el descote a los pies de media transparente» (p. 181). Like the body-painting image, this erotic use of a girl in a leotard is a bit surprising. A dialogue with this apparition follows, a dialogue of love and longing. She is, without a doubt, a version of Rebeca. «Tú has venido a esta pensión y mi puerta comunica con tu cuarto a través de este armario», the illusory woman says to him. To which he answers that, grateful as he is for the happiness she has brought him, he knows that apparitions, too, pass away. She, in turn, cautions as follows: «Todo muere, pero todo puede tener sorpresas en la vida.» It is as if the *greguería* itself were given voice, for if the flux of reality moves everything along, there can be the surprise of the 'split-second object'. As the apparition acquires the capital letter of intimacy, the Lost Man expresses feelings reminiscent of Bécquer's «Los ojos verdes»:

> La Aparición se acercó a mí y se sentó sobre mis rodillas como un gabán, ligera y suave.
> Se veía en ella lo que la mujer tiene de vampiro nocturno guardado en los guardarropas.

> Despertaba en mí, como ninguna otra mujer, la iracundia contra la muerte. Era la pimpante cebolla sonrosada hecha de capas superpuestas, fresca y rozagante como lo efímero.
> No se podía dudar de su esbeltez y de su reciencia y eso hacía más grave la evidencia de su desaparición.
> Los abstinentes, los que nunca han tenido cerca la Aparición, se han salvado de la gran contrición de la vida, que es la belleza en la mano y, sin embargo, la belleza ida, volando, desapareciendo. (p. 182)

In effect, the Apparition disappears (as in the previously discussed novel Rebeca, the illusion, disappeared so many times): «a la mañana siguiente... sólo encontré un ropero vacío...»

It is extremely difficult to assess the relative importance of the various «aphoristic» or «anecdotal» passages. They all are part of the kaleidoscopic novelistic structure. At times they give the impression of being «inserted» (as might be expected from what is known of Ramón's method of composition) but, in the last analysis, there is no doubt that the intent of composition prevails and that the seemingly disconnected or heterogeneous parts of the narrative are exactly the way they should be, according to the style of the greguería.

At this point in the book, the reader comes upon a long narrative episode divided into several chapters and very similar to the last part of ¡Rebeca! in that it deals anecdotally with the man-woman theme, the attraction exerted by amatory relationships on the Lost Man. It begins with his being invited by a nameless friend to dinner at the house of a rich man named Oriol. A certain ventriloquist is expected to attend with his papier-maché lady, in whose honor the dinner is being held. The Lost Man agrees to go: «Yo sabía que de esas bromas sale un resalte extraño y se descubren cosas insospechadas» (p. 183). The cardboard woman presides over the gathering, the words emitted by her mouth jokingly referring to Sr. Oriol's courtships. The Lost Man notices that the blonde sitting in front of him fits the description mouthed by the dummy: «La rubia que tenía frente a mí representaba en vivo la imitación sarcástica de la otra, y ella se sobreexcitaba al ver lo que hacía su doble» (p. 184). When the cardboard woman mimics the ruin of her life as a result of Sr. Oriol's seduction, the blonde across the table from the Lost Man faints: «Me asedió tanto que me perdió» (p. 185). Everyone rushes toward the casualty, including the Lost Man who now feels personally involved: «Me atraía aquella rubia, que como todas las rubias, era una aleación aurífera y carnal.» The blonde's name is Alcira; when she regains consciousness she asks the Lost Man to take her to her «domicilio de soltera» (p. 186), where she reveals her strange nature. Reminiscent of the episode in El Incongruente, in which Gustavo visits the city of the wax dolls (who speak because they are not actually wax dolls but wax women, whom one meets just before they become dolls),

Alcira explains as follows: «sol como la muñeca que hemos dejado en plena juerga, sino que yo lo soy de verdad y aquella lo es de mentira...» The interplay of reality and illusion naturally continues, with the added parallel between the doll[2] and the ideal woman (Rebeca). The implied pun brings together a «mujer perdida» turned into a doll and an «hombre perdido» turned into a ventriloquist: «Lo único que me faltaba en la vida sin orientación, pero con aventuras en laberinto, era hablar por mí y por ella en el diálogo del amor ¿en qué loco me iba a convertir? Ventrílocuo y no ventrílocuo» (p. 187). We have here another excellent example of the stylistic revolution which Ramón had in mind and practiced to a higher and higher degree as his techniques evolved. To the charge that unconventional syntax produces inferior works of literature, levelled by Martín Alonso, for example, there will be added that of Eugenio de Nora, who regards *El hombre perdido* as a novel (he still calls it a novel) of the most doubtful aesthetic viability. In this episode, the notion of reversibility, so attractive to Ramón's sense of humor, is superimposed on the basic plot of Délibes' ballet, *Coppélia*. Yet the image of vacuity prevails. Alcira, the woman-doll, asks the Lost Man if he finds her blonde enough. Yes, he answers, but also empty. But that should be an attraction, she retorts, for a man to have a woman he can «fill» as he wishes. Unfortunately, the Lost Man confesses, he is looking for a woman who can fill him, that is, who can give him consistency. Is this not another instance of literary self-awareness, the humorous admission of an empty image trying to pass for a novelistic character? The metaphysical mirror-image of Alcira is a talking emptiness: «Ha robado usted al señor Oriol su mejor juguete mecánico... Él se ha quedado haciendo el imbécil con la dama rubia, esa pobre imagen de vestir hecha de ortopedias baratas... A mí me puede usted libertar y convertirme otra vez en mujer...» The scene that follows is daring in its metaphors, as Alcira takes a bubble-bath and the amorous though nebulous adventure leads into the night.

The relationship with Alcira is ambivalent for the Lost Man: «Me atraía y me ponía triste. Era como esos topes de los trenes que no dejan ir más allá, pero no contestaba a ninguna de mis preguntas. '¿Cómo acercarse más a Dios?' '¿Cómo librarse de morir demasiado pronto?' '¿Cuál es el destino para quedarse tranquilo y quieto?'» (p. 189). The old preoccupations with life, death, and the hereafter are the preoccupations of this new Lost Man. Woman is what comes closest to solving the enigma but not completely, especially when the old green-eyed

---

[2] A story which Ramón might have known is entitled *La Femme endormie* (Paris, 1899) and tells how «a shy recluse, Paul Molaus, asks an artist to make him a lifelike female doll who will be in all respects like a real woman»; see PHYLLIS and EBERHARD KRONHAUSEN, *Erotic Fantasies* (New York: Grove Press, 1969), pp. 362-84.

monster rears its head: «¿Que está soñando conmigo? Muy crédulo se tiene que ser para pensar eso. Está hablando con caballeros o rufianes...» Is the Lost Man's Alcira a «modern» version of Don Quixote's Dulcinea? One's mate is perhaps someone else's mate while asleep, the Lost Man concludes, and he is about to depart when Alcira tells him that she dreamed that he was leaving. «Ante aquella conducción secreta entre los sueños y la realidad que me revelaban aquellas palabras», he says, «comprendí que hay un misterio que obliga a la compañía de los que se juró acompañar» (p. 190). He tells her to go on sleeping, while he takes care of his letter-writing. Finally, he too goes to sleep, wishing to find his way into her dreams, which he does. The consequence is unfortunate: «todo... me era desconocido comenzando por mi llamada mujer... Ver un sueño por dentro es una desolación monstruosa...» (pp. 191-92).

Modern society, the Lost Man muses, has tried to answer the age-old metaphysical questions with inventions such as the *apéritif*. In the meantime, the unknown remains unknown. Though turned into a commonplace, inanity is as real as it is illusory. The Lost Man's argument is whimsically irrefutable: «si no es el aperitivo, tampoco es el trabajo la justificación del vivir...» (p. 195). He and his blonde Alcira take in the high life and catch sight of the cardboard lady of the previous night. There is a reprise of *El Incongruente*: «Como continuación del aperitivo, aquella noche entramos en la *boîte* de la caja de la escalera, la *boîte* más pequeña del mundo. Tocaban el fox *Sus medias no armonizan*» (p. 196). Is the latter image a humorous yet transparent anticipation? The rest of the episode suggests aspects of autobiography. There is a falling out between the lovers: «Yo quería saber lo que iba a pasar. Quería tentar al destino, ver si un viraje fuerte se precipitaba sobre el certificado que yo quería tener» (p. 198). In anticipation of the final split, while Alcira is away visiting her sister, the Lost Man makes use of his imagination to turn his room into a Museum of Decapitated Ladies; the purpose is to delve into those images for an evaluation of his love. When the vision disappears, a letter is delivered; in it, Alcira says that she is not coming back and to wrap her belongings in two bed sheets so as not to betray her move with suitcases. The letter ends as follows: «Yo sé que tú sabrás morir solo y feliz. Yo moriré desesperada y así te liberto de mi desesperación» (p. 201). This letter, we are told finally, is a copy of a draft he wrote himself. Humorous paradox, the farewell note was preconceived in the mind of the Lost Man. One question remains: was Alcira (Rebeca) also thus preconceived?

The break with Alcira, no matter what her nature, is of itself significant. A transition is subtly recorded in the life of the Lost Man: «todo lo más grave me sucedía en aquel rincón de plaza... / Allí me fui a morir una tarde, allí compré unas flores a la mujer que se quería ir de mi lado... Siempre era en esa esquina donde se resolvía mi destino entre prisión y libertad, entre engaño de amigo y engaño de mujer, entre compra de sillón de mimbre ideal y medicina verde nueva» (p. 202). Here we have two Spanish words that mean «corner» and refer to the «in» and «out» of things; love and deceit are now associated with both sexes. A mystical image of blue vases beyond his possession is used to connote the Lost Man's sense of despair. (For Ramón's fondness of vases, see works as early as *Entrando en fuego* [pp. 13-14], as well as *¡Rebeca!* [pp. 59, 164]; for the symbolism of the color blue, see particularly *¡Rebeca!* [pp. 186, 194] and the work presently under discussion [pp. 20, 34, 129, 151, 202-07]; an attempt to interpret the symbol will be made at the end of the chapter.) An appeal to common sense, uttered by the Lost Man, is frustrated: «Volví la cabeza para ver si alguien me veía tambalear y me pareció que en la parada de taxis los chóferes se reían como caretas de la realidad... Yo me decía: 'Lógica, lógica, lógica', pero el disgusto de los jarrones azules no tenía lógica» (p. 203). The Lost Man remembers what his father (!) used to say about people being all caught in the rain of life with varying kinds of umbrellas. The memory sends the Lost Man to an umbrella shop: «Aquella tarde... vi la vida justificada y calma como no la he visto nunca, entre el olor grato a tela impermeabilizada y barniz de maderas finas» (p. 204). To become impermeable in the comparative security of memory and materialized tradition is, perhaps, what man, or at least the Lost Man, needs to defend him from the danger of metaphysical sickness: «salí con mi paraguas abierto porque estaba lloviendo —igual hubiera salido con él abierto si no hubiera llovido— encontrándome curado del vuelco al corazón que me habían dado los jarrones azules...»

Back in the rooming house, the Lost Man actually introduces the reader to a couple of guests by name. They are Don Práxedes, who manages to keep the house well stocked with freakish clientele, and Doña Estrella, who owns the establishment. The Lost Man confesses that, during his interminable walks along the streets of the city, he is looking for a woman with her own house who will take him in. What he is actually looking for is a young godmother who would show him the reverse side of family life and in whose house plain crackers would taste as good as wafers of moonlight. The Lost Man is interested in those aspects of human life most remote from politics. What he calls «el Museo de los Armarios de la luna» (p. 205) is the place (?) that most attracts him, because «vivir se vive con cualquier cosa, sacando en los trenes o en los cafés una pluma fuente eterna, que escribirá siempre sin cambiarle la tinta. Garantizada hasta el *post mortem*.» Such is the life and thought of the Lost Man until one night he refuses to go back to the boarding-house and yells «Doña Socorro!...» Like his predecessors (Gustavo, Andrés, Luis), the Lost Man is succored by a female manifestation of the destiny he has invoked: «Una mujer rubia y opulenta salió al balcón... Sólo una frutería o una mujer resuelven la vida que no resuelve nadie.» In a manner similar to that of Gustavo the Misfit, the Lost Man apparently is still drawn to woman as a solution to the enigma. He guesses her name, Matilde, entitling him to enter the «Museo de los Armarios de luna», one by one of which open and display feminine details that could realize the Lost Man's ideal. Matilde has an «encantadora manera de ensartar lo diverso» (p. 206). The ability to *greguerizar* would indeed be considered by Ramón to be a virtue in a theoretical mate (take, for example, the illusory Rebecas that appear in the previous nebular novels). The Lost Man wonders: «Quizá había llegado al final de mi vida de aventuras y de admirador de terráqueos y tijeras, habiendo encontrado en la heterogeneidad del mundo la mujer sana, plena de confianza en los geranios y los plumeros» (p. 207). The echo of former protagonists is loud and clear. Matilde agrees to be his godmother and invites him to move in with her, as simply as if she had put him down on her grocery list.

The Lost Man finds himself very much at ease in his new home; he even thinks that his new life will cure him of his lostness. He is in love with this woman, another illusion that elicits the themes of the Platonic halves and the *Doppelgänger*. Curiously, the Lost Man has joked about a certain Uncle Bernabé, whom he made up; one day such a person shows up and takes up residence with the happy couple. This blissful situation lasts barely three years (it is interesting that such an exact period of time is stipulated by the author): «Matilde me dominaba ya hacía tres años y no me dejaba buscar los museos de la casualidad, mi única aspiración seria en esta vida» (p. 209). The gregueristic «museums» where the 'split-second objects' are found have somehow come to be neglected by the Lost Man, due to the demands of domesticity. What is worse, the presence of his Unclé Bernabé annoys him: «me repugnaba como una vergonzosa coincidencia de la realidad con la suposición...» Coincidence is the enemy of the *greguería,* which presumes to create associations through anticipation. This turns out to be the case with the Lost Man's suspicions aroused by jealousy. His affection often becomes verbally sadistic, and he concludes that «lo que hay que hacer es perderse» (p. 210). Consequently, he one day slips up to Matilde's room and finds her in the arms of, alas, his Uncle Bernabé. The strangest part of this situation is not its complex irony but the Lost Man's simple belief that the woman involved is to be the last one in his life. Furthermore, he reasons that such an event was a sheer whim of Providence and, despite the accompanying disillusion, his faith allows him to confront a different destiny. His private life is negligible compared to his view of the universe: «Todo lo que sucede en el mundo es unánime y el mundo vive de esa unanimidad. / Se cruza con nosotros todo lo que sucede pero no lo vemos. Lo que no es visible es lo que más nos rodea de cosas y sucesos» (p. 211). This is Ramón's gregueristic vision of the world, of course, and the change to the third person, as well as to the first person plural, is significant: «El cretino no ve los pájaros muertos que llenan los días y los pisa al andar.» But the immediate reappearance of the first person singular is even more significant: «Yo sí los veo y por eso las mujeres que me acompañan por la calle se indignan con mi manía de cruzar de pronto de acera a acera porque he visto un montón de pájaros muertos y no quiero pisarlos» (cf. the first two pages of the novel and the quotations found at the end of this discussion). The reader will discover that the affective as well as the imagistic trajectory of the book has ended. What remains is a sort of coda apparently intended to give the narrative a proper novelistic close, as we shall see.

Once again in the rooming house, the Lost Man finds solace in what seems to be a fancy stained-glass window put there to hide the unattractive patio from view. The suicide motif reappears: «Aquellas vidrieras me ponían triste pero me ocultaban el infame patio con color de masa encefálica de suicida.» We are led to conclude that the Lost Man was Matilde's gigolo by these words: «Había vuelto a mi modestia de corredor de comercio, lo que me salva en los malos momentos después de mis aventuras con el eterno femenino» (p. 212). The whimsical allusion to Goethe's concept of the Eternal Feminine, in spite of its inversion, is indicative of an ideal shared by the two writers. An emphatic statement, attenuated by a humorous qualification, heralds the Lost Man's return to honest living: «Lo subversivo es pensar vivir sin trabajar. Yo he encontrado una situación intermediaria que es la de representante de vinos...» This is followed by much praise of the wine trade and its entrepreneurs, some of which, in view of what is related in the next chapters, cannot help suggesting a combination of two old-time Spanish «lost men», Don Quixote and Lazarillo de Tormes. Naturally, a routine that deprives him of adventure could not last long for the Lost Man: «Lo malo ha sido que cuando estaba ya normalizada mi vida he caído con una enfermedad de casa de huéspedes... En la convalecencia he vuelto a mirar a la mujer» (p. 213). Through the one clear glass pane in the large window he watches a young woman in the intimacy of her own room. The girl's physical charms work their magic on the Lost Man, whose expressed reaction leaves the reader in a state of bewilderment: «me ha parecido la ideal para una cosa que no había pasado nunca y a la que tengo derecho porque [sic] mi fe de soltería intacta y ese es un impreso que hemos de llenar alguna vez.» There is no sure way to deduce the intent of these words, and we may be doubtful once more of the correctness of our printed text. Is it an extreme example of Ramón's gregueristic shorthand or useful evidence on which to build a case against his method of composition? Whatever the answer, there is no doubt about having reached the apex of nebulosity: «Por otras ventanas he llegado

123

a persuadir de miradas y de breves palabras de patio a la joven del más allá y espero que en las primeras salidas se ordene por fin mi destino y ya no saque corbatas de la cuerda floja de mi armario de luna para colocarlas en la cuerda floja de otro armario de luna...» The punishment to which conventional syntax is subjected is staggering. Such syntax, however, conceals the essentially paratactic nature of the narrative; one might even say that it makes narrative what is actually not. With a mark of affirmation, the Lost Man decides to leave the rooming house.

If the search for the ideal woman and the faith in destiny, both so reminiscent of *El Incongruente* and *¡Rebeca!*, have a practical effect on what follows, it is either unclear or ironic. The transition is acute but not (nothing is) unexpected. «Después de la temporada más borrosa de mi vida», the Lost Man says, «ya estoy establecido en un lugar confortable porque mi mujer es rica. / Es la mujer del no sueño. Me he convencido a través de los mejores meses del idilio.» Again the Lost Man has been disillusioned by a woman; his pessimism grows: «Yo que no creía en la muerte comencé a pensar en ella y a temer irme tan perdido como siempre, escapado a la asamblea de ciclistas del domingo sin saber lo que significa el rodar de la vida» (p. 214). As this new relationship becomes brittle, the Lost Man's spirit tries to root itself in material objects. First there is a bedspread («si resolviese por medio de su apariencia o sus pliegues un problema, el problema de la vida, que sólo lo objetival, una cosa entre las cosas podría resolver, todo estaría arreglado...») and then a washbowl («fue mi último recurso y salvación...», p. 215). But this «third love» is apparently his undoing, and he comes to suspect its insidious qualities: «La virginidad de los lavatorios, a prueba de escándalos, vírgenes siempre, nos resarce y nos libera del no saber qué hacer en la incompatibilidad de almas, caracteres y sueños» (p. 216). The Lost Man stops trying to make a success of his home life. He gives up: «Mi insistente deseo de evasión no había encontrado oportunidad ni recodo pero ya estaba cansado de esa vida de creer ir a lograr lo que nunca se hacía efectivo.» He takes to walking aimlessly again. Late one afternoon he finds himself along a railroad track. The time is explicit: twilight, end of summer. We are presented with the last scene of the Lost Man's existence, as the first image of the narrative («papeles azules corrían detrás de papeles rosas», p. 19), casually recurs: «Como estaba en liquidación de pensamientos y proyectos, parecían también aquellas mariposas rojo oscuras como el escape y barreduría de los papeles rotos en menudos trozos que no podían remontar la altura, empujados por un viento rasero de la tierra» (p. 217). He hears the whistles of a train in the distance; his soul dreads another voyage. It seems that he has arrived at that particular place intentionally: «Fuera de los escapes absurdos de la vida, que no pudieron ser duraderos, porque nunca pude establecerme en ellos, sólo conocía un sitio estable, como fuera de la existencia en común, y, sin embargo, al lado de ella: las trochas muertas del ferrocarril... Siempre había mirado hacia ese intervalo entre la vida y el viaje con un mudo deseo de refugiarme allí algún día...» The Lost Man is at the novelistic counterpart of the 'para-real', that parallel reality conceived by Ramón as his personal Utopia where he wished to live. Actually, it has a classical precedent; the theme of the *beatus ille* is touched upon by the Lost Man: «de donde más difícil me era desprenderme era de ese cobijo verde de los miserables sabios.» He knows that Death is coming (but he does not know how): «¡Ya me podía esperar, atenta al reloj, la que en mis adentros llamaba 'la finada'!» (p.218). Yes, such is the out-of-the-way place he has been looking for, the spiritually comfortable nook where he can «get away from it all». Yet the reader must deal with yet another novelistic trick before the apocalypse, a hypothetical but tantalizing return «home»: «me volvía a casa dando largas a ese que debía ser penúltimo deseo de perdición. Antes había que agotar muchas cosas, esperar muchas esperas, contar con las novedades del progreso, encontrar un empleo sosegado y feliz.» No, it would be useless; moreover, the current version of the goldenhaired woman makes life impossible for him. Coming at this particular juncture, such a statement turns out to be the subtlest of puns (to make life impossible is to make death certain). With a sense of determination, the Lost Man sits down among the weeds and symbolically takes off his necktie. There are indications of the passing of Time: «Iba anocheciendo, y la decisión era marcada por los minutos que pasaban... A través de los años me había dado cuenta de que siguiendo una ley bíblica aquél era el único sitio de que no echaban» (p. 219). No more exile, no more sense of alienation, that «corner of the world» alone musters the only possibilities of safety from persecution: «Ante el llegar de la noche... me decidí a quedarme, y poniéndome en pie comencé a internarme con el pudor de quien da un paso pecaminoso... Ya dentro del paraje... se veía al mundo como desde otro mundo.» Again the pun is implicit in the final phrase. As the Lost Man stands there, Diogenes «the Cynic» walks by and verifies that the margins of the railroad tracks are the only spaces ignored by the builders of progressive society; he even admits eating now and then the unowned chickens lurking about such places. The *mostrenco* character of the surroundings is as much in keeping with the notion of the 'para-real' as their location, parallel or lateral with respect to the mainstream of human activity. The Lost Man becomes strangely aware of a satisfaction never before experienced: «Por fin encontraba a mano la mujer rubia y dadivosa, vestida de blanco y viéndosela los pendones de la camisa» (p. 220). He seems to have found his ideal, the impossible. Once again the first person singular pronoun becomes prominent: «Yo, que había tenido todos los gestos que permite hacer la vida, noté que en mi nueva actitud tenía un aire inédito, un afondamiento especial, como de

monolito del valle que vaca desde el principio del mundo hasta el final.»
The feeling of total liberation, nay, of eternal freedom is, for the Lost
Man, conducive only to sleep. A semiconscious thought that quickly
passes contains the warning of impending doom: «No acababa de cono-
cer bien las vías muertas, y eso podía costarme la vida o una pierna cer-
cenada, como hacía pocos días le había costado a un vagabundo que estaba durmiendo en esos parajes, por los que no pasa más que el silencio.»
Besides, even the «*nullius*» (p. 220) can have inhospitable dwellers or
dangerous interlopers. (M. Newmark, *Dictionary of Foreign Words and
Phrases* [New York, 1950] defines *res nullius* as «thing belonging to no-
body; previously unoccupied territory»; V. Blanco, *Diccionario latino-
español...* [Madrid, 1948] defines *res nullae* as «asuntos perdidos».) The
Lost Man lies down and, feeling his bones rearrange themselves within
his body, finds his eyes beginning to shut.

The last page of the book, entitled «Anexo Final», is the reproduction
of a newspaper clipping that tells the following story: «On the public
lands that border the Southern railroad tracks, the body of a man has
been found so mangled that he can not be identified. It appears that
while asleep he was run over by one of the freight trains composed of
innumerable boxcars which carry merchandise to Km. 5, where the final
shipments are made ready.» Did Ramón actually find such an item in
the newspaper? It is highly doubtful. Did the Lost Man merely go to
sleep and, hence, does the news item refer to another vagabond? Not
likely; what has happened is that the man who was looking for his
identity in life remains without it even in death, or, perhaps, in the moment of finding his identity for himself, he lost it as far as «reality» was
concerned.

As suggested earlier, a few words can be said about certain symbolic
images. The first line of the book, «Papeles azules corrían detrás de papeles rosas», simply denotes the twilights, thus telescoping all the life-
experiences suggested in the course of two hundred pages into an arbitrary and recurrent unit of time. Life, then, at least for the Lost Man,
has been —to borrow from Eugene O'Neill— «a long day's journey into
night». The rose of dawn is followed by the blue of evening. I have already
mentioned the passage in which the Lost Man sees through a shop window
a pair of blue vases which have been pawned: «Palpitaba mi corazón
como nunca había palpitado y miraba los jarrones como si me los hubieran robado con nocturnidad y alevosía. / Eran suntuosos y su azul estaba
hecho con el humo azul de la noche, luciendo rebordes y superposiciones
doradas» (p. 202). The above passage notwithstanding, and although blue
appears rather frequently in Ramón's narratives, it cannot be regarded
as suggestive of something unconditionally desirable. In *El alba y otras
cosas,* to which Ramón himself referred in its preface as «el libro que

más está hecho con la muerte en mí... el que más depuré...»,[3] the author includes this aphorism: «Las nubes están asustadas y por entre ellas hay un color de mirada providencial, un color que no es azul» (p. 621). The ethical aspect of color symbolism is not consistent in Ramón as it is, say, in Lorca where it has a systematic connotation; it is variable and subordinated to a different use of imagery; it is actually closer to Valle-Inclán's except that in the case of Ramón the imagery is, naturally, almost free-flowing. Certain objects present a different situation, however, because they do seem to elicit the potentiality of a fixed symbol. In his first book, as mentioned above, the youthful Ramón criticizes the Spanish older generation for keeping its heart covered like a vase, but even admits: «... aquellos objetos que se fueron amontonando en los jarrones por descuido, por capricho: aquellos retazos de tela, de objetos, con dejadez, yo he admirado este amor por las cosas colocadas en variedad dentro de los jarrones y que parece referirse a su alma oculta, desconocida, característica...»[4] It would seem that in 1904 or 1905, falteringly, rather carelessly, perhaps unconsciously, Ramón already outlined the whole range of his feeling and vision of the world. Such a vase as described in this passage is a miniature Rastro and, in turn, El Rastro is a microreflection of the human universe.

Of real significance to the present discussion is the fact that in *El alba* we find the genesis of *El hombre perdido.* The various key images and themes of this most nebulous of Ramón's nebular novels are all prominently used in the earlier book. In a total of fifty-one pages there are twenty-three references to emptiness and associated images, twenty-three to railroads and associated images, among which are the following, including those to the Lost Man, the Man of Dawn, and the Novel of the Nebula:

> ... (Un coche ha pasado y ha sonado la calle a vacío, con esa vaciedad *sui géneris* del alba). (p. 589)

> Si el suicida logra pasar el alba sin haber disparado sobre su sien, si la mira con audacia a los ojos de cráneo vacío, volverá a conseguir para sí los ojos que pueden seguir viendo y se sentirá resignado a vivir... (p. 590; also contains the idea of suicide vs. the will to live).

> En el alba estamos sin mujer, como si se nos hubiese muerto o se nos hubiese ido... Qué juego más macabro si nos empeñamos en que no sea esto verdad y jugamos con su espectro (p. 592; contains idea of loneliness).

> Mundo extinto, completamente extinto, el del alba; todo sin porqué, todo informe, nada con fisonomía; todo tendido, arrasado, tumbado, intimi-

---

[3] Madrid: Calleja, 1923. The first part of this book, *El alba,* is reproduced in RAMÓN GÓMEZ DE LA SERNA, *Obras completas,* Tomo I (Barcelona: Editorial AHR [1956]); all quotations are from this edition. I have been unable to find the 1918 first edition of this work.
[4] RAMÓN GÓMEZ DE LA SERNA Y PUIG, *Entrando en fuego,* p. 14.

dado, medido por un rasero común; mejor dicho, arrasado según un rasero común (p. 596; cf. last chapter of *El hombre perdido*).

No se puede pasear en parejas por el alba. Dos en el alba descomponen el alba... (p. 601; contains idea of ultimate metaphysical solitariness).

¡Cómo mira el alba por las ventanas vacías que dan al otro mundo! (p. 622; cf. last chapter of *El hombre perdido*).

Ahora se sabe los pájaros que hay, porque pájaro que no cante en el alba es que está muerto (p. 634; cf. image of dead birds in chapters I and L of *El hombre perdido*).

Asomándonos a la noche de vez en cuando, a sabiendas de que se camina hacia el alba, se ven las estaciones por que pasa el cielo, por que pasa la noche... El trac-trac del reloj en la noche es como el son monótono, constante, isócrono, del tren sutil, del tren que se mueve, del tren que marcha. (p. 590)

En el alba parece que llegamos a la ciudad como a una estación... si bajamos, vagabundeamos por la ciudad del alba... (p. 597)

Estación del alba: hemos llegado al mismo sitio en que estábamos. (p. 637)

En el alba todo hombre pierde su identificación... Se es en el alba cadáver sin identificar (p. 599; cf. the «Anexo Final» in *El hombre perdido*).

De los bancos públicos levanta el alba a los que están acostados y los empuja más allá... ¿Adónde?... (p. 601)

El alba... trae... algunos hombres que indudablemente no van a ningún lado de la ciudad, no se quedarán en ella, no viven ni están empleados aquí, sólo pasan arrastrados por el alba... (p. 607)

Pasa el hombre que se ha perdido, muy parecido al perro que ídem de ibídem anda extraviado a esas horas por la ciudad.
Parece que camina a alguna parte, pero está equivocado. No lleva dirección ni la tiene. Camina por caminar, por no sentarse en un banco, por no confesar su derrota y ya someterse a no encontrar ningún camino.
No quiere aparecer en el alba como el pobre niño perdido. Tiene esos escrúpulos del hombre al que parece que también le está prohibido llorar.
El hombre que se ha perdido en el alba y que camina muy chiquitín, muy en lo hondo de una civilización que comienza, como primer hombre de la tierra que va a ser repoblada, en cuanto llega la mañana se orienta y encuentra su portal, mirando mucho el número como misionero de sí mismo que se trajese una misiva.
¡Y pensar que he estado perdido como un niño de los que cogen los guardias de la mano y llevan a la Comisaría!
Avergonzado espera el hombre que ha estado completamente perdido en el mundo, no en la ciudad, que abran los portales para poder entrar en su casa y olvidar la pesadilla del alba, ocultándose con las sábanas la cabeza.
¡Qué alta columna de tiempo y espacio vio en el alba!... ¡Por qué sierra más profunda anduvo como pastor sin ninguna oveja!
El hombre extraviado durante el alba recurrirá ya siempre a su reloj para seguir su camino de vuelta. (pp. 611-12)

Sale el hombre más feo y se pasea durante el alba. Es la única hora en que puede gozar de la luz del día mirando a lo alto, parándose a ver las fachadas, mirándose sin miedo en los altos cristales.

Ese hombre terriblemente feo, monstruosamente feo, es el protagonista humano del alba, su tipo «shakesperiano», el que hace entrar en plena acción dramática las calles vacías por el alba, que echa sobre ellas una cosa así como la cal viva que se echa sobre los muertos. Son desatadas las varas de la constelación «el gran carro» y... bru-run-run... se vacía el carro en una caída de espaldas violenta y cubre la vida de pulverización que desinfecta la ciudad del día anterior y la llena del material nuevo (pp. 617-18; see also similar aphoristic sketches on pp. 618-19, 633).

Los hombres que hablan en el alba están en el estado de espíritu de saberlo todo. Parecen los dotados de mayor experiencia y de mayor instinto (pp. 620-21; it should be remembered that the Lost Man and the Man of Dawn, Gonzalo Herreros, walk and talk together at dawn when they first meet; in an aphorism quoted above, Ramón states that a couple cannot stroll at dawn, thus we must conclude that the two men are one).

No hay optimismo, ni fe, ni esperanza en el Paisaje... La Nada, la idea de la novela máxima, es lo que abunda. (p. 595)

En el alba el mundo vuelve a ser la nebulosa primitiva... (p. 606)

Estando de verdad dentro del alba comienza uno siendo fantasma y después se desarrolla en persona. (p. 640)

...Una mayor y más terrible incongruencia hay que dar al alba. Sus inmensos cielos de incongruencia vibran en su atmósfera, y todas estas imágenes que he escrito las he sentido y las he consultado, no con mi ansia de novedad, sino de verdad. (p. 624)

...El alba echa también sus cuerdas salvadoras al fondo del patio desgraciado... lleno de las cenizas del tiempo y del color ceniciento de lo perdido, de lo hundido, de lo miserable. (p. 630)

Beyond the anticipation or coincidence of the images just pointed out which suggest the «plot» and «setting» of the Lost Man's novel, it is worth mentioning that *El alba* is a marvelous though small laboratory in which Ramón experimented with narrative technique. Published again in 1923, it includes almost verbatim the principle on which *El novelista* is based: «Cómo se ven los cuartos desalquilados en el alba!... Sólo a mí que soy un ducho conocedor del alba no se le [*sic*] han ocultado los pisos estratégicos y baratos, y veo amanecer por distintos balcones en distintas casas de las que yo sólo tengo la llave y cuya posesión es mi único ideal, escribiendo en cada una de ellas una novela distinta...» (p. 619). *El alba* is a collection of aphorisms. Since it develops around a basic subject, however, there is a difference between it and the volumes entitled *Greguerías*. Apart from the sequential nature of language, these aphorisms, one following another on the same subject produce a kind of narrative. It would be simply wrong to suggest that the dawn emerges from this narrative as a protagonist emerges from a novel. But it can be asserted, because there is sufficient evidence, that now and then the narrative undercurrent of the aphorismatic series picks up momentum, and the author's impetus is shown to expand a given sketch into what might

129

have been the beginning of a novel. When this happens, both the third person referring to an object or phenomenon and the first person plural referring to a subjective human reaction disappear in favor of the first person singular. One example of this has already been quoted; another is as follows: «Yo he salido un alba por hielo para contener la sangre a una persona querida. Me acuerdo de aquella alba entre todas las albas... sólo un par de personas vieron mi figura presurosa como la de quien llega tarde al tren, con la corbata liada de cualquier modo. ¡Aquella alba fue extraordinaria!...» (p. 612). The author's will to narrative is evident, and the uchronic quality of the aphorism succumbs to the movement of the narrative *yo*, first person singular, that went on to produce *El hombre perdido.* Thanks to *El alba,* we can interpret more firmly what we had merely considered possible: the Lost Man and the Man of Dawn are one and the same (a veiled instance of the *Doppelgänger*), and this oscillating image is, in turn, a literary representation of the author himself as he lives and dies in the vacuum of «reality», searching for the ultimate meaning of life.

The implications of the title are many; the possibilities of ambiguity are, I think, intentional. Is the Lost Man actually lost or damned? The latter is unlikely. In spite of Ramón's actual though unorthodox Catholicism, his inmost beliefs respond to the ideas manifested in his literature. In this book he states: «Yo creía en el Dios que no quiere saber nada de la tierra y al que no le importan ni oraciones ni blasfemias...» (p. 144). Perdition, then, in the theological sense is not the issue. The sense of the image lies somewhere between the subjective and objective acceptations of the word *perdido:* lost to the world (helpless, alienated) and lost from view (in the regions of the 'para-real'). The first is manifested many times, in such statements as: «De un momento a otro poder ser inexistente que es más que pobre. Haberlo perdido todo, no sólo la sombra, sino el cuerpo que debía dar esa sombra» (p. 41). And «La soledad es absoluta. Nadie se ocupa de nadie» (p. 180). The second is suggested by such as «todo esto quiere decir que me pierdo más cada día que pasa y que sin depravarme lo que hay que hacer es acabar por perderse en absoluto» (p. 42) and «Ya sabe que yo vivo de estar extraviado» (p. 170). The quest of the Lost Man (=Gonzalo Herreros) is actually nothing more than his constant effort to reach the other side of the commonplace: «Me prestaba a toda investigación para ver si conseguía saber si la vida es trapo o zapato, caja de píldoras o botella de vino» (p. 57). But alienated modern man has surrounded himself with trivia of his own making, and the Lost Man's attempt to break out of the cage of the conventional is doomed to failure as any other quest for the impossible, no matter how admirable. *El hombre perdido* is a huge metaphor of this immemorial human concern, reinforced in recent times by the impact of a technologically oriented society.

VI

THE NOVELS OF THE NEBULA:
AN INTERPRETIVE SYNTHESIS

An examination, no matter how cursory, of representative studies of the novel leads to the conviction that this genre is largely undefined beyond its being a long prose fiction. Thus, no one would take issue with me for categorizing most of Ramón Gómez de la Serna's long prose fictions under the heading of novels. Most critics have done so unblinkingly. To be sure, these works are different from more traditional novels, but if we have read those by Ramón's contemporaries (even the older ones) such as Unamuno, Valle-Inclán, Baroja, Azorín, Gabriel Miró, Pérez de Ayala, and Benjamín Jarnés, we know that the novel in Spain had been evolving not very differently from the way it did in England with Joseph Conrad, James Joyce, D. H. Lawrence, and Virginia Woolf. In a study of these four writers,[1] David Daiches states that the experimentation in the writing of prose fiction which took place between the World Wars came about as a result of cultural crises and new concepts of time and human consciousness. The same reasons apply to Spanish literature, and the period of experimentation can be seen to stretch back to the turn of the century. Certainly by 1920 the psychological novel had come into its own and, with its extensive use of interior monologue, made not only possible but probable the overlapping of character and author. So, among Ramón's seventy-eight novels, including the long and the short, we are not surprised to find some in which the hero is something like a Ramón-physician or a Ramón-bullfighter and the heroine is a partial idealization. But what about the novels in which the protagonists elude every convention, the novels that lead to those which Ramón called «Novelas de la Nebulosa»? They are indeed different, even from Ramón's other novels, though naturally they share with them many stylistic traits, such as many aspects of syntax and imagery. How and why they are different is the subject of this discussion, which must include an explanation of what Ramón means by *nebulosa* and why the four novels are thus related.

---

[1] DAVID DAICHES, *The Novel and the Modern World* (Chicago and London: The University of Chicago Press, Phoenix Books [1970]).

In *El alba* (first published in 1918), Ramón says: «A los objetos se les busca en el alba el secreto como a objetos recién encontrados.»[2] His preoccupation with objects has been treated sufficiently in preceding chapters of this study and elsewhere,[3] but it must be stipulated that such a preoccupation has more to do with the imaginative than with the logical aspect of things. And Ramón continues: «En el alba el mundo vuelve a ser la nebulosa primitiva... Por eso se siente un vértigo reblandecido, incomprensible, con pérdida del conocimiento..., y después se recobra todo.»[4] Many other references can be found in his vast production that will further clarify the notion, but those just quoted should be sufficient to define Ramón's nebula or nebulosity as the invisible, true essence of all life, the origin and end-result of a universe in flux, the real chaos in which we live under the manifold deception of our common constructs. In *El alba* the specifically literary idea of a chaos-creation antinomy is also present. According to Ramón, one can verify in the dawn the fact that «la Nada, la idea de la novela máxima, es lo que abunda».[5] In *El novelista* (published between 1921 and 1923) this idea is further elaborated. And in the essay entitled «Las palabras y lo indecible» (first published in 1936, anticipating some aspects of Samuel Beckett by at least ten years), Ramón states: «el logro de la inspiración está... quizás en la estratósfera de las palabras, en plena nebulosidad».[6] It is this notion, based on his vision of the multifariously associated forms and substances which we experience, that eventually will lead Ramón to infuse a novelistic structure, as he had infused an aphoristic structure, with his style.

Ramón metaphorically applied the term *novela* to any process, provided it augured substantial length and sustained theme. Thus the novel may be regarded, and not inappropriately, as the opposite of the aphorism, but only formally. In his «Prólogo a las Novelas de la Nebulosa», which appears as preface to *El hombre perdido,* Ramón says: «La vida y la novela son una ilusión, la ilusión de encontrarse uno a sí mismo».[7] This particular feeling undoubtedly has been shared, a witness of which fact is Wayne Booth as he notes, in speaking of what he calls the «implied author», that «to some novelists it has seemed, indeed, that they were discovering or creating themselves as they wrote».[8] Ramón continues by asking the question: «¿Pero no están en uno mismo esas cosas

[2] RAMÓN GÓMEZ DE LA SERNA, *Obras completas,* I (Barcelona: Editorial AHR [1956]), p. 600.
[3] See, for example, CARDONA, pp. 113-30.
[4] *Obras completas,* I, p. 606.
[5] *Ibid.,* p. 595.
[6] *Lo cursi y otros ensayos,* p. 195.
[7] *El hombre perdido,* p. 7. A slightly different version of the first half of this preface appears in *Obras selectas,* pp. 1089-94.
[8] *The Rhetoric of Fiction,* p. 71.

que no se sabe lo que son y que aún no son cosas ciertas y creadas porque la naturaleza inventa el árbol pero no el armario?»[9] The relation between tree and cabinet here suggested becomes more significant when put in the actual context of Ramón's novels. As Ramón is known to use a language which I will call 'precognitive' to reveal unsuspected qualities of real objects through the flashing insights of his aphorisms; so we will see him try to delve into the unrealized through the enigmatic designs of his nebular novels. Is this actually possible? If the imagination is powerful enough, anything is possible for the mind. To see such marvels we must follow the author to a region of human experience which he distinguishes as follows: «Hay una realidad que no es surrealidad ni realidad subreal, sino una realidad lateral».[10] Between the real reality which lies beyond our ken and the illusory reality in which we live (and of which Surrealism presumes to show an unconscious part), there is something which is tangible and yet scarcely visualized, the region where our potential experiences are being forged before they are cast into either the relativity of life or the absoluteness of death. To explore such a region the writer must deal not only with natural objects, potentialities and displacements, but also with human desires, fulfillments and frustrations —in other words, with the elements of novelistic characters. That such characters in the nebular novels do not have the same consistency as in traditional novels should not be at all surprising. Ramón gives this explanation of his intent: «El sentido de estas novelas es buscar cosas menos convencionales, menos amaneradas, en otras dimensiones de la vida, escribiendo y escribiendo hasta acabar sin detective ni víctima, revelando cómo nos ataca el mundo confuso de hoy, librándonos así de su realidad y de sus esquinazos, superándolos por la queja o la invención».[11] And in the preface to *Ismos* he elaborates: «Ya que se contrae el mundo gracias a la telecomunicación, lo tenemos que ensanchar por la invención. El papel de la invención es cada día más importante».[12] In the four «Novels of the Nebula» the reader will find this intent to be the common denominator realized by means of varying structural designs, each more complicated than its predecessor.

From the fact that Ramón was not the first to experiment with novelistic structure we cannot infer that his contribution is not original. We can see in the «Novels of the Nebula» that his effort is to use their structures as he uses the aphoristic structure in his volumes entitled *Greguerías,* among others of similar nature. This explains the lack of conventional plot and exclusively linear development. The structure of these novels, particularly the last two, may bewilder the casual reader

[9] *El hombre perdido,* p. 7.
[10] *Ibid.*
[11] *Ibid.,* p. 10.
[12] *Obras completas,* I, p. 962.

133

because he is required to exercise new modes of perception in order to appreciate the plethora of interrelated images that vibrate in an atmosphere where time and space have been significantly altered. Literature has been traditionally recognized as a temporal art. From the «Novels of the Nebula» the reader sometimes derives a feeling akin to that of being surrounded by images, as in a museum. The reason is that the dynamics of the narrative, which ordinarily serve to delineate character through action, have been shifted almost exclusively to the language and the thought behind it, that is, to the verbal arrangement of the novel as a whole. It becomes evident, then, that structural design is more important to the author than the mere telling of a story; in fact such design becomes all-important. There are, to be sure, occasions in which the quasi-static elements of the narrative give way to the kind of image-movement typical of films, but one should remember, in compensation, that even in motion pictures there are techniques for structuralizing the narrative, such as the flash-back and flash-forward so successfully employed by contemporary film-makers. The common grounds of the narrators in both media are well described by Daiches when he says about modern novelists that

> They have become interested in those aspects of consciousness which cannot be viewed as a progression of individual and self-existing moments, but which are essentially dynamic rather than static in nature and are independent of the given moment. The present moment is specious; it denotes the ever fluid passing of the «already» into the «not yet», and therefore retrospect and anticipation constitute the very essence of consciousness at any specified time. In other words, the relation of consciousness to time is not the simple one of events to time, but is independent of chronological sequence in a way that events are not.[13]

This is not the place to elaborate on certain evident similarities between Ramón's narrative techniques and those variously practiced in films; the subject should provide an interesting study in itself. But it is pertinent to note that the question of the spatialization of time and its counterpart, the dynamization of space, have been studied with respect to the novel as well as the motion picture.

In a well-known essay entitled «Spatial Form in Modern Literature»,[14] Joseph Frank has shown that in relatively recent times literature, long regarded in the West as solely and inexorably dependent on the temporal order of sequence, has shifted significantly toward the spatial order of juxtaposition and reiteration. He points out that the reader is expected to apprehend the work of writers like Pound, Eliot, Proust, and Joyce spatially and instantaneously. And, because of its importance to the un-

[13] *The Novel and the Modern World*, pp. 15-16.
[14] *Sewanee Review*, 53 (1945), 221-40, 433-56, 643-53.

derstanding of modern literary structures he quotes the definition of an image given by Pound, erstwhile leader of the Anglo-American Imagists, as «that which presents an intellectual and emotional complex in an instant of time». To the student of Ramón this will seem all too familiar; one is dealing here basically with the same thing as the *greguería,* the limit to which man can project words beyond their mimetic function in search of the invention which is self-expression. In fact, Frank goes on to give the implications of this new poetic as follows: «image is defined not as a pictorial reproduction, but as unification of disparate ideas and emotions into a complex presented spatially in an instant of time».[15] The old plastic factor in literature which consists of naturalistic description is no more acceptable today than the imitative elements of decorative painting. Everyone is aware of the fact that the «isms» have been at work in the literary as in the graphic arts. For the painter an analogous task was much easier; it is no accident that the very vanguard of art has always been in the field of the visual. A parallel of the *greguería* is found in the simultaneity of the Cubists, for example, or of Marcel Duchamp's «Nude Descending a Staircase», when considered «a synthesis of movement in space carried to the limit of the abstract».[16] From his analysis of modern literature, Frank recommends that the reader do exactly what the *greguería,* of whatever length, expects him to do, namely, «suspend the process of individual reference temporarily until the entire pattern of internal references can be apprehended as a unity».[17] In other words, it is impossible to grasp the aesthetic meaning from a linear approach. The poem as a whole (poem in the etymological sense) forms a single image. This poetic, Frank believes, «runs through Mallarmé to Pound and Eliot» and «can be formulated only in terms of the principle of reflexive reference», which «is the link connecting the esthetic development of modern poetry with similar experiments in the modern novel». We all know that the technical boundaries between verse and prose fiction, lyric and narrative have been gradually fading. Daiches points out that the modern English novelists brought some of the techniques of poetry into prose fiction, and no Hispanist would deny that the same is true of the Generation of 1898 and its *epígonos.* It is precisely the 'principle of reflexive reference' that makes possible the apprehension of an entire modern literary work as one vast image, an image, furthermore, no longer «of manners and life» (as M. H. Abrams puts it[18]), which was the Classical model, but of the author's inmost personality. My own interpretation of

[15] *Ibid.,* p. 226.
[16] EMILE LANGUI, in CASCOU *et al., Gateway to the Twentieth Century* (New York: McGraw-Hill [1962]), p. 155. For a comparison of Ramón and Picasso, see Guillermo de Torre's preface to Ramón's *Obras completas,* II, pp. 9-29.
[17] *Sewanee Review,* 53 (1945), 230.
[18] *The Mirror and the Lamp* (New York: W. W. Norton [1958]), p. 236.

Ramón's «Novels of the Nebula» has been independently drawn along very similar lines.

Needless to say, the works to be discussed do not permit a suitable synopsis. That is why in the preceding chapters I have endeavored to provide annotated summaries. In this respect my purpose here is simply to keep the variant themes apart but within access of comparison. While the differences are considerable regarding structure, the similarities are equally considerable regarding motivation. The latter would seem to be somewhat trite and overused, the liquidation of a Romantic repertory, but we must bear in mind that, just as he revealed unusual aspects of isolated objects and situations in his aphorisms, Ramón was able to explore the paradoxical factors of human complexes. The universal concepts of individuality and duality, creativity and limitation, reality and appearance, communication and estrangement, free will and fate, all these are employed by Ramón as roads for his imagination, not as the highways of philosophical investigation, however, but as the by-ways of poetic response. In the last analysis, it is not in its content that the ulterior meaning, the beauty, of a work of art resides, but rather in its form.

The first of these novels, *El Incongruente* (1922), came to be considered by Ramón, in his own words, «la más innovadora de mis novelas... primer grito de evasión en la literatura novelesca al uso».[19] Such a statement undoubtedly reflects his conviction that this work was the initial step toward the eventual formulation of a gregueristic or nebular novel. The protagonist bears only a first name and a sobriquet. Gustavo «el Incongruente» is characterized by the incongruous adventures which he pursues while in search of the woman who would be right for him. From his birth at the Opera to the discovery of his destined mate at the movies (the modern heir to the Opera, where she happens to be sitting next to him watching a film in which the hero and heroine are none other than themselves), Gustavo proves to be a figure in an incongruous melodrama, the novelistic counterpart of the kind of whimsical image found constantly in Ramón's aphorisms. At the end of the first chapter, the narrator refers to his protagonist in this rather gratuitous yet deceptively meaningful statement that anticipates a substantial part of the development of later novelistic writing:

> Ni de la novela de esta misma época ni de la de después se pueden seguir con cierta cronología las peripecias. Tiene que ser una incongruencia la misma historia de su vida y la de la elección de capítulos.
>
> Además, es que no se podrían contar todas las incongruencias de su vida. No; yo sólo intento escalonar unas cuantas, y que se le vea vivir y producirse, y se imagine el lector todo lo que pudo pasar en los otros días que no se reseñan.

[19] *El Incongruente*, p. 7.

> Baste decir, para darse idea de este ser incongruente, que se vió mezclado a todos los enredos imaginables.[20]

The reader can already infer from the above paragraphs that in this book not just certain turns of phrase or the aphorisms mixed into the narrative are meant to be incongruous, but the whole story of Gustavo's life, in other words the entire novel, is intended as *greguería,* a *greguería* which the protagonist and the other characters serve to novelize. Equally important is the unexpected and, in this book, unrepeated use of the first person narration in a very brief but telling reference to the composition. The invitation to the reader to participate by extending the novel's open structure is retracted by the last words of the narrative: «a los pocos días se casaban... acabando en aquel mismo instante la incongruencia del Incongruente, la vida novelesca de Gustavo».[21] This does not constitute a contradiction but a corroboration of Ramón's concept of a nebular novel; when the incongruity vanishes, so does the novel.

There is no question about *El Incongruente* being related in theme and tone to the main currents of European artistic activity of the period. René Marill-Albérès describes the times as those of *les enfants terribles* whose most significant novelty is their *disponibilité* «devant le spectacle renouvelé et les saveurs nombreuses de la vie».[22] This goes beyond the earlier ideals of neutrality, impartiality, and impassivity[23] and sometimes runs counter to them. Marill-Albérès refers to such writers as Gide, Cocteau, Morand, Montherlant, Aldous Huxley, Werfel, and Ramón. That state of aesthetic availability was, of course, what gave rise to so many productive art schools and movements, among them Surrealism. This movement has long been associated with some aspects of Ramón's work, although in the end he seems to have clearly gone beyond it. Paul Ilie has dismissed *El Incongruente* as «an abortive attempt at a surrealist novel»,[24] contending that it is unstructured to the point of having no thematic recurrence. Rodolfo Cardona, on the other hand, extols the surrealistic aspects of the work, judging it superior to André Breton's *Nadja* (1928), and sums up the difference between Ramón's novel and earlier ones as follows:

> *El incongruente...* is... Ramón's first major attempt to find a way to bring to light the inexpressible... Ramón departs from the traditional form of the novel with its logical structure and slow transitions and becomes a recorder of unpredictable adventure... Gustavo lives in a world where factors of time and space do not count.[25]

---

[20] *Ibid.,* p. 14.
[21] *Ibid.,* p. 188.
[22] R. M. ALBÉRÈS, *L'Aventure intellectuelle du XXᵉ siécle* (Paris: Editions Albin Michel [1963]), pp. 123-25.
[23] Cf. BOOTH, *The Rhetoric...,* pp. 67-86.
[24] *The Surrealist Mode in Spanish Literature,* p. 156.
[25] CARDONA, *Ramón,* p. 101.

The time and space that do not seem to count for Gustavo do count for us, however; they do because ultimately their not counting is a part of the fiction which we cannot totally let go after our chronological experience of reading it. And yet it is chronology precisely that this narrative attempts to elude. The reiteration of an image in a disconnected, episodic narrative, that of Gustavo in a zig-zag pursuit of his destiny, is the thematic substitute which Ilie is not willing to accept. And this incongruous recurrence makes up the design of the novel in which the altered functions of time and space are those described by Joseph Frank. However, long before Frank or, to my knowledge, anyone else discovered these aesthetically substitutable factors of the space-time continuum, Ramón had advanced his notion of the inexpressible which, more than any such previous insight or anxiety, corresponds to that metaphysical longing in modern man to overcome the limits of perception and, consequently, of being as he is. So it appears that we can begin to glimpse an evolution of intuitive thought in Ramón: *la greguería, lo indecible, la nebulosa.*

Eugenio de Nora, who has written what at the present time is considered the standard history of the modern Spanish novel, believes that

> Con *El incongruente* acaba... la etapa que pudiéramos considerar de búsqueda en el arte narrativo de Ramón. En efecto, aunque gran parte de sus relatos sigan siendo acumulación o amplificación de temas típicos de su literatura personal de greguerías, disparates o caprichos, cabe situar hacia esa fecha —1922— el acceso del escritor a una época de madurez en la que los libros por él calificados como *novelas,* sin serlo acaso plenamente, se caracterizan porque un tema dado, o una intuición fundamental, al menos, dominan el relato y, más o menos a fondo, unifican y dan su estructura al conjunto.[26]

According to this critic, Ramón experiments with narrative technique and, at this point in his production, finds two different types of general novelistic structure: the one having an obvious theme which is more or less developed, the other having no obvious theme, at best having a fundamental intuition. Regarding the first type Nora says that, of Ramón's novels, the one exhibiting the most classic structure is his first, entitled *El Ruso* (1913), which has «ambientación, arranque, conflicto y desenlace, con hechos coherentemente eslabonados y conducidos en una acción lineal y sucesiva».[27] This evidently does not apply to *El Incongruente,* whose fundamental intuition I have equated with the protagonist's reiterative image. The evasion of conflict and climax in the second type is a result of the kind of character used as a basis for the narrative, and this kind of character, in turn, is a result of the author's point of view, which

[26] EUGENIO G. DE NORA, *La novela española contemporánea (1927-1960)* (Madrid: Editorial Gredos [1962]), p. 112.
[27] *Ibid.,* p. 105.

is not the traditional one that wrestles with moral concerns. In his *Ideas sobre la novela,* Ortega distinguishes between the relative importance of emotional enjoyment and absolute enjoyment of a work of art. Humor such as Ramón's, which is mental rather than emotional, may not seek moral commitments, but it does not avoid them. In fact, for all its aesthetic playfulness, *El Incongruente* can be seen casually dropping the simple lesson that in the flux of life the human being longs for stability. The same lesson is not so casual in the later «Novels of the Nebula».

The second of these is entitled, not surprisingly, *El novelista* (1923). Fragments of this work appeared in the Madrilenian literary journal *La Pluma* between December 1921 and October 1922, a fact which makes it perfectly contemporaneous with *El Incongruente.* According to Nora, the 1946 edition differs considerably from the original, giving the impression of having been expurgated. The protagonist is named Andrés Castilla. A writer who lives from his books, he is in constant search of materials, travelling as far as Paris and London. He rents four apartments in different parts of town in order to take advantage of the city's various perspectives. Of his novels, the reader is given no less than seventeen distinct samples. Although the controlling narrative, the story of Andrés Castilla himself, is written in the third person, two of the inserted novel-fragments are told in the first. Besides providing a crucible for a fictional amalgam, in which themes and techniques reflect the metamorphoses of the narrator and his characters (some of which are inanimate objects such as a street lamp and a Japanese screen) and the relations of the novelist and his characters (some of whom pay him a visit, as Augusto Pérez did Unamuno), *El novelista* offers this not so humorous assessment of Castilla's objective in his writing:

> Caminaba por la realidad supuesta como por una novela de magia en que hablan los cuadros y un plumero se convierte en un ramo de flores...
> La novela se puebla de lo inconcebible y se habla con las más dudosas palabras, las que no se esperan.
> El seguía en su barca por los subterráneos del mundo y sólo estaba entregado a la fidelidad de su imaginación. Lo que no tenía era técnica, aunque se reconociesen sus novelas por algunas repeticiones y por un aire arbitrario...
> El adoraba poner en pie toda la realidad...[28]

The phrases «realidad supuesta» and «novela de magia» are nearly synonymous in Ramón's vocabulary, a fact that would tempt us to apply the pictorial term *magic realism* to Ramón's work, were it not so misleading. The paragraphs just quoted probably constitute a retort to criticism from contemporaries. It might be noted, in passing, that H. G. Wells, a writer of powerful imagination but questionable aesthetic sense,

[28] *El novelista,* p. 102.

also boasted of having no technique. And the above reference to unthinkable things and unexpected words anticipates the metalingustic notions advanced in the essay «Las palabras y lo indecible», which is very much in keeping with the narrative contained in the next chapter of the book, significantly entitled «Vuelta a la nebulosa». In that chapter the narrator tells of Castilla's frustrated attempt to write a new kind of novel, superficially similar to what years later would be the so-called *nouveau roman.* «El novelista», the narrator says, «deseaba hacer una novela en que la vida entrase sin tesis y sin ser sectorizada ni demasiado individualizada».[29] Castilla cannot do it: «rompió las cuartillas de *Todos,* novela vana, hija del deseo estéril de la universalidad y de la totalidad».[30] At this point we would do well to recall the earlier quotations from *El alba,* in the 1923 edition of which, incidentally, the image of the writer with four apartments also appears. Andrés Castilla is not seriously affected by his failure to write a nebular novel; his collected works enable him to retire *à la bourgeoise* to a spacious residence in Italy. At the end of the book, the narrator ironically raises some pertinent questions: «¿Qué clase de novelista ha sido éste? ¿Es el tipo del novelista ideal?»[31] The answer is cautious: he has been both realistic and arbitrary. The reader cannot help noticing the nuance between the perfect and the present tenses. The book has closed on Andrés Castilla, but Ramón goes on. Emilio Gascó Contell calls *El novelista* «le roman subjectif de l'écrivain non pas qui 'se décrit', mais 'qui s'écrit soi-même', car il se recherche au moyen d'un effort d'immersion en soi, penché sur ses propres cellules et arrivant à un résultat si original qu'il n'en existe de comparable dans aucune littérature».[32] The *novelas intercaladas* in *Don Quijote* are, of course, just one precedent in the use of narrative inserted in narrative. But it is *Les Faux-Monnayeurs* (1926), Gide's most extensive and elaborate fiction, that bears the most remarkable resemblance to *El novelista;* both are about the writing of novels and each chapter seems to be the beginning of a new one. Thus the effect of disjunction is as much a part of Gide's design as it is of Ramón's. There are in both novels apparently meaningless expressions, the significance of which is up to the reader to decipher, but while Ramón offers brief paragraphs on his theory of the novel, Gide devotes a whole chapter to the topic, besides keeping a separate notebook on the writing of his narrative.

There is no doubt that *El novelista* is an outstanding work. Nora thinks of it as «la obra maestra de Ramón, ... su más auténtica novela (como que es *su* novela, la confesión verídica del escritor y del hombre

---

[29] *Ibid.,* p. 110.
[30] *Ibid.,* p. 117.
[31] *Ibid.,* p. 268.
[32] «Ramón Gómez de la Serna», *Revue de l'Amérique Latine* (Paris), XV (1928), 192.

siempre personal, refractario siempre al 'conformismo' de la objetividad: llamado así al acierto máximo, naturalmente, en la novela del novelista)».[33] As accurate as this observation may be, the literary confession to which it refers is, nevertheless, superficial and therefore slippery; it does not represent the author's deepest penetration into his own personality. The truth is that this kaleidoscopic narrative, this cluster of embryonic novels within a novel (Cansinos-Asséns calls Ramón's early works «libros urdidos por un procedimiento madrepórico»[34]), is best described as an organic or cohesive anthology of Ramón's experiments in prose fiction.

With *¡Rebeca!* (1936) the «Novels of the Nebula» really come into their own. It is quite probable that, as in the case of *El novelista,* the 1947 edition of *¡Rebeca!* varies from the original. The protagonist, whose name is Luis, lives in constant expectation of finding the ideal he has forged in his mind and arbitrarily calls Rebeca. The materialization of this ideal, on which depends what the narrator calls «la solución de su vida»,[35] should be an ominous entity taking shape within a cabinet where Luis deposits sundry things of his peculiar interest; it could be an object, such as a teapot, with which he seems to converse; it actually though accidentally turns out to be a woman among the many he meets. Like Gustavo in *El Incongruente,* Luis is a well-to-do *señorito* who does not have to earn a living and has no family ties, although we do briefly come across some of his relatives. Also like Gustavo, Luis has many love-affairs before unexpectedly finding his Platonic other half. From the beginning, the awaited Rebeca is described as «la ideal catalizadora nebulosa».[36] As exemplified by the two novels previously discussed, *El Incongruente* and *El novelista,* it is a fair assumption that woman and literature, dream and fiction are often for Ramón interchangeable ideals. Their difference lies in that, whereas the idealization of woman almost always turns out to be an illusion, that of literature remains as a plumbing into some human reality.

In many respects *¡Rebeca!* is a new version of *El Incongruente.* It repeats many basic images of the earlier work, but it also adds new ones, such as that of Luis's apolitical stand. It also emits echoes of *El novelista,* notably the relation between life and literature. The notions of nebulosity and 'para-reality' are even more evident in this novel. Luis, the narrator tells us, «quería leer los libros que no se habían escrito, que no había podido encontrar, donde se dijesen las cosas que quizás abriesen brecha en esta vida».[37] The novels which Luis would like to find are described

---

[33] Nora, p. 120.
[34] RAFAEL CANSINOS-ASSÉNS, «Ramón Gómez de la Serna», *Poetas y prosistas del novecientos* (Madrid: Editorial América, 1919), p. 254.
[35] *¡Rebeca!*, p. 104.
[36] *Ibid.*, p. 10.
[37] *Ibid.*, p. 56.

as «novelas que oliesen a claraboyas grises llenas de polvo antiguo, esas claraboyas de patio sobre las que se está al otro lado del mundo, del lado de los ratones y de los abortos».[38] Thus Ramón's 'para-reality' can be judged to exist not just in the mind of the author, as a poetic hetero-cosm (to use M. H. Abrams's term) but in the consistency of all observ-able phenomena relegated by convention to oblivion or unthought. There is a further indication of the genealogical ties between this nebular novel and the preceding one in the narrator's statement that Luis «tenía que encontrar la cifra de la posible llegada de la escondida».[39] For among the works attributed to Andrés Castilla, although a sample of it is not given, there appears the title «La escondida». I suspect that the original idea, perhaps even a first draft or sheaf of notes pertinent to ¡Rebeca!, dates back to the early 1920s.

If El Incongruente can indeed be considered an innovation in the art of the narrative and El novelista, a highly original approach to variegated fiction in the tradition of Cervantes and Laurence Sterne, ¡Rebeca! is a deeper and better integrated achievement of the author's purpose to employ the novelistic structure in a way that is essentially the same as with the aphoristic structure which he had already used successfully. This novel ends, like the preceding ones, on a «happy» note; Luis finds his Rebeca in the person of a woman named Leonor. In a last thematic re-prise of El Incongruente, the narrator tells how Luis shows sudden con-cern about «aquella amenaza del destino» (always the ambivalent attitude toward fate), but then becomes utterly resigned because «al escoger mu-jer hay que acertar con que sea la verduga».[40] How is Rebeca to fulfill her function as executioner, in the «tying down» implicit in her Hebrew name? The death of illusion is the only lasting illusion, the most for which a man can hope.

Cardona, too, points out the similarities between ¡Rebeca! and El Incongruente. For Luis, he says, «woman is the holder of life's mysteries; for him the experience of love is the knowledge of immortality...»; while «the idea of the importance of woman as the agent for reconciling man with the universe was also present in El Incongruente».[41] And with res-pect to narrative technique in ¡Rebeca!, Cardona believes that «the lack of nexus between scenes is an important factor... in bringing about the impression of mystery and the 'marvelous' which Ramón is striving to stir in us».[42] Evidently, among the readers that remained unstirred is Nora, whose principal objections to ¡Rebeca! are the following:

[38] Ibid., pp. 57-58.
[39] Ibid., p. 102.
[40] Ibid., p. 214.
[41] CARDONA, Ramón, p. 102.
[42] Ibid.

... una falta absoluta de cohesión o continuidad, una conciencia en estado gaseoso de sueño, en plena libertad imaginativa, pero tomada no como delirio, sino como plasmación del proceso vital del personaje.

... aquí la fantasía funciona... en total libertad, y el «extravío imaginativo» del autor se confunde por completo con la «vida» fantasmagórica de sus personajes inexistentes, disueltos en el humo de un ensueño sin despertar. Nada tienen que ver, en efecto, con el verdadero «contenido» del libro, ni el supuesto «protagonista», Luis (un nombre sin hombre), ni siquiera que su problema (sin planteamiento ni solución) sea la obsesión por Rebeca *(la* mujer; es decir, *una* mujer que se supone, aunque no existe; pero la vida entera de «Luis» es buscarla)...[43]

It is interesting to note that this critic, after performing a rather acute analysis, suddenly does not know quite what to do with the results. His conclusion is the following:

Imposible valorar este libro con los criterios normales, o decidir incluso a qué se acerca más: si a fruto de una inspiración genial o a borrador confuso de un alienado. Más parece en todo caso el resultado «final» (final como principio del fin, aunque no último) de la disolución de un gran talento, que un punto de partida aceptable como tentativa o como descubrimiento de un modo nuevo de novela. Para ser obra que dure le falta (aun admitido el «principio» de la novela como pura fiesta imaginativa) lo que la «nebulosa», claro está, no puede tener (sin dejar de serlo): concreción, densidad, forma, *unidad* de cosa «terminada». Es el apunte, el borrador caótico, amorfo; es decir, lo opuesto a toda obra de arte. Libro artificioso, pero negligente; creación imaginativa, pero no acabada de expresar; insuficientemente dominada o defectuosamente captada por la inteligencia.[44]

The fourth and last of the «Novels of the Nebula» is *El hombre perdido* (1947). Nora gives the date of publication as 1946, which is borne by the preface. This narrative is in the first person. The narrator-protagonist does not give himself a name; therefore I shall begin by calling him the Lost Man. The Lost Man has no permanent home or family; only a brother appears in one episode. At different times we are surprised by the intervention of various women in the narrative, but we cannot be sure that they are real and, if they are, whether they are really different or merely different manifestations of a single one, who is perhaps his wife. The Lost Man is never seen at, going to or coming from work, although on several occasions he mentions either having an occupation or the need of returning to it; the occupation is that of salesman. The Lost Man spends his time in aimless wandering; his constant preoccupation is to find the meaning of life and some proof of his having lived. After numerous misadventures either alone or in the company of friends or *apparent* strangers, he decides to leave his last respectable abode, the

[43] NORA, *La novela...*, p. 142.
[44] *Ibid.*, p. 143.

143

house in which he has lived for several months with his wealthy wife, and goes wandering again until he comes to a deserted railroad spur track out in the country. This is the kind of place which he has always both feared and longed to find, a vacant and neglected place, set aside from the mainstream of human activity. There the Lost Man lies down in utter abandon and goes to sleep. The story closes with a newspaper report of a man's body which was found smashed beyond recognition by a train which stopped on that very spur track for loading.

If a man is truly lost, it matters little whether he is alive or dead. Henry Drummond, in his *Natural Law in the Spiritual World,* defined death as «a falling out of correspondence with environment».[45] The sum total of the Lost Man's life-experience is to have glimpsed «un promedio de lo diferente, de lo hallado, de lo no hallado, de lo concebido como posible y del goce de lo inconcebible que es uno de los mayores goces de la vida». His wandering is a mixture of «busca, desopilación, vago movimiento, exasperación traslaticia, deseo de ir a *otro sitio,* otro sitio que no es la fantasía confeccionada de siempre».[46] This we know because we have the author's testimony. The Lost Man dies; it is of no consequence, because we also have Ramón's testimony to the effect that «el hombre, en definitiva, vive perdidamente perdido».[47] The novel of the Lost Man (which, rather than the dissolution viewed by Nora, represents in my estimation the final coalescence of Ramón's multiple talents) is an excellent case in which to study Joseph Frank's theory of the spatialization of time and the 'principle of reflexive reference'. We can begin our interpretation backwards because it is with the ending that we get the key to what otherwise must seem like an insoluble puzzle. The newspaper reports the death of an unidentified man on the railroad tracks. This man could have been someone other than the Lost Man for, as narrator, he takes care to mention, just before the end of the book, that he has heard of another vagabond who has been run over by a train a few days before; he does not clarify whether this man was actually killed or simply maimed. Where, then, is that key? It is found in the fact that even at the very end of the novel, which is his life story, the Lost Man, as narrator, has not been able to identify himself, in the same way that the dead man found on the railroad tracks cannot be identified by the newspaper. The novel ends with the narrator-protagonist killed by a train. We have the key; but how do we turn it?

Trains, locomotives, railroad stations, and railroad tracks are mentioned reiteratively in the novel almost from beginning to end. As we remark on this, we come to realize that such imagery serves as a reflexive

---

[45] New York: James Pott & Co., 1884, p. 177.
[46] *El hombre perdido,* p. 11.
[47] *Ibid.,* p. 12.

factor in the structural design, and design must have meaning. Those images are vague symbols of material instability. And then we discover that what happens with the railroad imagery also happens with the human imagery. At the end of the narrative we have two unidentified men who are presumably the same. At the beginning, we have two vagabonds. One is presented as the narrator-protagonist (the Lost Man); the other (a hobo who appears casually in the dawn) is not given a name in the first chapter but eventually does acquire a surname (Herreros) and later a first name (Gonzalo). There is dialogue between them from the start; initially they both use the polite *usted;* subsequently they switch to the familiar *tú* (the Man of Dawn in chapter one, the Lost Man in chapter forty). Soon after the beginning of the novel, the hobo introduces himself by saying (presumably to the Lost Man): «Yo soy la radiografía que salió mal.»[48] When the Lost Man, almost at the end of the book, lies down (like a hobo) by the railroad tracks, he says: «me desperecé de tal modo que varié de sitio mi esqueleto en el fondo de la carne y sentí un descanso supremo preconizador de buenos sueños...»[49] Furthermore, there is an early hint of the identity of these two human images, a hint which, while disconcerting at the outset, becomes quite evident after the novel is finished. When in the first chapter the Man of Dawn agrees to let him spend part of the day in his company, the narrator records the following: «Los dos hombres perdidos íbamos pensando lo mismo y volvíamos la cabeza para ver el puente despedirse, porque los puentes que se quedan atrás se despiden desgarradoramente porque por ellos se pasa una verdadera medida de espacio y tiempo.»[50] There also appears, though briefly, a third vagabond who is a bald philosopher. He shares a unique experience with the narrator (that of seeing a fantastic vision in the sky) and he shares baldness with Herreros, the Man of Dawn, who, upon introducing himself to the narrator, «se quitó el pelo viéndose que era completamente calvo».[51] In terms of gregueristic imagery, these constitute equations and, since two quantities which are equal to a third are equal to each other, this third image axiomatically corroborates the basic identity. All three vagabonds are one and the same, or they are different aspects of the same one. Thus the name of the narrator-protagonist, whom we were induced to call the Lost Man, is none other than Gonzalo Herreros. This is by no means a kind of *anagnorisis,* since the narrator does not directly reveal his identity; it is a device based on the afore-mentioned 'principle of reflexive reference' which enables the reader to deduce the total design of the novel and appreciate its meaning. In this novelistic structure the human images are vague symbols of spiritual instability.

[48] *Ibid.,* p. 22.
[49] *Ibid.,* p. 220.
[50] *Ibid.,* p. 23.
[51] *Ibid.,* p. 22.

The element of time in this work is amazingly resilient. The reader must use his imagination analytically to follow the chronological presentation of the more significant events, a presentation that extends through some two hundred pages in which the narrator morosely explores and attempts to describe the 'para-real'; and then the reader must use his imagination synthetically to telescope all those events into a single final image at the end of the book, despite the narrator's very casual mention of days, months, and years. For it all could have happened during the deceiving temporality of a dream or as a blinding flash of revelation. Thus in this very modern example of modern literature the aesthetic topology proposed by Frank, and effectively employed by him to explicate Djuna Barnes's *Nightwood,* is amply demonstrated. The inevitable segments of the narrative, first spread out in sequence, later fold into one another, presenting an ulterior arrangement. The effect is one of moving, to use Daiches's words again, «backward and forward with a new freedom to try to capture the sense of time as it actually operates in the human awareness of it».[52] But while even *Nightwood* exhibits a pluralistic use of character, *El hombre perdido* comes close to being a one man show. The human element, like every other in the narrative, is given only in images. All these images are produced by the narrator, naturally, but the narrator is also the protagonist and, in turn, the protagonist unfolds in numerous projections of self and ideal. Such an exaggerated 'stream of consciousness' results in the absorption by the protagonist of all the human images, in the same way that the protagonists of *El Incongruente, El novelista,* and *¡Rebeca!* absorb all the human images in their novels. The reader cannot think of the human images in any of these novels without thinking of the protagonist; they are simply not developed as are characters in good conventional novels. Even the protagonist does not develop with an individual plastic consistency. We do not know what Gonzalo Herreros looks like; one single feature, his baldness, turns out to be a metaphor. But he does have aesthetic consistency, and this within the psychological consistency of the narrator. So there is no question that such an iridescent cluster of images constitutes a character, for it represents a personality, a fictionalization of the author, to be sure, but a fictional entity nonetheless, since Ramón is not run over by a train, Gonzalo Herreros is. Just before this sensitive wanderer, in disharmony with his surroundings and unable to find answers to his questions, is finally destroyed by chance and returned to the void, he acknowledges that

> Fuera de los escapes absurdos de la vida, que no pudieron ser duraderos, porque nunca pude establecerme en ellos, sólo conocía un sitio estable, como fuera de la existencia en común, y, sin embargo, al lado de ella: las

---

[52] DAICHES, *The Novel...,* p. 7.

trochas muertas del ferrocarril, como ancha orilla de los primeros kilómetros junto al terraplén de la plataforma viva de la estación central, un plus de terreno que las grandes compañías adquirieron para aumentar algún día sus trazados de líneas, cruces y empalmes.[53]

The plight of Gonzalo Herreros, incognito, is shared by Herman Hesse's *Steppenwolf* and Colin Wilson's *Outsider*. He is also a victim of what Alvin Toffler would call *Future Shock,* for he warns that «con lo que hay, tenemos necesidad de fomentar lo que no hay. La vida no es cierta en ningún momento y lo único cierto que hay es que hay algo que nos empuja como un torrente a una velocidad inconcebible».[54] The Lost Man reflects what is known and anticipates what is emerging in a modern world where, devoid of meaning, fullness is the equivalent of emptiness. His actions correspond to Surrealist and Existentialist concepts of irrationality and absurdity, and since Gide, if not before, gratuitousness has been the artist's primary reaction to the lack of true meaning in society. How close the implied author comes to explicit identification with his creation is revealed by this briefest of narrative segments:

> Me iba convirtiendo en el hombre al que exigen los demás que escriba, pero yo sólo quería lograr un destino fijo y meditar, ver venir a la que se esconde detrás de biombos, poder estar sentado en el jardín de invierno de un gran hotel, viendo entrar a los que se han citado para comer y se creen los dueños del mundo.[55]

To see the woman hiding behind the screen, an event that takes place in the lives of Gustavo and Luis, is a lost hope for the Lost Man, much to his chagrin since he admits to his incidental lover and her psychiatrist husband: «La mujer es lo que contesta algo al enigma.»[56]

The four «Novels of the Nebula» have in common the theme of quest, which is an ancient narrative device. The first two are novels in which the description of environment follows the presentation of character, at least to the extent that we are told from the start that Gustavo is an incongruent individual and Andrés Castilla is a professional writer. Of these two narratives, *El Incongruente* contains more action, in the sense that Gustavo's adventures, whether fantastic or merely absurd, are fairly explicit; *El novelista* exhibits more coherence, since in the master fiction Andrés Castilla goes from one writing project to another and finally retires. The last two are novels in which the revelation of character emerges from reaction to and as adjunct of an environment described. It is with *¡Rebeca!* and *El hombre perdido* that Ramón makes a truly radical

[53] *El hombre perdido,* p. 217.
[54] *Ibid.,* p. 32.
[55] *Ibid.,* p. 178.
[56] *Ibid.,* p. 62.

departure from traditional novelistic structure. The conventional norms of plot and character do not get as much as token recognition. Neither Luis nor Gonzalo Herreros is presented with even minimal credentials. They are neither flat nor round characters (to use E. M. Forster's famous terms[57]); they are actually of no shape or density because, like their fictional habitat, they are totally dynamic. Of these latter two novels, the first is less successful, perhaps because of a less effective network of imagery and the ultimate subordination of the fiction to a historical reality, namely, that Leonor, the materialization of Rebeca, represents the author's wife, Luisa Sofovich.[58]

Nevertheless, the four novels are related through what Ramón calls *la nebulosa,* the novelistic manifestation of *la greguería* and a more ambitious and concentrated attempt to reach *lo indecible.* Although they can be read as separate books, together they constitute what we might call Ramón's personal novel, his autoideography, as opposed to his official autobiography. In this respect, the first three serve as steps that lead to the formulation of a consummately gregueristic novel. *El hombre perdido* subsumes all predecessors and epitomizes everything that Ramón ever wanted to write. In the «Prólogo a las novelas de la nebulosa», he refers thus to *El hombre perdido* specifically:

> Esta novela está en mi camino desde hace muchos años, porque no en vano yo escribí y publiqué..., en el año 1922 mi novela *El incongruente* —Kafka moría ese año y sus obras no iban a ser conocidas sino muchos años después—, y en 1936 apareció... mi más nebúlica novela titulada ¡*Rebeca!*...
>
> En mi *Novelista,* escrito hace veintitrés años en plena juventud... está ya el atisbo de esta realidad desesperada... y allí en el capítulo XVIII donde intenté una novelita titulada *Todos,* escribía ya: «En esta cuartilla se detuvo... No podía ser... La nebulosa se traga las novelas y por deseo de dar capacidad a la novela la perdía en la masa cosmogónica primera, desprovista de formas, de géneros, de salvedades, de concepciones, de concreción.»
>
> Sin embargo, abortada entonces, después de esos veintitrés años, aparezco con nueva fe en la nebulosa e intento mi primera novela completa nebulosal.[59]

Clearly, at least in the author's own mind, this fourth nebular novel is the true one. It succeeds where the fragmentary «Todos» failed; it goes far beyond the other three in the gradual fulfillment of a literary Nebula that reflects the world in flux, the real chaos in which we live. What Ramón says about the evolution of these works is borne out by the recurrence of both simple and complex images (the idea of destiny,

[57] Cf. *Aspects of the Novel,* p. 67.
[58] Cf. Luis S. Granjel, *Retrato de Ramón* (Madrid: Ediciones Guadarrama [1963]), p. 218.
[59] *El hombre perdido,* p. 12.

for example, as that which man both fears and desires, or the spiritual tension between the flight from convention and the quest for truth). Perhaps the most significant evidence of this lineage comes from the notion of self-eclipse which is found in Ramón's work, from *Morbideces* (1908) which he attributes to «un poeta perdido en las sinuosidades de un laberinto»,[60] all the way to *El hombre perdido*, in which the protagonist-narrator recalls already having lived «treinta y cinco años como un hombre perdido».[61] The images of a lost man, a man of the dawn, and railroads are first associated in *El alba* (1918). Also in this book we find an aphorism on the relation between death and identity: «En el alba todo hombre pierde su identificación... Se es en el alba cadáver sin identificar»[62] (the fate of Gonzalo Herreros), a notion which is projected into the novel by means of these words from *El hombre perdido:* «La identidad del tiempo es de lo más desconcertante porque vivimos lo que ya está muerto.»[63] The optimism prevalent in the first two nebular novels and the gradual change through the third (ca. 1936!) to a stark pessimism in the fourth reflect, at least in part, the shift in the general world mood between the end of the first world war and the foreboding and realities of the second.

The specifically structural evolution of the nebular novels is most evident in the similar but gradually more effective use of language. Cardona believes that *El hombre perdido* «is essentially an experiment with language...».[64] And so it is, especially as it represents an effort to give linguistic expression to an experience far beyond the bounds of ordinary language. This, however, is equally true about the very first use of the *greguerías,* Ramón's aphorisms, whose aim is to transcend the stereotype and try to catch a reality before it leaves behind an empty form. But the aphorism aspires to stasis; the novel aspires to kinesis. In the novel that spatializes time, the aspiration to kinesis is modified by a new concept of narrative structure. Does Ramón provide a transfer of such images that is actually suitable for a novelistic structure? Nora does not think so; he looks upon *El hombre perdido* as a «novela de lectura trabajosa, monótona en su orgiástico desbarajuste de temas y vivencias (sueño y realidad, conciencia y objetos, en el más abrumador e incoherente desorden)». And he goes on to question the notion of 'para-reality':

[60] *Morbideces* (Madrid: Imprenta «El Trabajo», 1908), p. 14.
[61] *El hombre perdido,* p. 27. The above data point to the «final» composition of this work as taking place circa 1943, a deduction corroborated by the appearance in the text of the following lines: «Entonces vi el subsuelo y revés del gran campo de aviación con los aparatos en estertor, como después de una traición japonesa» (p. 76), an image probably suggested by a 1941 newsreel. See supplementary note No. VII (Ramón at the movies).
[62] *Obras completas,* I, p. 599.
[63] *El hombre perdido,* p. 51.
[64] CARDONA, *Ramón,* p. 159.

Esa nueva «realidad lateral» que Ramón pretende descubrir por cansancio o desprecio del mundo de todos, no parece que sea mucho más que la escombrera de una conciencia saturada de literatura, en pleno «terremoto mental»: espectáculo interesante, impresionante, incluso, pero de más que dudosa viabilidad estética.[65]

It is not completely clear whether Nora denies the success of *El hombre perdido,* as he does that of *¡Rebeca!,* or the very aesthetic principles on which these works are grounded. The latter possibility seems to be the case; which means that, while conceding that it is a novel, he does not recognize *El hombre perdido* as the novelistic counterpart of *Greguerías,* although he refers to certain fragments of *El novelista* as «esbozos de novelas-greguerías».[66] Cardona, on the other hand, is convinced that the «psychic and linguistic phenomenon which has produced the *greguerías,* and which has so deeply affected the style of Ramón reaches its maximum expression in his last novels. In a sense, these last novels, and in particular *El hombre perdido*..., are the ultimate consequences...».[67] He further elaborates as follows:

> Not having a body of inherited, *accepted* beliefs, the artist needs to create his own unity by means of the effort to express himself. Ramón has done this by means of a new creative style, one in which words can have a new and authentic value because they have been liberated from their ordinary context. How else can things —including man— have any meaning in this chaos except through an explanation according to a dialectical system which brings two things together into a new and comprehensible whole. We saw the system work in the *greguerías*... then it began to permeate more and more Ramón's style, until... it culminated in *El hombre perdido.*[68]

Those words which «have been liberated from their ordinary context», which transcend the stereotype and surprise reality in flux, producing new and strange configurations, make up the peculiar kind of language employed by Ramón which I call 'precognitive', because it anticipates through metaphorical imagery what later becomes a «comprehensible» unified vision. The «Novels of the Nebula», then, are novels whose designs spring from imagery and, if the reader is unable to share in the author's vision (like the Doppelgänger in *El hombre perdido*), those designs will naturally dissolve in imagery. Guillermo de Torre calls *El hombre perdido* «la novela de la imagen continua, del supremo extra-

---

[65] NORA, *La novela...,* p. 147. Ronald Daus echoes this general opinion in his otherwise very well documented and helpful *Der Avantgardismus Ramón Gómez de la Sernas* (Analecta Romanica, Heft 29). Frankfürt am Main: Vittorio Klostermann [1971], pp. 304-06.
[66] *Ibid.,* p. 121.
[67] CARDONA, *Ramón,* p. 155.
[68] *Ibid.,* p. 164.

vío imaginativo».[69] It is a pity that this critic, who in other instances so well elucidated Ramón's work, did not see fit to grapple with the stylistic problems posed by the «Novels of the Nebula».

There are two questions which I will discuss but briefly. First, the inevitable remark, such as that of Luis Granjel, concerning the «'novelas de la nebulosa' en las que algo hay que recuerda a las 'nivolas' de Unamuno».[70] The profound differences and the subtle similarities between the two writers are quite evident. Suffice it to say that, apart from the enormous influence which Unamuno exerted, like it or not, on his contemporaries, Ramón admired him implicitly as a novelist. In his *Retratos contemporáneos,* he says:

> Como novelista, don Miguel de Unamuno es un laberinto, un laberinto admirable.
> En ese remezclado azar de sus invenciones la realidad le dejaba ver sus intimidades...
> En la puerta del laberinto está escrita la palabra *nivola,* su invención original...
> La vida de novelista de Unamuno es un puro lío, un lío fértil de novelería, porque la novela es más novela cuanto más puro lío sea.[71]

The second question is that of how Ramón anticipates Samuel Beckett and how he compares with the objectivism of the *nouveau roman.* To begin with, the coincidence of Ramón and Beckett on the subject of inexpressibility should not be emphasized, or it will become deceptive because their views are contradictory. Simply put, Ramón contends that not everything has been said because there are unexplored realms of language, while Beckett asserts that nothing has been said because saying anything is a fruitless enterprise. With regard to Robbe-Grillet, Sarraute, Butor, and the like, a similar polarization exists. Although these writers, too, are interested in objects, they are the enemies of metaphor and «improvisation». If nothing else, however, the concern for form over content warrants the placing of Ramón alongside the acknowledged progenitors of the *nouveau roman.*

> From Flaubert to Kafka, a line of descent is drawn... That passion to describe, which animates them both, is certainly the same passion we discern in the new novel today. Beyond the naturalism of Flaubert and the metaphysical oneiroticism of Kafka appear the first elements of a realistic style of an unknown genre, which is now coming to light.[72]

These are the words of Robbe-Grillet. To claim kinship with Kafka, a master of the fantastic and the absurd, is already a significant conces-

---

[69] GUILLERMO DE TORRE, preface to R. GÓMEZ DE LA SERNA, *Antología; 50 años de vida literaria,* p. 22.
[70] LUIS S. GRANJEL, *Retrato...,* p. 220.
[71] *Obras completas,* II, pp. 1759-60.
[72] ALAIN ROBBE-GRILLET, *For a New Novel* (trans. Richard Howard; New York: Grove Press [1966]), p. 14.

sion on his part (which, if held to specifics, flatters him more than it does Kafka). One detail, the incomplete nominality of the protagonist, is common to Kafka, Ramón, and the practitioners of the New Novel; another is the revelation of the narrator's mind through the description of things and events. But it is Flaubert's casual theorizations that are best realized, whether consciously or not, in both the «Novels of the Nebula» and the works of the new French novelists. If for no other reason, we can venture to describe their individual techniques as variants of 'poetic realism'; this applies particularly to Ramón. In a letter of Flaubert's we find this beautifully daring statement, which foreshadows the twentieth century:

> There are in me, literally speaking, two distinct persons: one who is infatuated with bombast, lyricism, eagle flights, sonorities of phrase and the high points of ideas; and another who digs and burrows into the truth as deeply as he can, who likes to treat a humble fact as respectfully as a big one, who would like to make you feel almost *physically* the things he reproduces; this latter person likes to laugh, and enjoys the animal sides of man...
>
> What seems beautiful to me, what I should like to write, is a book about nothing, a book dependent on nothing external, which would be held together by the strength of its style, just as the earth, suspended in the void, depends on nothing external for its support; a book which would have almost no subject, or at least in which the subject would be almost invisible, if such a thing is possible. The finest works are those that contain the least matter; the closer expression comes to thought, the closer language comes to coinciding and merging with it, the finer the result. I believe that the future of Art lies in this direction. I see it, as it has developed from its beginnings, growing progressively more ethereal, from the Egyptian pylons to Gothic lancets, from the 20,000-line Hindu poems to the effusions of Byron. Form, as it is mastered, becomes attenuated; it becomes dissociated from any liturgy, rule, yardstick; the epic is discarded in favor of the novel, verse in favor of prose; there is no longer any orthodoxy, and form is as free as the will of its creator. This emancipation from matter can be observed everywhere: governments have gone through similar evolution, from the oriental despotisms to the socialisms of the future.
>
> It is for this reason that there are no noble subjects or ignoble subjects; from the standpoint of pure Art one might almost establish the axiom that there is no such thing as subject, style in itself being an absolute manner of seeing things.[73]

Since a comparison of Ramón with the various authors just mentioned is really beyond the limits of the present discussion, the mere implications of the preceding side lights, despite their unscholarly nature, must here suffice. The same would apply to Sartre, Camus, and in the general framework of prose fiction, Borges.

---

[73] Letter to Louise Colet [Croisset, January 12 or 14, 1852], included in *The Selected Letters of Flaubert* (Trans. and ed. Francis Steegmuller; New York: Farrar, Straus and Young [1953]), pp. 127-28.

To sum up: Ramón's «Novels of the Nebula» are the best examples of his personal style within a novelistic structure. They also reveal gradual stages in the evolution of that style. For these reasons they represent a more original contribution to the modern novel than has commonly been recognized. Among the many problems that face the modern novelist are the limitations of language imposed on nonverbal experience, the logical inability to capture movement through a static medium, the simultaneous perception of an object and its transfer to an image, the pitfalls of autobiographical fiction.[74] These last apparently raised grave doubts in E. M. Forster; commenting on Gide's *Counterfeiters,* for instance, he states: «The novelist who betrays too much interest in his own method can never be more than interesting; he has given up the creation of character and summoned us to help analyse his own mind, and a heavy drop in the emotional thermometer results.»[75] This is a dilemma faced by every modern novelist. When, earlier on, Ramón faced it, he used his natural bent for humor as the radical solution of dissolution. Hence, *El hombre perdido* came much too late, when he had already become typed as a humorist and an aphorist. But the *Künstlerromanen* which are *¡Rebeca!* and *El hombre perdido* are humorous only in a dismally ironic and almost apocalyptic way. The latter (and not *El novelista,* as Nora suggests) is the book which Ramón calls his «confesionario atrevido y displicente de la vida».[76] This confessional, this novel of the artist, is truly both things at once because Ramón was able to invent another Ramón and to discover his possibilities of autonomous behavior, living and dying under the ultimate guise of Gonzalo Herreros, whose flesh and blood are, from beginning to end, sheer language. Thus the author has fictionalized himself to the point of casting his unique verbal process at full capability into an absolute invention. Critics with varied backgrounds will continue to speculate on the phenomenon of expression. In closing, I shall quote one such critic. Joseph Church, a psychologist, thinks that

> Although the perfect stylist is the invisible one who allows the listener or reader to look right through him to the subject matter of his discourse, our means of expression always have some degree of opacity. It is only the most banal statements in the most neutral situation that ever attain transparency. As soon as we try to describe a new phenomenon, a new relationship, a new way of looking at something, our medium thickens and becomes prominent. Indeed, much of the innovator's time is taken up with means of expression rather than with what is being expressed. It is not quite accurate, for instance, to say that one can write about writing but cannot paint about painting. The many artistic innovations of the last

---

[74] Cf. HOWARD MUMFORD JONES' review of *The Psychological Novel: 1900-1950,* by LEON EDEL, in *Saturday Review,* XXXVIII (April 25, 1955), 19.

[75] *Aspects of the Novel,* p. 80 (cf. also pp. 97-102).

[76] *El hombre perdido,* p. 14.

century are as much statements about the medium as about any subject matter. It is this very reversal, this making form dominant over content, that puts people off and makes them complain of the «lunacy» of modern art...[77]

A very interesting observation, indeed; but what people is he talking about? The average reader or spectator? Evidently; yet unknowingly he is also including other people, maybe even Nora and Forster. As for Ramón, he long ago had chosen intuition over contrivance, and, particularly in the «Novels of the Nebula», he did what even today is thought by some to be impossible for prose fiction, if not for pictorial fiction: he managed to fuse together the content and the form. And this is particularly true of ¡Rebeca! and El hombre perdido because art and life intermingle to such a degree. It, however, is not a question of something like the autobiographical or confessional novel of the nineteenth-century romantics.

When I first read Wylie Sypher's Loss of the Self in Modern Literature,[78] I was impressed by how so many of his observations seem to apply to the above-mentioned novels. Sypher presents the reader with a general scenario. Around the middle of this century, three forces have impelled artists and writers to search for «selfless» creations: 1) the liquidation of collective romanticism, including orthodox religion, from the realm of art, 2) the almost inevitably parallel development of art and science as world-views in which anthropomorphic and anthropocentric values have been significantly diminished, and 3) the creation through technology of a mass consumer society, in which individual human identity is blurred to near-extinction and is replaced by dehumanized figures much like statistical data. Of course, this is in many ways an updating and elaboration of Ortega y Gasset's well-known caveat, and the consequences suggested by Sypher are idealistically though not summarily attacked by Robert Langbaum in The Modern Spirit: Essays on the Continuity of Nineteenth- and Twentieth-Century Literature.[79]

Ramón's last two «Novels of the Nebula», the nebula being life as seen by the eye of the author's mind, have for their theme the human condition in the middle of the twentieth century. Although the reader is able finally to perceive that such a theme is dismally negative, it is hardly exploited in a conventionally narrative manner. What little actually happens, as I have said before, is inconsequential in terms of ordinary

[77] JOSEPH CHURCH, Language and the Discovery of Reality (New York: Vintage Books, n.d.), p. 191.
[78] WYLIE SYPHER, Loss of the Self in Modern Literature and Art. New York: Vintage Books [1962].
[79] ROBERT LANGBAUM, The Modern Spirit: Essays on the Continuity of Nineteenth- and Twentieth-Century Literature. New York: Oxford University Press, 1970.

prose fiction. It is only a mood sustained by the author's use of reiterative metaphor, the staple of his style, with a tenuous though clever and ultimately decisive plot-design (Luis repeatedly going to and from his cabinet in *¡Rebeca!*, the narrator-protagonist meeting his doubles in *El hombre perdido*) superimposed on the loose text for symbolical as well as structural reasons, a framework which, upon considerable scrutiny, appears to bring together the referential action of the many discontinuous episodes.

As Lukács pointed out long ago, purely subjective works of literature, like satirical tracts, cannot achieve effective reality at the level of the epic. In *The Theory of the Novel* (written to give a look at the history of ideas through the development of the novel and criticized by the author himself in a 1962 preface), Lukács traces a typology of the genre depending «to a large extent on whether the chief protagonist's soul is 'too narrow' or 'too broad' in relation to reality».[80] What he means by narrow and broad is how badly or how well the protagonist's soul or capacity for transcendence relates to the outside world comprehensible to the reader at any given time. Paradoxically, Lukács says, the subjectivity of a great epic novel can be so creative and lyrical that it can «transform itself into a purely receptive organ of the world» and «partake of the grace of having the whole revealed to it».[81] Thus Dante, Cervantes and Goethe are saved, while Laurence Sterne and Jean-Paul Richter «offer no more than reflexions of a world-fragment which is merely subjective and therefore limited, narrow and arbitrary».[82] What would this great Marxist critic have said about our «Novels of the Nebula» either in 1914 or 1962? If, in 1914, Lukács did not accept the fact that Dostoevsky wrote novels, despite his suggestion of the novel as a genre always in the process of becoming, his early typology clearly cannot encompass modern literature. And yet there are concepts there more helpful than later ones when used experimentally. The romanticism of disillusionment, for example, is certainly not the exclusive patrimony of the nineteenth-century novel, but Lukács's climaxing of the tradition with Flaubert's *L'Education sentimentale* is not only a lesson in itself but a point of far-fetched contact with *El hombre perdido* as its realist counterpart, since Frédéric Moreau and Gonzalo Herreros are both estranged seekers of the meaning of existence who ultimately withdraw from all meaningful action.

The intermingling of art and life in *¡Rebeca!* and *El hombre perdido* is such that is comes very close to fitting John Stuart Mill's self-evalua-

[80] GEORG LUKÁCS, *The Theory of the Novel: A Historico-Philosophical Essay on the Forms of Great Epic Literature.* Translated from the German by Anna Bostock. Cambridge, Massachusetts: The M.I.T. Press [1971], p. 13.
[81] LUKÁCS, *ibid.*, p. 53.
[82] LUKÁCS, *ibid.*, p. 54.

tion in the fifth chapter of his *Autobiography*. Without anything personal left to live for, his life no longer seemed to be his own, instead only
a consequence of the society which had produced it. He felt like an
empty being whose pleasures, passions and virtues had been subverted.
Mill's statement, in turn, makes us think of the reification of the human
being reduced to a quantifiable object by industrial and political proces-
ses, as discussed by Lukács in his *History and Class Consciousness*
(1923). The parallels with themes from T. S. Eliot and Robert Musil
should not be surprising. Indeed, as Sypher has pointed out, this represents a crisis in romantic-liberal thought and, I might add, it applies
to the artists and writers of the last one hundred and fifty years, even
those not so liberal, since Thomas Carlyle asked the not so rhetorical
question: «Who am I? The being who calls himself I?»

We are confronted here with the ultimate mystery of identity, of
the name and nature of the individual human being, especially when
subjectively rooted as a center of consciousness and conscience. It is
something we do not generally accept as a mystery in everyday life,
thanks to our defensive epistemological capacity, and yet it lurks in the
depths of our psyche. It is, in effect, the philosophical preoccupation
at the bottom of *El hombre perdido*. Being and existence are not the
only concerns of the Lost Man. His relations with other people and
things, the relation between his interiority and the ouside world, as
Lukács would say, are his problem, and they are a problem because he
has no handles on them: he does not know why he feels guilty, he does
not know whether or not he is really alive, *ergo* he does not know who
he is. Furthermore, his interiority is riddled with morbid curiosity
because he does not know what crime or sin he has committed. At times
he resembles a character from Albert Camus and at others he seems
to suffer from the Kierkegaardian «sickness unto death». His is a lonely,
agonizing experience of a man's inner solitude which only reflexively
refers to the possibility of God and finds solace in the most ironical
and almost banal ways of meeting death at a not totally unexpected
time. Because he does not know who he is, he cannot tell us.

Langbaum makes the following observation concerning the general problem of individuality and identity in twentieth-century literature:

> Individuality, which was for the romanticists the one sure thing, is now
> treated as only a concept and a problematical concept. In attempting to
> liberate the individual from the social and moral categories that define
> him, literature somehow dissolved him out of existence. Writers nowadays,
> who want to face the problem, can... face it in two ways. They can deny
> the existence of a free and knowable self and —like Beckett, Sarraute
> and Robbe-Grillet in Paris— take soundings of characters only to make
> us hear the hollow ring within. Or they can —like Mann, Joyce, Yeats,

Eliot, Lawrence— reaffirm the authenticity of the self by finding that individual identity emerges... from an archetypal identity.[83]

What Langbaum is prescribing, of course, is the wisdom of the older writers over that of the *nouveau roman,* a rather unfair if not petty piece of advice. There is no doubt that, were he to pass judgment on Ramón, he would find him inferior still. But there is in his observation a curiously fortuitous part of which I will take advantage and which says: «literature somehow dissolved him out of existence». I, in turn, may seem unfair taking this out of context, but it happens to constitute a good lead for a trick with which I would like to end this disquisition.

Does the Lost Man exist «as an isolated, unique, pure, and therefore abstract interiority»,[84] in Lukács's alternative description, or does he not exist at all? To be sure he exists in some way that we can apprehend his existence, even if it is, as with all characters in fiction, through the means of a verbal configuration. But then the question arises whether within such literary medium that gives him existence as a reference, is he substantial enough to merit our acknowledgment of him as a fictive entity or is he an out-and-out lie, the invention of the author's novelistic voice and persona? Is he a Doppelgänger or wraith of Ramón, as other character-figures were of him? Being, existence and identity: three critical concepts of our times, when everything has been placed in doubt, are involved here. To cease to be and the fear of such, possibilities or certainties and fears as poetized by Keats and Rubén Darío, are not only natural to the human being but have become a philosophical preoccupation since Hamlet anticipated the Existentialist concept of dread. Assuming that the Lost Man does exist at least as a fictional reference, how does he cease to be and what does that signify in terms of his former habitat, the literary structure that bears his non-name?

Let me suggest, but barely suggest an answer, an appreciation of the pseudo-dramatic device that ends the narrative. The medium in which the Lost Man has lived his «life» is no more real than a utopia. If topography, even imaginary topography, is the realm in which conventional narrative unfolds, topology is that in which this narrative hovers. I use the term topology as it is used in modern mathematics: «the study of the properties of geometric configurations invariant under transformation by continuous mappings.»[85] Topologists often speculate on the physical properties of an object in imaginary situations, perhaps in other

[83] LANGBAUM, *ibid.,* p. 171.
[84] LUKÁCS, *ibid.,* p. 152.
[85] *The American Heritage Dictionary of the English Language.* Boston-New York: American Heritage Publishing Company and Houghton Mifflin Company [1975].

dimensions such as, for example, the plane without a surface.[86] Does this sound like a contradiction, an absurdity? The inevitable result would be the disappearance of the object. Some of the hypothetical demonstrations of this notion are the so-called Möbius strip and the Klein bottle, whose surfaces seem to be continuous and suggest the shapes to be incapable of having a surface since it has become two which cancel each other. Some drawings and engravings by M. C. Escher illustrate this notion and his artistic elaborations.

There are many other works of fiction in which a character disappears into thin air. It is, of course, a fantastic event; supernatural tales are full of them, but these are not what we are interested in here. In Galdós's *La sombra,* the protagonist's morbid jealousy temporarily hypostatizes a fictive character found in a painting and in *El amigo Manso,* the protagonist-narrator announces and consummates a vanishing act as only a fictive entity can. In *Niebla,* Unamuno employs a different device, the author presently telling his character he will have to kill him. In *El hombre perdido,* however, we have something totally different. The narrator-protagonist does not disappear on his own, and yet the novel is deliberately written in the first person, the only novel by Ramón written in the first person. What happens is that the narrator-protagonist does not disappear all of a sudden; first he disappears only as narrator. We are led to believe that this protagonist has been smashed beyond recognition by an unexpected train. But another narrator has to tell us that, since the original narrator has ceased to be. Thus we have a shift from the first to the third person. When we are informed by the new impersonal narrator that someone who indirectly fits the description of the original narrator-protagonist has been killed, we accept the disappearance of that fictive entity in his second guise, that of protagonist. Everything folds one into another, as earlier I referred to Joseph Frank's aesthetic topology in his exegesis of Djuna Barnes's *Nightwood.* Ramón had prepared the way for this in his text. He not only bases his novel on his notion of the nebula, he has his initial narrator-protagonist morosely explore and attempt to describe the lateral reality which is his vision of the world and which very well could resemble a plane without a surface or the continuous space of his imagination. «Esta realidad», he says, «que acabo de tocar y que puede desaparecer de un momento a otro... no me convence como motivo de escrituración.»[87] He is looking for a reality which is «una cosa que no esté ni en el realismo de la imaginación ni en el realismo de la fantasía,

[86] DOUGLAS R. HOFSTADTER, *Gödel, Escher, Bach: An Eternal Golden Braid.* New York: Random House (Vintage Books) [1980].

[87] RAMÓN GÓMEZ DE LA SERNA, *El hombre perdido.* Madrid: Espasa-Calpe [1962], p. 7.

*otra* realidad, ni encima ni debajo, sino sencillamente *otra*».[88] Disappearance, whether vital, physical or ontological is much on his mind, as these quotations show: «Yo seguía comprendiendo el regreso al revés que es la vida, la risa de desaparecidos que debíamos tener y el teatro de desaparecidos que debíamos ir a ver... Teatro de desaparecidos en un gran teatro que se podría llamar el Teatro de la Desaparición».[89] And, finally, this dialogue:

> «Yo lo que quiero es un vaso de leche de junquillos.»
> «Con esas ideas se va a volver un desaparecido.»
> «No es que vaya a ser un desaparecido —no es que vayamos a ser unos desaparecidos— es que lo soy ya —es que lo somos ya.»
> Aquel amigo que se había acordado de mí de pronto —presagio de nichos— y me había hecho una visita inesperada se fue en seguida no pudiendo aguantar mi teoría de los desaparecidos en que figuraba él en primer término. No quería darme la razón y me la dio entera al desaparecer.[90]

Of course, Ramón is here playing with words as usual and *desaparecer* can mean not only to disappear but also to die. In any event, it is still a valid point, I think, to consider what happens to the Lost Man as a topological case,[91] even if this, in turn, is judged to be a humorous criticism —I would call it an appreciation— of Ramón's final literary rope trick.

---

[88] *Ibid.*
[89] *Ibid.*, p. 40.
[90] *Ibid.*, p. 44.
[91] For a tongue-in-cheek example of topology applied to literary fiction, see MARTIN GARDNER, «No-Sided Professor», in Clifton Fadiman (ed.), *Fantasia Mathematica* (New York: Simon and Schuster, 1958), pp. 99-109. There too may be found some references to articles and book-chapters on topology, othrewise called *Analysis Situs*. See also DOUGLAS R. HOFSTADTER, *Gödel, Escher, Bach*, under «Loops» «Möbius Strips», and «Klein Bottle» (New York: Random House, Vintage Books [1980]). There is also another interesting and very humorous piece of fiction about a man who gets rid of his wife by tying her up in a topological knot in IAN McEWAN, «Solid Geometry», *First Love, Last Rites* (New York: Random House [1975]), pp. 31-52.

# EPILOGUE

I have purposely avoided even attempting to deal with the many aspects of Ramón's *novelas de la nebulosa* using the specific methods of fashionable literary criticism. To begin with, though I find them interesting, I also find them confining, somewhat presumptuous, and ultimately transitory when not already *demodés,* as methods are always likely to become in time. Literature being an eclectic, non-specific approach to life, I think that the best approach to it is also eclectic. There is simply no one way to deal with it, no matter the current fashion.

When it comes to semiotics, I suggest that the methods derived from Charles Sanders Peirce might be particularly fruitful to someone disposed to such a task, since Ramón's writing seems to fulfill the requirements of what is called iconic discourse, that is, one structured through analogies and juxtapositions instead of through cause-and-effect and massive continuity systems (for a further suggestion of advantages and disadvantages of this method, see Paul Ricoeur, *The Rule of Metaphor,* pp. 187 ff.). That is why I have referred to Ramón's language as static even though it reflects his perception of a world in constant flux. His expressive mechanism is geared by intuition to the meshing of endless patterns of change as they occur in life into a sort of discrete cinematography of language-acts, giving those patterns a new, albeit illusory, form. Art, after all, is the relentless pursuit of new forms.

In the course of my investigation I have found that, among the nearly eighty works of prose narrative which Ramón considered novels and which best fit into that extremely flexible genre of fiction, the four *novelas de la nebulosa* are, in my estimation as well as in the author's, the least conventional and most obviously designed to convey his aesthetic awareness of the animate and the inanimate. Thus what the *greguería* is to aphoristic writing, the *nebulosa* is to novelistic writing, revealing all the metaphorical, whimsical, humorous, and ultimately tragicomic qualities of which Ramón was capable.

Although critics have long paid a great deal of attention to the *greguerías,* relatively little has been done with the novels and hardly any substantial commentary on the *novelas de la nebulosa* has been available up to now. Some critics have considered all of Ramón's novels as either hypertrophic *greguerías* or long strings of the capsular type. Such critics have not remarked on the particular designs of these structures. In turn, I hope to have demonstrated that Ramón's style or idiolect or otherwise verbal process, which I prefer to call *ramonismo*, articulates these novelistic structures in basically the same way as the short texts.

It is wrong to believe that nothing «happens» in Ramón's *novelas de la nebulosa,* even though such a «happening» may be regarded as taking place exclusively in the author's mind, as a sort of elliptical behavior-action. My contention is that, at least in *El hombre perdido,* the author has fictionalized himself completely; he has taken over the far reaches of invented action with his own psychic behavior. Granted that these are by no means conventional novels; yet the narrative segments can and must be brought together by means of a thread of imagery, thus revealing their structural design. In Ramón's other novels there is a story line, albeit a vague one. The *novelas de la nebulosa,* however, should be regarded as narratives in which an on-going image (that of the protagonist) is reiterated at varying radii of a nautilus-like structure, a process reinforced by the constant juxtaposition of other sympathetic images, thus creating an actual yet labyrinthine situation.

In «conventional» narrative the situational development has the nature of evolution, especially with respect to character. It is essentially linear, at least its impetus is linear, although there may be retrospective and anticipatory factors and involutions of thought and reference. Modern literature through its prevalent use of the interior monologue has been shown to tend toward the simultaneity of consciousness through devices which suggest the spatialization of time. But in Ramón's *novelas de la nebulosa,* particularly the last two, the development may be regarded as a convolution. The main resemblance that these works bear to «conventional» novels is the inevitable requirement for the author to write and for the reader to read one word after another on the page; and this, in a way, is due only to another accident of nature, which is the length of the narrative instead of what might have been that of, say, a concrete poem. This is what makes *¡Rebeca!* and *El hombre perdido,* in my estimation, remarkably original pieces of prose fiction cast in the unconventionally employed narrative structures which represent the acme of what we have called *ramonismo.*

As for Gómez de la Serna in general, I have examined here the springs of his vision, disposition, and psychological activity; his propensity for the image, his humor (which gradually changes from the merely witty and playful to the ironic and pessimistic), his method of composition, and his unique style as the product of an aim to express the inexpressible, with its beguiling hypomythology of unexpectedly related and disconformed images of objects (things, animals, and people no

161

longer «seen as through a glass darkly») that reveal what Ramón calls a «lateral reality».

It is undoubtedly incumbent upon the conscientious critic to put the author's work in perspective and yet also to maintain the lines of communication open to that work as a living organism of aesthetic independence. Though we are related to the past we do not actually live from it or in it. My main concern has thus been to interpret the meaning and to assess the importance of Gómez de la Serna's *novelas de la nebulosa* as they should be seen today. Despite the presence of universal values in great works of art, the reader (or spectator) must accommodate himself to the epochal factor. After all, a work of art is a response to a human concern as perceived and moulded by its own time yet projected toward a future. Timelessness, however, is not a reality but rather a concept which merges with the sometimes unconscious convention of timeliness to make the stream of human life not only comprehensible but indeed viable.

As Joaquín Marco has succinctly put it in his *La nueva literatura en España y América* (p. 50): «Bien es verdad que Gómez de la Serna había inventado una literatura próxima a los futuros movimientos. Si alguien se anticipó en muchas cosas fue él.»

# SUPPLEMENTARY NOTES

## I. Page 1: IMAGERY IN PROSE NARRATIVE.

René Wellek and Austin Warren in their *Theory of Literature* (New York: Harcourt, Brace and Company, 1949, p. 16) state that «one common misunderstanding must be removed: 'imaginative' literature need not use images. Poetic language is permeated with images, beginning with the simplest figures and culminating in the total all-inclusive mythological systems of a Blake or Yeats. But imagery is not essential to fictional statements and hence to much literature... Imagery, besides, should not be confused with actual, sensuous, visual image-making... But much great literature does not evoke sensuous images, or, if it does, it does so only incidentally, occasionally, and intermittently. In the depiction even of a fictional character the writer may not suggest visual images at all. We scarcely can visualize any of Dostoevsky's or Henry James's characters, while we learn to know their states of mind, their motivations, evaluations, attitudes, and desires very completely»; and so on. Obviously, these critics do not have Gómez de la Serna in mind (and it is a pity that so many non-Hispanist literary critics and theorists do not become better acquainted with at least the better-known modern Spanish writers) —but they do make some interesting statements, some of which apply to Ramón, conditionally, and some of which do not.

Richard Jackson is right when he says that Ramón wants to turn everything into imagery; although Jackson refers primarily to the aphorisms. Sister Albert Mazzetti is also right when she says that it is the image rather than the gregueristic aphorism that is ever-present in Ramón's writings; she is, of course, referring primarily to the biographies. But how does Ramón turn everything into imagery, as in fact he does in his novels, and why is the image ever-present in his writing? Because he tries to think in images —images that will retain in words the various phenomena— to the extent that he starts off his novels from nothing but an image. And in fact it is that image —the total image but also the initial image— that is left with us when we finish reading his novels: Gustavo el Incongruente being born at the opera or ending at the movies with a leg of his bride-to-be entwined with one of his own; the Novelist writing all the time and in different places or talking to his characters; Luis in *¡Rebeca!* searching for his 'para-real' woman or the mythical greyhound (symbolizing the chase?) hiding under the table; the Lost Man lost, lying down by the railroad spur, or the «blue papers streaking behind pink papers» (symbols? or also mere images of nothing but color and velocity? —a favorite notion of Ramón's).

In Ramón's «Novels of the Nebula» the «protagonist»

(a)  is A
(b)  goes from B to C
(c)  does D,

but A, B, C, and D do not have the same functions they have in «conventional» novels. The same is true of the other «characters». A, B, C, and D are not really «people, places, and actions» that flow one from another with logical motive producing a true (if hazy) story-line and a psychological development; they are primarily excuses for imagistic description, all of which have the same level of aesthetic and narrative value. The actual motive behind the verbal surface is the expression of the author's own literary life at a given time of creativity: his vision of the world *through* his awareness and use of language. Names are simple grammatical categories.

Ramón's vision must not be regarded as merely picturesque. His vision strives to enfold the multilateral, which associates him with Cubism. As early as 1902, Azorín had anticipated something of this sort in *La voluntad,* but his ideological bent did not allow him to go very far toward the strictly imagistic.

Azorín writes novels of ideas (even ideas of things), while Ramón writes novels of perceptions; neither writer really cares to develop characters as people. That is why one might refer to both as writers who practice dehumanizing techniques. But actually both are concerned with the only knowable attitude, the only possible viewpoint —the human, though perhaps only their own. (Regarding Ramón's «humanization of things», see Cardona, p. 130.)

## II. PAGE 5: NARRATIVE STATEMENT (creative vs. constructive).

Philip Stevick asserts that «no one, with the possible exception of the practitioners of the 'new' French novel, has ever attempted to define a 'pure' novel» (p. 2). Leave it to the French; were they not the first to advocate «la poésie pure»? I believe that there is no need for such a definition, because there is no such thing. One might even think of literature as comprising two great divisions: scientific literature (which many would not regard as literature at all) and artistic literature. Scientific literature is primarily intended to make us «think»; artistic literature is primarily intended to make us «feel». The first is essentially discursive, while the second is essentially direct. The first includes the history, the treatise, and the formal essay, all of which purport to be objective. The second includes the lyric, the drama, and the tale, none of which purports to be objective. Naturally there are many kinds of mixtures, including didactic poems and plays, biography, and prose fiction. These mixtures can make us either «think» more or «feel» more, and they can alternate the two, depending on the amount of commen-

tary; by commentary I mean anything that is neither lyrical nor dramatic, anything that is either historical or critical. It follows, then, that to
be narrative a literary work does not have to be discursive.

For a parallel comparison of prose and poetry values, see the scheme
which (following S. Alexander, Herbert Read, Ogden and Richards, etc.)
Charles Seltman offers in his *Approach to Greek Art* (London and New
York: The Studio Publications [1948], p. 27) with respect to both literature and the plastic arts.

III. Page 94: THE DOUBLE IN LITERATURE.

Because of its title, the story which first comes to mind is Dostoevsky's (1846) followed by Gogol's *Diary of a Madman* (1835), a title Eugenio
de Nora would have us give to Ramón's *El hombre perdido.* But *Don
Quixote* is in a way this kind of story if we place the emphasis on
madness where it really does not belong. The notion of a shared identity,
such as that afforded by twins goes back to ancient mythology, where
it takes on the value of natural verisimilitude far above the level of
mental illness. The examples of Castor and Pollux, Romulus and Re-
mus, Cain and Abel, and even Adam and Eve have yielded all kinds
of possibilities. Antiquity provided the basis for legends of supernatural
transformations precisely because not much was known then about the
workings of the mind, though a philosopher like Plato can, in the *Phaedrus*,
give us a figure of duality which applies to the human soul for both its
ethics and aesthetics. And we must remember also that in the *Symposium*
we have the humorously grotesque and hence morbid explanation of the
origin of love, namely, the split halves constantly looking for each other.

«The origin of prose fiction», H. T. Peck tells us, «is to be sought
in the history of the Fable, and the Fable grows out of a desire to
explain the phenomena of nature and to give to the explanation a concrete form... Pure fiction, as distinct from religious and semi-religious
myth, first took on a definite shape in the Beast Fable... It is not alone,
however, the Beast Fable that arose out of humanity's ignorance in the
days of its childhood. A swarm of superstitions that are as universal as
human life itself all found their utterance in the folklore of Greece and
Rome» (Petronius Arbiter, *Trimalchio's Dinner.* Edited with an introduction by Harry Thurston Peck. New York: Dodd, Mead and Company,
1898, pp. 4-6). Thus was born the ghost story which, after all, deals
with mankind's most prevalent concern: death and life after death. It
is not surprising that the inability to explain the violent consequences of
a neurological failure in the human organism would lead to a superstitious notion, such as that of lycanthropy as presented in the *Cena Tri-
malchionis* by Petronius. The transformations, produced by a «split personality» reveals a second self, and thus the double in literature emerges
from a combination of myth, ethical regard, fearful superstition, and
abnormal psychology misunderstood.

Of course, imagination develops as rapidly as any other human trait.

165

The literary works which employ the double as a theme or motif continually become more sophisticated. The heyday of the literary double has been, as pointed out by C. F. Keppler in *The Literature of the Second Self* (Tucson, Arizona: The University of Arizona Press [1972]), the nineteenth and twentieth centuries, «whether because during this period writers of creative literature have been influenced by psychologists or (as seems more probable) because both writers and psychologists have been giving expression to a greatly increased sense of the complexity of the human mind» (p. xii). Keppler, whose book is probably the best overview on the subject, does not pretend to analyze the literary works themselves; rather he uses those works synthetically to compose an «anatomy» of the Double, beginning with the nymph Echo, whose voice was left behind as a moral and a mystery. We might add the young Narcissus, whose reflection in the water plays upon his morbidity causing his death by drowning at the same time it merges the two halves, the real and the illusory. Calderón presents the motif in *El Purgatorio de San Patricio,* when the protagonist, intending to kill a cloaked adversary, comes to the realization it is his own skeleton). These have been precisely the attraction the theme has held for writers of all times, especially the modern; whether in comedy or tragedy or something in-between, the moral lesson and the fascinating mystery have been conveyed by the use of the double in a great variety of combinations and permutations, from Plautus's *Menaechmi* to Shakespeare's *Comedy of Errors, The Tempest, Twelfth Night* and *Hamlet,* from Spenser's *The Faerie Queene* to the present day, in writers like Borges, Cortázar, Fuentes and Onetti, Barth, Bellow, Capote, Malamud, Patrick White and Updike, and the films *The Passion of Anna* (Ingmar Bergman) and *2001: A Space Odyssey* (Stanley Kubrick). Below is a short and highly selected list of nineteenth- and twentieth-century writers (older) who have made particular use of the theme or motif of the double:

| *Nineteenth Century* | *Twentieth Century* |
|---|---|
| Honoré de Balzac | Samuel Beckett |
| Emily Brontë | Walter de la Mare |
| Edward Bulwer-Lytton | Friedrich Dürrenmatt |
| Anton Chekhov | William Faulkner |
| Arthur Hugh Clough | André Gide |
| Joseph Conrad | Ramón Gómez de la Serna |
| Charles Dickens | Franz Kafka |
| Fedor Dostoevsky | Ernest Hemingway |
| J. W. von Goethe | Hermann Hesse |
| Nikolai Gogol | James Joyce |
| Thomas Hardy | Thomas Mann |
| Nathaniel Hawthorne | José Martínez Ruiz (Azorín) |
| Heinrich Heine | Vladimir Nabokov |
| E. T. A. Hoffmann | Flannery O'Connor |
| Henry James | Eugene O'Neill |

| *Nineteenth Century* | *Twentieth Century* |
|---|---|
| Rudyard Kipling | Horacio Quiroga |
| Matthew Gregory Lewis | Alfonso Reyes |
| Charles Maturin | Rainer Maria Rilke |
| Herman Melville | Osbert Sitwell |
| Friedrich Nietzsche | John Steinbeck |
| Benito Pérez Galdós | August Strindberg |
| Edgar Allan Poe | Miguel de Unamuno |
| Jean Paul Richter | Edith Wharton |
| Mary Shelley | Charles Williams |
| Robert Louis Stevenson | William Butler Yeats |
| Oscar Wilde | |

I have included in the bibliography a substantial though certainly not exhaustive section of the literature dealing with the Double. The basic difficulty of the relationship of the self to itself, the motive behind much of the creative literature here involved as well as the origin of the most overwhelming problem in abnormal psychology, is succinctly treated by R. D. Laing in his book *The Divided Self.*

IV. Page 118: THE MODALITIES OF ILLUSION.

Bécquer's fundamental theme of the ideal and its impossible attainment is well known by now. The reader is referred, in particular, to EDMUND L. KING, *Gustavo Adolfo Bécquer: From Painter to Poet* (México: Editorial Porrúa, 1953).

Concerning the reference to finding only an empty wardrobe the next morning when the «Apparition» has vanished, as also concerning the evidently very significant and repeated image of a cabinet or wardrobe in *¡Rebeca!* (from which the ideal is supposed to emerge but never does), it would be interesting to know if such images were by any chance impressed on Ramón's mind by having seen «The Cabinet of Dr. Caligari», an outstanding product of the early German cinema and a masterpiece of the morbid and grotesque. An Expressionist film made in 1919, it was written by the scenarists Carl Meyer and Hans Janowitz, and directed by Robert Wien. The story is simple but weird, the latter quality being explained at the end when the viewer realizes he has been seeing the action through the eyes of a madman. Such a device that requires the semantic rearrangement of the narrative in the viewer's mind (which, incidentally, is dramatically self-destructive) is somewhat reminiscent of the gregueristic or nebular novel, particularly with its «surprise» ending. The nebular novel, unlike the dramatic novel, does not build up to a climax; unlike most psychological novels, it does not even create anxiety or excitement; more than anything else, it is a sort of mystery that plays on the reader's curiosity like a puzzle.

## V. Page 272: THE USE OF COLOR IN IMAGERY.

If anything symbolic can be deduced from the appearance of the color blue in Ramón's work, it is to be found in *El alba,* where blue seems to represent Time. According to the chromatics of this book, blue surrounds the dawn (the dark blue of night followed by the light blue of day) but the dawn itself is not blue, it is another color, «un color de mirada providencial» (p. 621), that of Eternity. Ramón tells us that «se muere un azul y renace otro» (p. 627) and that «cuando clarea el día, cuando despunta, cuando surge el llamado rosicler, ya no está el alba, este alba creatriz» (p. 633). Of course, it is not surprising that Ramón also employs the strange precision of humor: «El alba no es color rosa, sino color salmón cocido» (p. 636). And he presents this exciting image of the phenomenon of daylight: «la madrugada del día de ayer —el de hoy aún— se va metiendo en la carpeta azul claro del día de hoy —que todavía no es el día de hoy» (p. 637). At the moment of dawn, Ramón submits, is when «la idea compacta, prevalida y testaruda del tiempo se deshace porque se la ve la trampa» (p. 622), and «mirando fijamente el alba se ve que no hay sutura entre un día y otro» (p. 636). In other words, the blue of day and the blue of night, that is, a chromatic representation of Time, is a continuum as illusory as life itself. The ultimate reality, as represented by the dawn, is Eternity, a flash across the sky which ideally can be glimpsed by the rare mortal who survives metaphysical hunger. Perhaps this is not so remote, after all, from the feelings of a poet whom Ramón very much admired, Mallarmé, when one recalls the exclamation uttered by him: «Je suis hanté: l'Azur, l'Azur, l'Azur!»

Regarding the symbolism of other colors in Ramón, one can mention that of white and black in *La viuda blanca y negra,* generally considered to be his first novel. But it must be noticed that this is hardly symbolism at all, for the author tells us in a given passage what the colors represent: «Lo que se acentuaba mucho en ella, era su viudez y el contraste entre lo blanco y lo negro. Lo blanco que representaba aquella sinceridad, aquel entregarse que disfrutaba Rodrigo, y lo negro, que era lo que no se sabía, aquella especial astringencia de su espíritu, su no creer y no esperar en nada, su imposibilidad para la ingenuidad y el amor» (see *Obras completas,* I, p. 1371).

## VI. Page 135: AVANT-GARDE IMAGERY.

There is a connection between Ezra Pound, Wyndham Lewis, and the Vorticist Movement founded by the latter in 1914 with the publication of *Blast,* a manifesto. Based on Cubist and Futurist theories with a bearing on the literary and social problems of the times, its general objectives have much in common with Ramón's as stated in *Prometeo* (1908-1913), including *El concepto de la nueva literatura* (1909) and *Mis siete palabras* (1910). As a revolutionary program, destructive force, and social dissolvent, it has a parallel in Ramón's work, particularly when limited to the field of aesthetics, for if Ramón was ever really interested in social problems (cf. *Entrando en fuego, Prometeo,* etc.), he soon struck out toward a new horizon of pure theoretics in literature.

By 1940, when Lewis published in *The Kenyon Review* an article on Picasso, our society was already «so visibly dropping to pieces beneath our eyes, that destructive agents have lost their point» (Walter Michel and C. J. Fox, *Wyndham Lewis on Art,* p. 351). Ramón must have sensed all this ahead of time. There are other points of comparison. Lewis was against «intellectual» painting; Ramón was against «intellectual» writing. And Lewis advocated an artistic vision that placed what he called «super-nature» above «super-real», reminiscent of Ramón's notion of 'para-reality'.

Pound coined the name Vorticism, which finds its closest artistic Spanish parallel in *Ultraísmo,* though this was primarily directed to poetry. Ramón is commonly acknowledged to be a forerunner of *Ultraísmo.*

## VII. Page 149: RAMÓN AT THE MOVIES.

I have cited in note IV the possibility of a prefiguration of Ramón's mysterious wardrobe in the film «The Cabinet of Doctor Caligari». More probable is the influence of the moving pictures on Ramón in other instances. It is, of course, obvious in *El Incongruente,* particularly its ending, as I have demonstrated. In *El novelista* (pp. 167-68) there is another interesting reference to the cinema screen. But the most interesting and least obvious is found in *El hombre perdido.* Not only is the mention made of an airfield with warplanes vibrating on the ground after a Japanese sneak attack, but the climactic image of the Lost Man's perhaps accidental death and many devices leading up to it, such as the bums he encounters throughout the book and finally imitates, might have been suggested by a film released at a time when Ramón could have seen it along with the Pearl Harbor newsreels. The film is «Sullivan's Travels» (1941), written and directed by Preston Sturges and featuring Joel McRae. Its plot revolves around the life of a wealthy young man and his concern for the downtrodden, which makes him travel across the country to see how the poor live. In the course of his association with bums who ride the rails, the film narrates the accidental death of one of these unfortunate «lost men» who goes to sleep on the railroad tracks and is run over by a train. The visual effects devoted to this incident in the film are so graphic and so moving that it is easy to imagine why Ramón would have taken this idea from the film for the central and climactic images in his book. I have no documentary proof of this, so that I can only offer it critically as a suggestion. The internal evidence, however, seems to me so strong that I am personally persuaded of its truth.

I have employed the term «iconic discourse» at the end of my discussion of Ramón's particular style of writing. In connection with the cinema, it can be pointed out (see, for example, Peter Wollen, *Signs and Meaning in the Cinema*) that a filmmaker such as Joseph von Sternberg has been conceptually excluded from the doctrines of filmic representation centered around the indexical and the symbolic favored by André Bazin and Sergei Eisenstein, respectively. Von Sternberg can be considered an iconic filmmaker; the stylization of dialogue in his films creates an interaction of word and image similar to their relationship in dreams. This iconic discourse is structured through analogues instead of through the relation between cause and effect as in conventional discourse. So much in *¡Rebeca!* and *El hombre perdido* is grounded in this kind of narrative technique with all its subtle and, at the same time, slippery qualities. The passage on the «cuñadas de las paredes» *(El hombre perdido,* pp. 163-64) is a prime example of the «iconization» of the verbal in literature. Despite the unconventional grammar associated with *ramonismo,* I cannot help considering the word «hallado» which appears in this passage as a typographical error in the original. Although a case could be made for its meaning «found = surprised», I tend to think of the correct word being «hollado» (humiliated), more in keeping with the tone of the passage which forms its context (see Chapter V, page 113).


VIII.  Page 154: FORM AND CONTENT IN ART.

Useful sidelights may be derived from comparing my views on my particular subject with some of Bernard Berenson's on the general subject of art, as stated in his book *Aesthetics and History in the Visual Arts* (New York: Pantheon, 1948). The outstanding topics for our interest here are the following (page numbers are his): the absolute in art (18), concepts as fictions (124-125), incongruity and the grotesque (93), novelty (139), realism (131), revelation (219-220), sensations (67), style (147-157, 225). I quote the following lines which, because they refer to the visual arts in particular, are of special significance at this point: «It has been a commonplace of the ages to say that form and content are inseparable and even indistinguishable. Yet few are those who perceive them so» (125).

# LIST OF WORKS CONSULTED

WORKS BY RAMÓN GÓMEZ DE LA SERNA

*Antología; 50 años de vida literaria.* Selección y prólogo de Guillermo de Torre. Buenos Aires: Editorial Losada, Espasa-Calpe Argentina, Editorial Poseidón, Emecé Editores, Editorial Sudamericana [1955].

*Automoribundia.* Buenos Aires: Editorial Sudamericana, 1948.

*Biografías completas.* [Madrid]: Aguilar [1959].

*Cartas a las golondrinas; Cartas a mí mismo.* [Madrid]: Espasa-Calpe (Colección Austral) [1962].

*Diario póstumo.* Barcelona: Plaza & Janés, Editores [1972].

*El alba y otras cosas.* Madrid: Editorial Calleja, 1923.

*El hombre perdido.* [Madrid]: Espasa-Calpe (Colección Austral) [1962].

*El Incongruente.* Buenos Aires: Editorial Losada (Biblioteca Contemporánea) [1947].

*El novelista.* Buenos Aires: Editorial Poseidón [1946].

*Entrando en fuego; trabajos literarios.* Segovia: Imprenta del Diario de Avisos, 1905.

*Guía del Rastro.* [Madrid]: Taurus Ediciones [1961].

*La quinta de Palmyra/El chalet de las rosas.* Estudio preliminar de María Martínez del Portal. Barcelona: Editorial Bruguera [1968].

*La Sagrada Cripta de Pombo* (Tomo II). Madrid: Imprenta G. Hernández y Galo Sáez [1924].

«Las cosas y el 'ello'», *Revista de Occidente* (Madrid) XLV (1934).

*Lo cursi y otros ensayos.* Buenos Aires: Editorial Sudamericana, 1943.

*Morbideces.* Madrir: Imprenta «El Trabajo», 1908.

*Museo de reproducciones.* (With an introductory essay by Francisco Ynduráin.) [Barcelona] Ediciones Destino (Colección Destinolibro, Vol. 97) [1980].

*Nuevas páginas de mi vida (Lo que no dije en mi Automoribundia).* Alcoy: Editorial Marfil, 1957.

*Obras completas.* (Two volumes published.) Barcelona: Editorial AHR, 1956-1957.

*Obras selectas.* Madrid: Editorial Plenitud, 1947.

*Piso bajo.* [Madrid]: Espasa-Calpe (Colección Austral) [1962].

*Pombo.* Madrid: Imprenta Mesón de Paños, 1918.

*¡Rebeca!* Barcelona: José Janés, Editor, 1947.

*Retratos completos.* [Madrid]: Aguilar [1961].

WORKS ON RAMÓN GÓMEZ DE LA SERNA

CALLEJA, RAFAEL: «A propósito de *El torero Caracho*», *Revista de Occidente,* XVI (1927), 381.

CAMÓN AZNAR, JOSÉ: *Ramón Gómez de la Serna en sus obras.* Madrid: Espasa-Calpe, S. A., 1972.

CANSINOS-ASSÉNS, RAFAEL: «Ramón Gómez de la Serna», *La nueva literatura, IV: La evolución de la novela*. Madrid: Editorial Páez, 1927.

— «Ramón Gómez de la Serna», *Poetas y prosistas del novecientos (España y América)*. Madrid: Editorial América, 1919.

CARDONA, RODOLFO: *Ramón: A Study of Gómez de la Serna and His Works*. New York: Eliseo Torres and Sons, 1957.

CHABÁS, JUAN: *Literatura española contemporánea, 1898-1950*. La Habana: Cultural, S. A., 1952.

DAUS, RONALD: *Der Avantgardismus Ramón Gómez de la Sernas. Analecta Romanica, Heft 29*. Frankfürt am Main: Vittorio Klostermann [1971].

FERNÁNDEZ ALMAGRO, MELCHOR: «Esquema de la novela española contemporánea», *Clavileño*, No. 5 (septiembre-octubre 1950), 15-28.

— Review of *Cartas a las golondrinas, Clavileño*, No. 10 (1951).

GÓMEZ DE LA SERNA, GASPAR: *Ramón (Obra y Vida)*. Madrid: Taurus, 1963.

GONZÁLEZ-GERTH, MIGUEL: «Aphoristic and Novelistic Structures in the Works of Ramón Gómez de la Serna», doctoral dissertation presented in Princeton University, 1973.

— «Ramón Gómez de la Serna's Faded Image», *Essays on Hispanic Literature in Honor of Edmund L. King*. Edited by Sylvia Molloy and Luis Fernández-Cifuentes. London: Tamesis Books Limited [1983], pp. 91-95.

GRANJEL, LUIS S.: *Retrato de Ramón*. Madrid: Ediciones Guadarrama, 1963.

ILIE, PAUL: *The Surrealist Mode in Spanish Literature*. Ann Arbor: The University of Michigan Press, 1968.

JACKSON, RICHARD L.: «The *Greguería* of Ramón Gómez de la Serna: A Study of the Genesis, Composition and Significance of a New Literary Genre.» (Ph. D. dissertation, Ohio State University, 1963).

MARÍAS, JULIÁN: «Ramón Gómez de la Serna», *Diccionario de Literatura Española*. Edited by Germán Bleiberg and Julián Marías. Madrid: Revista de Occidente, 1949.

MARICHALAR, ANTONIO: *Mentira desnuda (hitos)*. Madrid: Espasa-Calpe, 1933.

— Review of *El alba y otras cosas, Revista de Occidente*, III, 7 (1924), 119-25.

MAZZETTI, SISTER M. ALBERT: «Poetic Biography: A Study of the Biographical Works of Ramón Gómez de la Serna.» (Ph. D. dissertation, Indiana University, 1968).

NORA, EUGENIO G. DE: «Ramón Gómez de la Serna», *La novela española contemporánea (1927-1960)*. Madrid: Editorial Gredos [1962].

ORTEGA Y GASSET, JOSÉ: *La deshumanización del arte*, 9.ª edición. Madrid: Revista de Occidente, 1967.

PAZ OCTAVIO: «Una de cal...», *Papeles de Son Armadans* (Palma de Mallorca) CXL (November 1967); reprinted in Octavio Paz/Juan Marichal, *Las cosas en su sitio* (sobre literatura española del siglo xx). [México]: Finisterre [1971].

PÉREZ MINIK, DOMINGO: «Ramón Gómez de la Serna», *Novelistas españoles de los siglos XIX y XX*. Madrid: Ediciones Guadarrama [1957].

RÍO, ANGEL DEL: *Historia de la literatura española* (edición revisada), Vol. II. New York: Holt, Rinehart and Winston [1963].

SÁINZ DE ROBLES, FEDERICO CARLOS: *La novela española en el siglo XX*. Madrid: Pegaso [1957].

SALINAS, PEDRO: *Literatura española, siglo XX*. México: Editorial Séneca, 1941.

— «Ramón Gómez de la Serna», *Columbia Dictionary of Modern European Literature*. New York: Columbia University Press, 1947.

SAZ, AGUSTÍN DEL: *Novelistas españoles*. Barcelona-Buenos Aires: Librería Editorial Argos, 1952.

LIST OF WORKS CONSULTED

TORRE, GUILLERMO DE: *Historia de las literaturas de vanguardia*. Madrid: Ediciones Guadarrama [1965].
— *Problemática de la literatura*. Buenos Aires: Losada, 1958.
— «Ramón y Picasso: paralelismos y divergencias», *Hispania*, XLV, 4 (December 1962), 597-611.
TORRENTE BALLESTER, GONZALO: *Panorama de la literatura española contemporánea*. Madrid: Ediciones Guadarrama, 1956.
VALBUENA PRAT, ANGEL: *Historia de la literatura española, II* (segunda edición). Barcelona: Editorial Gustavo Gili, 1946; fourth edition of the new version with the collaboration of Agustín del Saz under title *Historia de la literatura española e hispanoamericana*. Barcelona: Editorial Juventud [1969].


WORKS THAT REFER TO THE NOVEL

ALBORG, JUAN LUIS: *Hora actual de la novela española*. Madrid: Taurus, 1958.
AYALA, FRANCISCO: *Reflexiones sobre la estructura narrativa*. Madrid: Taurus, 1970.
BARNET, BERMAN, and BURTO: *A Dictionary of Literary Terms*. Boston-Toronto: Little, Brown, 1960.
BAROJA, PÍO: *La nave de los locos*. Prólogo. Madrid: Caro Raggio, 1925.
BLACKMUR, R. P.: *The Lion and the Honeycomb: Essays in Solicitude and Critique*. New York: Harcourt, Brace [1955].
BOOTH, WAYNE C.: *The Rhetoric of Fiction*. Chicago and London: The University of Chicago Press, 1965.
CAUDWELL, CHRISTOPHER: *Illusion and Reality: A Study of the Sources of Poetry*. New York: International Publishers [1973].
COMFORT, ALEX: *The Novel in Our Time*. London: Phoenix House Limited, 1948.
COOK, ALBERT S.: *The Meaning of Fiction*. Detroit: Wayne State University Press, 1960.
DAICHES, DAVID: *The Novel and the Modern World*. Chicago and London: The University of Chicago Press (Phoenix Books), 1970.
FERNÁNDEZ, RAMÓN: *Messages*. Paris: Gallimard, 1926; English translation, New York: Harcourt, Brace, 1927.
FLAUBERT, GUSTAVE: *The Selected Letters of Flaubert*. Trans. and ed. Francis Steegmuller. New York: Farrar, Straus and Young, 1953.
FORSTER, E. M.: *Aspects of the Novel*. New York: Harcourt, Brace and World [1966].
FRANK, JOSEPH: «Spatial Form in Modern Literature», *Sewanee Review*, LIII (1945); collected in *The Widening Gyre (Crisis and Mastery in Modern Literature)*. Bloomington and London: Indiana University Press (Midland Books) [1968].
FRIEDMAN, ALAN: *The Turn of the Novel: The Transition to Modern Fiction*. New York: Oxford University Press, 1970.
FRYE, NORTHRUP: *Anatomy of Criticism*. Princeton: Princeton University Press, 1957.
GIDE, ANDRÉ: *The Counterfeiters*. Translated by Dorothy Bussy and Justin O'Brien. New York: Modern Library, n.d.
GIRARD, RENÉ: *Deceit, Desire and the Novel, Self and Other in Literary Structure*. Trans. Yvonne Freccero. Baltimore: The Johns Hopkins University Press, 1976.
GOLDKNOPF, DAVID: *The Life of the Novel*. Chicago and London: The University of Chicago Press [1972].

HARVEY, W. J.: *Character and Novel.* Ithaca, N. Y.: Cornell University Press, 1965.

HEISERMAN, ARTHUR: *The Novel before the Novel: Essays and Discussions about the Beginning of Prose Fiction in the West.* Chicago and London: The University of Chicago Press [1977].

HOWE, IRVING: *Politics and the Novel.* [New York: Avon Books] Discus Books [1970].

HUMPHREY, ROBERT: *Stream of Consciousness in the Modern Novel.* Berkeley: University of California Press, 1958.

JAMES, HENRY: *The Art of the Novel.* With an introduction by R. P. Blackmur. New York-London: Charles Scribner's Sons [1970].

JONES, HOWARD MUMFORD: Review of *The Psychological Novel: 1900-1950,* by LEON EDEL, *Saturday Review,* XXXVIII (April 25, 1955), 19.

KUMAR, RAJ: *The New Concept of the Novel. The Research Bulletin (Arts) of the University of the Panjab,* XXIX, 3 (1959). Hoshiarpur: Vishveshvaranand Book Agency [Folcroft Library Editions, 1973].

KUMAR, SHIV K.: *Bergson and the Stream of Consciousness Novel.* [New York]: New York University Press, 1963.

LUBBOCK, PERCY: *The Craft of Fiction.* New York: The Viking Press (Compass Books), 1957.

LUKÁCS, GEORG: *The Theory of the Novel: A Historico-Philosophical Essay on the Forms of Great Epic Literature.* Translated by Anna Bostock. Cambridge, Mass.: The M.I.T. Press [1971].

MADDEN, DAVID: *The Poetic Image in 6 Genres.* Carbondale and Edwardsville. Southern Illinois University Press [1969].

MENDILOW, A. A.: *Time and the Novel.* Introduction by J. Isaacs. New York: Humanities Press, 1972.

MYERHOFF, HANS: *Time in Literature.* Berkeley: University of California Press, 1960.

MUIR, EDWIN: *The Structure of the Novel.* New York: Harcourt, Brace and World, n.d.

O'CONNOR, WILLIAM VAN (Ed.): *Forms in Modern Fiction (Essays Collected in Honor of Joseph Warren Beach).* Bloomington: Indiana University Press [1964].

ORTEGA Y GASSET, JOSÉ: *Meditaciones del Quijote; Ideas sobre la novela.* Madrid: Espasa-Calpe, Colección Austral, 1964.

PETRONIUS ARBITER: *Trimalchio's Dinner.* Translated from the original Latin with an introduction and bibliographical appendix by Harry Thurston Peck. New York: Dodd, Mead and Company, 1898.

ROBBE-GRILLET, ALAIN: *For a New Novel.* Trans. Richard Howard. New York: Grove Press, 1966.

ROSENHEIM, EDWARD W., Jr.: *What Happens in Literature: A Guide to Poetry, Drama, and Fiction.* [Chicago]: The University of Chicago Press [1963].

SCHOLES, ROBERT (Ed.): *Approaches to the Novel.* Rev. ed. Scranton, Pa.: Chandler Publishing Co., 1966.

SCHOLES, ROBERT, and ROBERT KELLOGG: *The Nature of Narrative.* Oxford-London-New York: Oxford University Press [1968].

SMITTEN, JEFFREY R., and ANN DAGHISTANY (Eds.): *Spatial Form in Narrative.* With a Foreword by Joseph Frank. Ithaca and London: Cornell University Press [1981].

STEINER, GEORGE: *Language and Silence. Essays on Language, Literature and the Inhuman.* New York: Atheneum, 1972.

STEVICK, PHILIP (Ed.): *The Theory of the Novel.* New York: The Free Press, 1968.

TRILLING, LIONEL: *The Liberal Imagination: Essays on Literature and Society.* New York: The Viking Press, 1950.

WELLEK, RENÉ, and AUSTIN WARREN: *Theory of Literature.* New York: Harcourt, Brace [1949].

ZEKOWSKI, ARLENE, and STANLEY BERNE: «When Will You Understand That In So Far As Present Use Is Concerned, The Novel As We Know It Is Dead?», *Trace,* 47 (1962), 262-63.


WORKS THAT REFER TO THE DOUBLE

APTER, T. E.: *Fantasy Literature: An Approach to Reality.* Bloomington: Indiana University Press [1982].

BRONTË, EMILY: *Wuthering Heights.* With preface by Charlotte Brontë. Edinburgh: John Grant, 1924.

BROOKE-ROSE, CHRISTINE: *A Rhetoric of the Unreal: Studies in Narrative and Structure, especially the Fantastic.* New York: Cambridge University Press, 1981.

BUBER, MARTIN: *I and Thou.* Translated by Ronald Gregor Smith. Edinburgh: T. & T. Clark, 1953.

CHIZEVSKY, DMITRI: «The Theme of the Double in Dostoevsky», *Dostoevsky: A Collection of Critical Essays.* Edited by René Wellek. Englewood Cliffs, N. J.: Prentice-Hall, 1962.

CRAWLEY, A. E.: «Doubles», *Encyclopaedia of Religion and Ethics.* Edited by James Hastings. Volume IV. Edinburgh and New York: T. & T. Clark, 1911.

DESSOIR, MAX: *Das Doppel-Ich.* Leipzig: Ernst Gunthers Verlag, 1890.

ELIADE, MIRCEA: *Mephistopheles and the Androgyne: Studies in Religious Myth and Symbol.* Translated by J. M. Cohen. New York: Harper & Row, 1965.

— *The Two and the One.* Translated by J. M. Cohen. New York: Harper & Row (Harper Torchbooks) [1965].

FODOR, NANDOR: *The Search for the Beloved.* New York: Hermitage Press, 1949.

FRAZER, JAMES GEORGE: *The Golden Bough: A Study in Magic and Religion.* Twelve volumes. Third Edition, Revised and Enlarged. New York: The Macmillan Company, 1935.

GUERARD, ALBERT J.: «Concepts of the Double», *Stories of the Double.* Edited by Albert J. Guerard. Philadelphia and New York: J. B. Lippincott Company, 1967.

HARTLAND, E. SIDNEY: «Twins», *Encyclopaedia of Religion and Ethics.* Edited by James Hastings. Volume XII. Edinburgh and New York: T. & T. Clark, 1911.

HOWE, IRVING: «Dostoevsky: The Politics of Salvation», *Politics and the Novel.* New York: Horizon Press, 1957.

JUNG, CARL GUSTAV: *Collected Works.* Second Edition. Eighteen Volumes. [Princeton]: Princeton University Press (Bollingen Series XX) [1976].

KEPPLER, C. F.: *The Literature of the Second Self.* Tucson, Arizona: The University of Arizona Press [1972].

KOHLBERG, LAWRENCE: «Psychological Analysis and Literary Form: A Study of The Doubles in Dostoevsky», *Daedalus* 92 (Spring 1963), 345-62.

KRAUSS, WILHELMINE: *Das doppelgängermotiv in der romantik; studien zum romantischen idealismus.* Berlin: E. Ebering, 1930.

LAING, R. D.: *The Divided Self: An Existential Study in Sanity and Madness.* [Harmondsworth]: Penguin Books [1971].

MAY, ROLLO: «The Daemonic: Love and Death», *Psychology Today,* I (February 1968).

MYOSHI, MASAO: *The Divided Self.* New York: New York University Press, 1969.

NIETZSCHE, FRIEDRICH: *The Birth of Tragedy,* in *The Philosophy of Nietzsche.* New York: Modern Library, 1954.

PACHMUSS, TEMIRA: *F. M. Dostoevsky: Dualism and Synthesis of the Human Soul.* Carbondale: Southern Illinois University Press, 1963.

PEARCE, RICHARD: *Stages of the Clown: Perspectives on Modern Fiction from Dostoevsky to Beckett.* Preface by Harry T. Moore. Carbondale and Edwardsville: Southern Illinois University Press [1970].

PLATO: *Symposium and Other Dialogues.* Translated by Michael Joyce. New York: Everyman's Library, 1964.

PRINCE, MORTON: *The Dissociation of a Personality.* New York: Longmans Green and Company, 1905.

RAHV, PHILIP: «Dostoevsky in 'Crime and Punishment'», *Partisan Review,* 27 (Summer 1960).

RANK, OTTO: *The Double: a psychoanalytic study.* Translated and edited with an introduction by Harry Tucker, Jr. Chapel Hill: University of North Carolina Press [1971].

ROGERS, ROBERT: *A Psychoanalytic Study of the Double in Literature.* Detroit: Wayne State University Press, 1970.

— «The Psychology of the 'Double' in 2001», *Hartford Studies in Literature,* I (1969).

ROSENFIELD, CLAIRE: «The Shadow Within: The Conscious and Unconscious Use of the Double», *Daedalus,* XCII (Spring 1963).

SCHMIDTBONN, WILHELM: *Der Doppelgänger.* Berlin: Deutsche Buch-Gemeinschaft, 1928.

SHUMAKER, WAYNE: *Literature and the Irrational: A Study in Anthropological Backgrounds.* New York: Washington Square Press [1966].

SIEBERS, TOBIN: *The Romantic Fantastic.* Ithaca and London: Cornell University Press [1984].

STARBUCK, EDWIN D.: «Double-Mindedness», *Encyclopaedia of Religion and Ethics.* Edited by James Hastings. Volume IV. Edinburgh and New York: T. & T. Clark, 1911.

SUGARMAN, SHIRLEY: «Sin and Madness: The Flight from the Self», *Cross Currents,* XXI (Spring 1971).

TODOROV, TZVETAN: *The Fantastic: A Structural Approach to a Literary Genre.* Translated from the French by Richard Howard. Cleveland/London: The Press of Case Western Reserve University, 1973.

TYMMES, RALPH: *Doubles in Literary Psychology.* Cambridge: Bowes and Bowes, 1949.

— *German Romantic Literature.* London: Methuen and Company, 1955.

VIVAS, ELISEO: «The Two Dimensions of Reality in *The Brothers Karamazov*», *Dostoevsky: A Collection of Critical Essays.* Edited by René Wellek. Englewood Cliffs, N. J.: Prentice-Hall, 1962.

WIMSATT, W. K., Jr., and MONROE C. BEARDSLEY: «The Intentional Fallacy», *Sewanee Review,* 59 (1946).

GENERAL WORKS

ABRAMS, M. H.: *The Mirror and the Lamp*. New York: W. W. Norton, 1958.

ALBÉRÈS, R. M.: *L'Aventure intellectuelle du XXᵉ siècle*. Paris: Editions Albin Michel, 1963.

ALEXANDER, HUBERT GRIGGS: *Language and Thinking: A Philosophical Introduction*. Princeton: D. Van Nostrand Company [1967].

ANDERSON-IMBERT, ENRIQUE: *Historia de la literatura hispanoamericana*. México: Fondo de Cultura Económica, 1961.

BACHELARD, GASTON: *On Poetic Imagination and Reverie*. Translated, with an introduction, by Colette Gaudin. Indianapolis-New York: The Bobbs-Merrill Company (The Library of Liberal Arts) [1971].

— *The Poetics of Space*. Translated by Maria Jolas. Foreword by Etienne Gilson. Boston: Beacon Press [1969].

BARNES, DJUNA: *Nightwood*. Introduction by T. S. Eliot. [New York]: A New Directions Book [1961].

BARSACQ, LÉON: *Caligari's Cabinet and Other Grand Illusions: A History of Film Design*. Revised and edited by Elliott Stein. Boston: New York Graphic Society [1976].

BARZUN, JACQUES: *The Energies of Art: Studies of Authors Classic and Modern*. New York: Vintage Books [1962].

BEARDSLEY, MONROE C.: *Aesthetics: Problems in the Philosophy of Criticism*. New York and Burlingame: Harcourt, Brace and World [1958].

BECKETT, SAMUEL: *Three Novels (Molloy, Malone Dies, The Unnamable)*. New York: Grove Press [1965].

BENÉT, WILLIAM ROSE (Ed.): *The Reader's Encyclopedia* (Second Edition). New York: Thomas Y. Crowell [1969].

BERENSON, BERNARD: *Aesthetics and History in the Visual Arts*. [New York]: Pantheon [1948].

BLANCO, VICENTE: *Diccionario latino-español*. Madrid: Aguilar, 1948.

BLUESTONE, GEORGE: *Novels into Film*. Berkeley-Los Angeles-London: University of California Press, 1971.

BRADBURY, MALCOLM, and JAMES MCFARLANE (Eds.): *Modernism: 1890-1930*. [Harmondsworth]: Penguin Books [1978].

CASSIRER, ERNST: *An Essay on Man: An Introduction to a Philosophy of Human Culture*. New York: Doubleday and Company (Doubleday Anchor Books), 1953.

CASSOU, JEAN et al. (Eds.): *Gateway to the Twentieth Century*. New York: McGraw-Hill, 1962.

CAWS, MARY ANN: *The Eye in the Text: Essays on Perception, Mannerist and Modern*. Princeton: Princeton University Press [1981].

CHAUCHARD, PAUL: *Le Langage et la pensée*. Paris: Presses Univesitaires de France. (Qué sais-je?) Tenth ed. [1976].

CHURCH, JOSEPH: *Language and the Discovery of Reality*. New York: Vintage Books, n.d.

CLIPPINGER, JOHN, Jr.: *Meaning and Discourse: A Computer Model of Psychoanalytic Speech and Cognition*. Baltimore: Johns Hopkins University Press, 1977.

DORSON, RICHARD M. (Ed.): *Folklore and Folklife: An Introduction*. Chicago and London: The University of Chicago Press [1972].

DRUMMOND, HENRY: *Natural Law in the Spiritual World*. New York: James Pott & Co., 1884.

DUPIN, JACQUES: *Joan Miró: Life and Work.* New York: Harry N. Abrams [1962].

DURGNAT, RAYMOND: «Film Theory: From Narrative to Description», *Quarterly Review of Film Studies,* VII, 2 (1982).

DURGNAT, RAYMOND, and ALLAN HOBSON: «A Dream Dialogue», *Dreamworks: An Interdisciplinary Quarterly,* II, 1 (Dream and Film. Fall 1981), 76-86.

DURR, R. A.: *Poetic Vision and the Psychedelic Experience.* [New York: Dell Publishing Co.] A Delta Book [1970].

EAGLETON, TERRY: *Literary Theory: An Introduction.* Minneapolis: University of Minnesota Press [1983].

FADIMAN, CLIFTON (Ed.): *Fantasia Mathematica: Being a Set of Stories, Together with a Group of Oddments and Diversions, All Drawn from the Universe of Mathematics.* New York: Simon and Schuster, 1958.

GOOCH, STAN: *Total Man: An Evolutionary Theory of Personality.* New York-Chicago-San Francisco: Holt, Rinehart and Winston [1972].

GROHMANN, WILL: *Paul Klee.* New York: Harry N. Abrams [1955].

HOBSON, JOHN ALLAN: «Film and the Physiology of Dreaming Sleep: The Brain as a Camera-Projector», *Dreamworks: An Interdisciplinary Quarterly,* I, 1 (Spring 1980) 9-25.

HOFSTADTER, DOUGLAS R.: *Gödel, Escher, Bach: An Eternal Golden Braid (A metaphorical fugue on minds and machines in the spirit of Lewis Carroll).* New York: Random House (Vintage Books) [1980].

HOFSTADTER, DOUGLAS R., and DANIEL C. DENNETT: *The Mind's I: Fantasies and Reflections on Self & Soul.* New York: Basic Books [1981].

HOROWITZ, MARDI JON: *Image Formation and Cognition.* New York: Appleton-Century-Crofts, 1978.

HOWE, IRVING (Ed.): *The Idea of the Modern in Literature and the Arts.* New York: Horizon Press [1968].

IHDE, DONALD: *Experimental Phenomenology.* Pittsburgh: Duquesne University Press, 1973.

KAHLER, ERICH: *The Tower and the Abyss.* New York: The Viking Press [1969].

KING, EDMUND L.: *Gustavo Adolfo Bécquer: From Painter to Poet.* México: Editorial Porrúa, 1953.

KRONHAUSEN, PHYLLIS and EBERHARD: *Erotic Fantasies.* New York: Grove Press, 1969.

LANGBAUM, ROBERT: *The Modern Spirit: Essays on the Continuity of Nineteenth and Twentieth Century Literature.* New York: Oxford University Press, 1970.

LEVIN, HARRY: *Contexts of Criticism.* New York: Atheneum, 1963.

LUKÁCS, GEORG: *Writer and Critic, and Other Essays.* Edited and translated by Arthur D. Kahn. New York: Grosset and Dunlap [1971].

MARCO, JOAQUÍN: *La nueva literatura en España y América.* Barcelona: Editorial Lumen [1972].

MAY, ROLLO: *Love and Will.* [New York: Dell Publishing Company] A Laurel Edition [1969].

MICHEL, WALTER, and C. J. FOX (Eds.): *Wyndham Lewis on Art: Collected Writings 1931-1956.* New York: Funk and Wagnalls [1969].

MIRÓ, GABRIEL: *El humo dormido.* Edited with an introduction by Edmund L. King. New York: Dell Laurel Library, 1967.

MITCHELL, W. J. (Ed.): *The Language of Images.* Chicago and London: The University of Chicago Press [1980].

MOLINER, MARÍA: *Diccionario de uso del español.* Madrid: Editorial Gredos, 1966.

# LIST OF WORKS CONSULTED

NELSON, CARY: *The Incarnate Word: Literature and Verbal Space.* Urbana-Chicago-London: University of Illinois Press [1973].

NEWMARK, MAXIM: *Dictionary of Foreign Words and Phrases.* New York: Philosophical Library, 1950.

PANOFSKY, ERWIN: «Style and Medium in the Moving Pictures», *Transition*, No. 26 (1937) 121-33.

PAZ, OCTAVIO: *El arco y la lira.* México-Buenos Aires: Fondo de Cultura Económica [1956].

— *Los hijos del limo: Del romanticismo a la vanguardia.* Barcelona: Editorial Seix Barral [1974].

— *Children of the Mire: Modern Poetry from Romanticism to the Avant-Garde.* Translated by Rachel Phillips. Cambridge, Mass.: Harvard University Press, 1974.

PEIRCE, CHARLES: *Collected Papers.* Eight volumes. Cambridge: Harvard University Press, 1931-1958.

PIGNATARI, DÉCIO: *Semiotica & literatura: icônico e verbal, oriente e occidente.* 2. ed., revista e ampliada. São Paulo: Cortez & Moraes, 1979.

POGGIOLI, RENATO: *Teoria dell' arte d'avanguardia.* Bologna: Società editrice il Mulino, 1962.

READ, HERBERT: *The Philosophy of Modern Art.* New York: Meridian Books, 1955.

SARRIS, ANDREW: *The Films of Josef von Sternberg.* New York: Museum of Modern Art (distributed by Doubleday) [1966].

SEBEOK, THOMAS A.: *Structure and Texture: Selected Essays in Cheremis Verbal Art.* The Hague-Paris: Mouton, 1974.

SEBEOK, THOMAS (Ed.): *Sight, Sound and Sense.* Bloomington: Indiana University Press, 1978.

SELTMAN, CHARLES: *Approach to Greek Art.* New York-London: The Studio Publications [1948].

SHATTUCK, ROGER: *The Banquet Years: The Origins of the Avant-Garde in France, 1885 to World War I.* Garden City, New York: Doubleday and Company (Anchor Books), 1961.

— «The Poverty of Modernism», *The New Republic*, 188, No. 10 (March 14, 1983), 25-31.

SLOTE, BERNICE (Ed.): *Myth and Symbol: Critical Approaches and Applications.* Lincoln: University of Nebraska Press [1967].

STALLMAN, ROBERT WOOSTER (Ed.): *Critiques and Essays in Criticism, 1920-1948.* New York: The Ronald Press [1949].

STEINER, GEORGE: *Extraterritorial (Papers on Literature and the Language Revolution).* New York: Atheneum, 1971.

SYPHER, WYLIE: *Loss of the Self in Modern Literature and Art.* New York: Vintage Books [1962].

TABUCCHI, ANTONIO: *Donna di Porto Pim e altre storie.* Palermo: Sellerio Editore [1983].

TATE, ALLEN (Ed.): *The Language of Poetry.* (Essays by Philip Wheelwright, Cleanth Brooks, I. A. Richards, Wallace Stevens). Princeton: Princeton University Press [1942].

TIBÓN, GUTIERRE: *Diccionario etimológico comparado de nombres propios.* México: Unión Tipográfica, Editorial Hispano Americana, 1956.

TOFFLER, ALVIN: *Future Shock.* New York: Random House [1970].

TOURNIER, PAUL: *The Meaning of Persons.* New York and Evanston: Harper & Row [1957].

MIGUEL GONZALEZ-GERTH

WILSON, COLIN: *The Outsider.* New York: Dell [1967].
WIMSATT, W. K., Jr.: *The Verbal Icon.* [Lexington]: The University of Kentucky Press [1954].
WOLLEN, PETER: *Signs and Meaning in the Cinema.* Bloomington: Indiana University Press, 1969.
WORRINGER, WILHELM: *Abstraction and Empathy: A Contribution to the Psychology of Style.* Translated by Michael Bullock. New York: International Universities Press [1967].